LESSONS FROM AQUINAS

MERCER
UNIVERSITY PRESS

Endowed by
TOM WATSON BROWN
and
THE WATSON-BROWN FOUNDATION, INC.

LESSONS FROM AQUINAS

A RESOLUTION OF THE PROBLEM

OF FAITH AND REASON

Creighton Rosental

MERCER UNIVERSITY PRESS
MACON, GEORGIA

MUP/H829

© 2011 Mercer University Press
1400 Coleman Avenue
Macon, Georgia 31207

First Edition

Books published by Mercer University Press are printed on acid-free
paper that meets the requirements of American National Standard for
Information Sciences—Permanence of Paper for Printed Library
Materials.

Mercer University Press is a member of Green Press Initiative
(greenpressinitiative.org), a nonprofit organization working to help
publishers and printers increase their use of recycled paper and decrease
their use of fiber derived from endangered forests. This book is printed
on recycled paper.

Library of Congress Cataloging-in-Publication Data
Rosental, Creighton.
 Lessons from Aquinas : a resolution of the problem of faith and reason
/ Creighton Rosental. -- 1st ed.
     p. cm.
 Includes bibliographical references and index.
 ISBN 978-0-88146-253-1 (hardcover : alk. paper)
 1. Thomas, Aquinas, Saint, 1225?-1274. 2. Faith and reason—
Christianity—History of doctrines. I. Title.
 B765.T54R673 2011
 231'.042092--dc23
                                                        2011024546

"The things that we love tell us who we are."
—Thomas Aquinas

To Carolyn

CONTENTS

DETAILED TABLE OF CONTENTS

PREFACE

This book presents a thorough, careful, and clearly explained account of faith as understood by Thomas Aquinas. This is done by a close reading of primary texts, with a careful consideration of the account of faith Aquinas had in mind. There is also a detailed exposition of Aquinas's account of reason. Following these accounts, Aquinas's conception of the relation between reason and faith is presented and explained, as is his resolution of the problem of faith and reason.

That there might be some sort of problem of faith and reason is perhaps easier to recognize than it is to formulate—certainly there is some sort of tension between the two, even if it is only superficial. The first chapter of the book takes some time to survey examples of the historical tensions between faith and reason, and discusses positions held by various theologians and philosophers on this issue. These examples illustrate three ways in which the tension between faith and reason about divine matters may be identified. First, either having faith or reasoning about divine matters could be held to be morally bad (or at least dangerous). Second, either having faith or reasoning about divine matters (or matters relevant to claims about the existence of God or the veracity of Scripture) could be held to involve adherence to false propositions. Finally, either having faith or reasoning about divine matters could be held to be epistemically irresponsible. This book focuses on this third problem of faith and reason, and is thus concerned with Aquinas's epistemological solution to this problem. The book also explores a number of epistemological approaches to the problem of faith and reason, which provide an intellectual backdrop for Aquinas's own solution.

Aquinas's resolution of the epistemological problem of faith and reason is interesting for a number of reasons. First, Aquinas is a doctor of the Catholic Church and remains an influential Christian theologian: his views (or neo-Thomist approximations) are still endorsed by many. That Aquinas reconciled faith and reason is well known; exactly *how* he did so is not. Thus, a careful philosophical examination of Aquinas's views can help illuminate philosophical and theological positions held, but not necessarily clearly understood, by many. Second, Aquinas was a scholar from the mid-thirteenth century, a period where Aristotle was just beginning to be widely read by theologians. Aquinas's reputation and influence, conjoined with his being one of the first Christian theologians to fully confront Aristotle, makes his account of particular historic interest. As presented in this book, Aquinas's accounts of faith and reason are what one might call "Christian-ized Aristotle" or perhaps "Aristotelian Christian theology"—and Aquinas's account represents a very early, thorough and influential attempt to reconcile Aristotle's philosophical views with Christian theological doctrine: something of a "founding father" of Scholasticism. Third, the problem of faith and reason remains a thorny issue to this date (consider, for example, the arguments surrounding teaching creationism/evolution in American public schools): as discussed in this book, part of the difficulty with the contemporary approach to faith and reason is that reason and faith are often placed in mutually exclusive epistemic categories, making them not only radically different, but difficult to reconcile. Aquinas's solution to the problem of faith and reason is to find a sort of middle position for faith, in which it counts as stronger than opinion supported by evidence, but is strong for different reasons than *scientia*, or the knowledge that results from deductive reasoning, or proof. This "in between" solution, much overlooked today, brings an interesting voice to the discussion;

and Aquinas's reputation, quality and influence make his solution all the more worth considering.

This book is primarily a work in the history of philosophy and examines closely and carefully the account Aquinas actually provided, primarily analyzing his own writings rather than interpretations by Thomists or of the Catholic Church. The book is philosophical in that it carefully presents his philosophical positions, particularly his epistemological solution to the problem of faith and reason. Aquinas's own theological arguments based on scriptural interpretations, as well as historical arguments provided by others which utilize the context in which Aquinas lived and worked, can both be helpful in understanding Aquinas's position on the reconciliation of faith and reason; however, these are only of secondary concern in this project. Of primary concern are the philosophical positions which can largely be understood without expert knowledge of the historical setting and without theological training.

Though the scholarship in Thomistic thought has had many examples of extraordinary quality in the last 70+ years, work on faith and reason in Aquinas has tended to be limited in one of two ways.

First, works on Aquinas written for students often present broad overviews of his thinking on faith and reason, and though these presentations are often very good and quite accurate, they often lack detail. Two common and very general explanations that are seen in texts on Aquinas hold that he considered faith to be compatible with reason because: (1) God would not let them conflict with each other; or (2) reason serves as "handmaiden" to faith and its role is to provide evidence or proof in support of faith. Neither of these interpretations is entirely inaccurate: Aquinas *did* believe (1), and he also believed something like (2). However, (1) is a theological explanation, and (2) is a practical one; neither accurately expresses Aquinas's carefully and thoroughly developed philosophical and epistemological solution. The broad reasons behind Aquinas's views on the reconciliation of faith and reason are often presented, but the detailed philosophical arguments that would justify his position are often absent.

Second, works written for scholars (typically published in academic journals) often have focused narrowly on aspects of faith and/or reason in Aquinas. Some of these works have presented a view of Aquinas's thinking that does not accurately represent him, particularly when a broader range of primary texts are considered. Other scholars have held Aquinas guilty of not having explained his views and/or not given a careful enough account of them. This is a possible, but an ultimately inaccurate interpretation of Aquinas. Though he does not directly confront the problem of faith and reason much in his writings, components of its solution can be found throughout: much of his work is in disputed question format, which does not easily yield to direct presentations of philosophical positions. I believe, and I endeavor to show in this book, that Aquinas has fully developed accounts of faith and reason, and of their reconciliation, and I support my interpretation by examining the extensive and wide-ranging texts written by him.

Part of the reason for the loose and general (and perhaps incorrect) interpretations of Aquinas by many scholars is, I believe, that adequate and careful expositions of Aquinas's account of reason (*scientia*) have rarely been made, and are frequently overlooked. Further, though in the past thirty years more scholars have attempted to explain Aquinas's account of faith than his account of reason, I find (and argue in my book) that many of these interpretations are inadequate or incorrect. I argue that Aquinas held that faith did not involve proof, nor require evidence in support of it, despite many scholars who have interpreted him as holding views to the contrary. By offering careful and detailed accounts of Aquinas's views of reason and of faith, I show that faith and reason are wholly separate (though similar) epistemic categories, and that many of the proffered interpretations of Aquinas are incorrect. Some of these incorrect interpretations include: that faith requires reason (e.g., the Five Ways), or faith is strengthened by reason (e.g., by evidence of miracles), or faith *is* a form of knowledge, or knowledge is impossible without faith.

ACKNOWLEDGMENTS

Many people were instrumental in helping me understand Aquinas, his peers, his commentators, and the issues discussed in this book. Several deserve particular notice. I'd like to acknowledge and thank Gary Matthews, Vere Chappell, Bob Sleigh, and Eileen O'Neill at UMass Amherst for their invaluable teaching, advice, and suggestions. I'd also like to thank Lynne Rudder Baker at UMass who first suggested that I could write a book on Aquinas. Also of great assistance were Scott MacDonald and Terry Irwin at Cornell: without their assistance, I would not have gotten very far at all in my attempts to understand Aquinas. I'd like to collectively thank the participants who provided me very valuable discussions, wisdom, and feedback at the various Augustine Lectios, Cornell Summer Colloquia in Medieval Philosophy, and Society of Christian Philosophers meetings that I attended and presented at over the years. Finally, I'd like to thank friends and colleagues who provided both intellectual and emotional support: Dan Kaufman, Susan Brower-Toland, Jim Wetzel, Bernd Goehring, Neil Sullivan, Kyle Fischer, and Carlos Hortas.

ABBREVIATIONS

CT   Aquinas, Thomas. *Light of Faith: The Compendium of Theology*. Translated by Cyril Vollert. Manchester, NH: Sophia Institute Press, 1993.

DA   Aquinas, Thomas. *Commentary on Aristotle's De Anima*. Translated by Robert Pasnau. New Haven: Yale University Press, 1999. (Cited by book, lecture, and numbered paragraph.)

DAM   Aquinas, Thomas. "De Aeternitate Mundi." In *St Thomas Aquinas, Siger of Brabant, St. Bonaventure: On the Eternity of the World*, edited by Cyril Vollert, Lottie H. Kendzierski and Paul M. Byrne, 19-25. Milwaukee: Marquette University Press, 1964. (Cited by numbered paragraph.)

DPD   Aquinas, Thomas. 1964. "De Potentia Dei, Question 3, Article 17." In *St Thomas Aquinas, Siger of Brabant, St. Bonaventure: On the Eternity of the World*, edited by Cyril Vollert, Lottie H. Kendzierski and Paul M. Byrne, 45-59. Milwaukee: Marquette University Press, 1964. (Cited by question and article.)

DPN   Aquinas, Thomas. "On the Principles of Nature." In *Selected Writings*, 18-29. New York: Penguin Books, 1998. (Cited by chapter.)

DT   Translations from questions 1-4: Aquinas, Thomas. *Faith, Reason and Theology: Questions I-IV of His Commentary on the De Trinitate of Boethius*. Translated by Armand Maurer. Toronto: Pontifical Institute of Medieval Studies, 1987. (Cited by question and article.)

       Translations from questions 5-6: Aquinas, Thomas. *The Division and Methods of the Sciences: Questions V and VI of His Commentary on the De Trinitate of Boethius*. Translated by Armand Maurer. Toronto: Pontifical Institute of Medieval Studies, 1963. (Cited by question and article.)

LC   Aquinas, Thomas. *Commentary on the Book of Causes*. Translated by Vincent A. Guagliardo, Charles R. Hess and Richard C. Taylor. Washington DC: Catholic University of America Press, 1996. (Cited by proposition and numbered paragraph.)

M   Aquinas, Thomas. *Commentary on Aristotle's Metaphysics.* Translated by John P. Rowan. Notre Dame, Indiana: Dumb Ox Books, 1995. (Cited by book, lecture, and numbered paragraph.)

P   Aquinas, Thomas. *Commentary on Aristotle's Physics.* Translated by Richard J. Blackwell, Richard J. Spath, and W. Edmund Thirlkel. Notre Dame: Dumb Ox Books, 1999. (Cited by book, lecture, and numbered paragraph.)

PA   Aquinas, Thomas. *Commentary on the Posterior Analytics of Aristotle.* Translated by F.R. Larcher. Albany NY: Magi Books, Inc., 1970. (Cited by book, lecture, and numbered paragraph.)

QDC   Aquinas, Thomas. *On Charity.* Translated by Lottie H. Kendzierski. Milwaukee: Marquette University Press, 1960.

QDV   Aquinas, Thomas. *Truth: De Veritate* Translated by James V. McGlynn. Chicago: Henry Regnery Company, 1953. (Cited by question and article.)

Sent   Aquinas, Thomas. *Commentary on the Sentences of Peter Lombard.* Sources for translations of passages from this text are provided as cited.

SCG   Translations from Book I: Aquinas, Thomas. *God.* Volume 1 of *On the Truth of the Catholic Faith: Summa Contra Gentiles.* Translated by Anton C. Pegis. Garden City NY: Image Books, 1955. (Cited by book, chapter and numbered paragraph.)

     Translations from Book II: Aquinas, Thomas. *Creation.* Volume 2 of *On the Truth of the Catholic Faith: Summa Contra Gentiles.* Translated by James F. Anderson. Garden City NY: Image Books, 1956. (Cited by book, chapter and numbered paragraph.)

ST   Translations from II-II.1-16: Aquinas, Thomas. *On Faith: Summa Theologiae, Part 2-2, Questions 1-16.* Translated by Mark D. Jordan. Notre Dame: University of Notre Dame Press, 1990. (Cited by book, question, and article.)

     All other sections: Aquinas, Thomas. *Summa Theologiae,* 2 volumes. Translated by Fathers of the English Dominican Province, revised by Daniel J. Sullivan. Great Books edition. Chicago: Encyclopedia Britannica, 1952. (Cited by book, question, and article.)

1

INTRODUCTION TO THE PROBLEM OF FAITH AND REASON

1.1. The problem of faith and reason

That there might be some sort of "problem" of faith and reason is perhaps easier to recognize than it is to formulate—certainly there is some sort of tension between the two, even if it is only superficial. Part of the difficulty in explicating the nature of this tension resides in the fact that opinions about what constitutes faith and what constitutes reason have changed over the last 2,000 years, and the tension has been observed for nearly as long as there has been Christian faith. Is the tension between faith and reason in the twenty-first century the same as in the second or the thirteenth? A further difficulty is that what counts as an acceptable solution has also changed, and such changes are not completely explicable in terms of changing accounts of faith and/or reason. For instance, some contemporary philosophers or theologians (e.g., contemporary creation science advocates) may hold that the beliefs of faith are "rational" because they meet the standards of modern science; however, to Medieval theologians who had very different standards for "science" such a solution would be unacceptable.

Even though there is no uniform account of faith amongst religious believers, we shall try to limit the scope of the problem of faith and reason by constraining our consideration of faith to *Christian* faith (even though there is also much disagreement among Christians about the nature of faith). And though it seems that nearly every theological or philosophical text that surveys accounts of faith has its own metric for categorizing accounts, we shall further limit the scope of the problem by following John Hick in observing that there are fundamentally two types of Christian faith: the first, from the Latin *fiducia*, is a trusting and confident attitude toward God, the second, from *fides*, is identified with a cognitive act or state in which one is said to know God or have knowledge about Him.[1] We shall take as a minimum criterion for any account of faith that it encompass either one or both of these meanings.

A common response to the tension between faith and reason is to find one side at fault and to excoriate it. Early critics of Christianity accused Christians of all sorts of moral failures related to their faith (including drinking babies' blood, having orgies, and even engaging in incest!).[2] Later secular critics found moral fault with Christianity in that faith was held to prevent Christians from achieving true or real goods. Karl Marx, for instance, exemplified this later view when he claimed, "[Religion] is the *opium* of the people. The abolition of religion as the *illusory* happiness of the people is required for their *real* happiness."[3] On the part of early Christians, reliance on philosophical reasoning was perceived as a diminishment of trust in God (faith as *fiducia*), and it was believed to have contributed to viciousness. Tatian (c. 150–170) exemplifies this position when he says, "What noble thing have you produced by your pursuit of philosophy? Who of your most eminent men has been free from vain boasting?"[4] And he continues, providing a

---

[1] Hick, "Faith," in *The Encyclopedia of Philosophy*, ed. Edwards (1967) 165.

[2] See Hoffman's introduction to Celsus's *On the True Doctrine*, trans. Hoffman (1987) 12-24.

[3] Marx et al., "Contribution to the Critique of Hegel's Philosophy of Right: Introduction," in *On Religion* (1964) 41-42.

[4] *Address of Tatian to the Greeks*, ch. 2.

list of notable philosophers and their vices, implying that the practice of philosophy in each case has contributed to moral turpitude. And, of course, Christians have always held that salvation requires faith, so that if one, as a result of reasoning, loses or fails to have *fiducia*, one would also fail to be saved.

Of more interest, perhaps, to philosophy are the arguments that reject either faith or reason on epistemic rather than moral grounds. Early Christian writers criticized reason precisely because (they argued) it yielded an intellectual failure. Tertullian (c. 200) observed that reason (exemplified by Greek philosophy with its dialectical methods) conflicted with faith as *fides* because its conclusions were incompatible with what was known or claimed to be true about God.

> ...Indeed heresies are themselves instigated by philosophy. From this source came the Aeons, and I know not what infinite forms, and the trinity of man in the system of Valentinus, who was of Plato's school.... Then, again, the opinion that the soul dies is held by the Epicureans; while the denial of the restoration of the body is taken from the aggregate school of all the philosophers; also, when matter is made equal to God, then you have the teaching of Zeno; and when any doctrine is alleged touching a god of fire, then Heraclitus comes in. The same subject-matter is discussed over and over again by the heretics and the philosophers; the same arguments are involved. Whence comes evil? Why is it permitted? What is the origin of man? and in what way does he come?... Unhappy Aristotle! who invented for these men dialectics, the art of building up and pulling down; an art so evasive in its propositions, so far-fetched in its conjectures, so harsh, in its arguments, so productive of contentions—embarrassing even to itself, retracting everything, and really treating of nothing!...[5]

---

[5] *The Prescription Against Heretics*, ch. 7.

Not only did Tertullian recognize that philosophical reasoning produces heresies, but he noticed that Scripture recognized this as well, and that the exercise of philosophy was explicitly proscribed therein:

> From all these, when the apostle would restrain us, he expressly names *philosophy* as that which he would have us be on our guard against. Writing to the Colossians, he says, "See that no one beguile you through philosophy and vain deceit, after the tradition of men, and contrary to the wisdom of the Holy Ghost." He had been at Athens, and had in his interviews (with its philosophers) become acquainted with that human wisdom which pretends to know the truth, whilst it only corrupts it, and is itself divided into its own manifold heresies, by the variety of its mutually repugnant sects. What indeed has Athens to do with Jerusalem? What concord is there between the Academy and the Church? What between heretics and Christians? Our instruction comes from "the porch of Solomon," who had himself taught that "the Lord should be sought in simplicity of heart." Away with all attempts to produce a mottled Christianity of Stoic, Platonic, and dialectic composition! We want no curious disputation after possessing Christ Jesus, no inquisition after enjoying the gospel! With our faith, we desire no further belief....[6]

According to Tertullian, there is a problem of reason and faith because the operation of reason that is philosophy often yields conclusions that contradict the propositions that are to be believed under faith. Faith as *fides* and philosophical reasoning are incompatible because *fides* holds certain propositions to be true whereas philosophy rejects them, or vice versa. Tertullian's recommendation: abandon Greek philosophy in favor of Christian *fides*.

---

[6] Ibid.

The tension between philosophy and *fides* identified by Tertullian represents an attitude that has persisted among a subset of Christians throughout the history of Christianity. Etienne Gilson, in *Reason and Revelation in the Middle Ages*, identifies Tatian, St. Bernard, and Peter Damiani as also holding Tertullian's position,[7] and in more contemporary times, the rejection by some Christians of scientific "theories" such as evolution is a result of a perception of tension between a product of reason (in this case, a scientific theory) and *fides*. Just as Christian philosophers have found there to be a conflict between faith and the products of philosophy and/or science, so too have secular philosophers and scientists found a similar conflict. Philosophers and non-Christians have long argued that the articles of faith should not be accepted because they cannot be true. There is an extensive philosophical tradition in which problems such as the problem of evil, the incoherence of the Trinity, and the problem of divine foreknowledge and human freedom have been advanced to demonstrate that the articles of faith are, in fact, false. Scientific accounts of evolution, cosmology, and geology are also often advanced to disprove specific claims of faith made in Scripture.

A second sort of epistemic tension between faith and reason does not involve identifying faith and/or reason to have produced false beliefs, but rather, to have produced beliefs that fail to be formed according to acceptable epistemic norms. A famous early attack of this sort on faith is made by Celsus (c. 175). In his work *On the True Doctrine*, we find a substantial and systematic attack on Christian faith in which he criticizes Christians for their failure to abide by the epistemic norms of reason:

> Now I would not want to say that a man who got into trouble because of some eccentric belief should have to

---

[7] Gilson, *Reason and Revelation in the Middle Ages* (1938) 11-13.

renounce his belief or pretend that he has renounced it. But the point is this, and the Christians would do well to heed it: One ought first to follow reason as a guide before accepting any belief, since anyone who believes without testing a doctrine is certain to be deceived.... Just as the charlatans of the cults take advantage of a simpleton's lack of education to lead him around by the nose, so too with the Christian teachers: they do not want to give or to receive reasons for what they believe. Their favorite expressions are "Do not ask questions, just believe!" and: "Your faith will save you!" "The wisdom of this world," they say, "is evil; to be simple is to be good."[8]

William Clifford is perhaps a paradigmatic later example of this view when he argues that "it is wrong always, everywhere, and for anyone, to believe anything upon insufficient evidence."[9] Clifford has in his sights faith in the existence of God that does not depend on evidence nor strive to find any. He continues:

If a man, holding a belief which he was taught in childhood or persuaded of afterwards, keeps down and pushes away any doubts which arise about it in his mind, purposely avoids the reading of books and the company of men that call into question or discuss it, and regards as impious those questions which cannot easily be asked without disturbing it—the life of that man is one long sin against mankind.[10]

Clifford even warns that favoring the form of faith that is *fides* to reasoning can itself put in jeopardy the trust one places in God, that is, the *fiducia* form of faith. He quotes Coleridge: "He who begins by loving Christianity better than Truth, will proceed by loving his own sect or Church better than Christianity, and end loving himself better than all." Views held by many contemporary philosophers and scientists are often as extreme as Clifford's, if

---

[8] Celsus, *On the True Doctrine*, 54.
[9] Clifford, *Ethics of Belief* (1877) ch. 1.
[10] Ibid.

not more, and the attitude expressed by Richard Dawkins in the following passage is common:

> But insofar as theology studies the nature of the divine, it will earn the right to be taken seriously when it provides the slightest, smallest smidgen of a reason for believing in the existence of the divine. Meanwhile, we should devote as much time to studying serious theology as we devote to studying serious fairies and serious unicorns.[11]

The views expressed by Celsus, Clifford, and Dawkins call for rejecting faith for different reasons than Tertullian's call to reject philosophy. According to Tertullian, philosophy should be rejected because it yields false conclusions; on the other hand, Celsus et al. have not claimed (at least in these passages quoted) that faith involves accepting false premises as true. Instead, these secular views argue that faith fails some sort of epistemic norms of belief. Some Christians, on the other hand, have held that reasoning about matters pertaining to the divine without having faith is itself epistemically irresponsible. Augustine (and many Christians following him) famously held that, due to sin, our reasoning faculties were damaged and could only be repaired through faith. For instance, "The eye of the mind is healthy when it is pure from every taint of the body, that is, when it is remote and purged from desire of mortal things. And this, faith alone can give in the first place. It is impossible to show God to a mind vitiated and sick. Only the healthy mind can see him. But if the mind does not believe that only thus will it attain vision, it will not seek healing."[12]

These examples provide three ways in which the tension between faith and reason about divine matters can be identified. First, either having faith or reasoning about divine matters could

---

[11] Dawkins (1998).
[12] *Soliloquies*, 12, in Augustine (1953) 30.

be held to be morally bad (or at least dangerous). Second, either having faith or reasoning about divine matters (or matters relevant to claims about the existence of God or veracity of Scripture) could be held to involve adherence to false propositions. Finally, either having faith or reasoning about divine matters could held to be epistemically irresponsible.[13] Let us dub the position which holds that either faith or reason has failed in any of these three ways the *incompatibilist* position. *Secular incompatibilists* will hold faith at fault for the tension, and *Christian incompatibilists* will hold reason at fault. Further, *secular moral incompatibilists* claim that believing on faith is morally bad (or at least dangerous), *Christian moral incompatibilists* claim that reasoning about the divine is morally bad (or at least dangerous), *secular truth incompatibilists* claim that the articles of faith are false, *Christian truth incompatibilists* claim that reasoning about divine matters (or matters relevant to claims about the existence of God or veracity of Scripture) leads to falsehood, *secular epistemic incompatibilists* claim that believing on faith is epistemically irresponsible, and, finally, *Christian epistemic incompatibilists* claim that believing on the basis of reasoning about the divine is epistemically irresponsible.

No Christian will accept secular moral or truth incompatibilism, for these positions would imply that Christianity is either immoral or false. Some Christians could, however, accept secular epistemic incompatibilism, as long as epistemic "irresponsibility" is understood correctly. James Kellenberger presents a model of faith discussed by Kierkegaard in *Fear and Trembling*. This model of faith, rather than hold that belief in or about God is certain, holds that faith is precisely uncertain and

---

[13] These three ways may not always be independent: on some occasions, epistemic irresponsibility can be construed as a moral failure, and it can lead to one to believe false propositions.

doubtful. Under this view, faith is explicated as follows: "It cannot be, all reason is against it; yet I believe!"[14] This provides the grounds for one response to the tension between faith and reason—at least for some varieties of faith, the faithful can concede that there is a tension between faith and reason when it comes to epistemic norms and as a result, faith is irrational, but simultaneously, the faithful can hold that faith is worthwhile and the propositions believed are true. On the other hand, no one who rejects the truth of the Christian faith would accept Christian truth incompatibilism, for the latter position entails holding that the beliefs of Christian faith are true, and that any contradicting evidence (scientific or otherwise) is false. Most non-Christian scientists and philosophers would similarly not accept Christian epistemic incompatibilism (which implies that our reasoning faculties cannot function reliably about matters relevant to the divine).[15]

A typical passage from Scripture that is often adduced in support of claims of the moral danger of reasoning (in this case, philosophy) and thus in support of Christian moral incom-

---

[14] Kellenberger, "Three Models of Faith," in *Contemporary Perspectives on Religious Epistemology*, ed. Geivett and Sweetman (1992) 322.

[15] I can easily imagine, however, that some non-Christians could accept Christian epistemic incompatibilism. Some might concede that our reasoning faculties are permanently damaged or somehow limited, and thus we cannot reason correctly about matters relevant to the divine. One specific view along these lines is that of Keller (2003). She argues that the human mind (brain) is a product of evolution and is naturally selected for evolutionary success, not for unlimited access to the truths of the natural world. It is unlikely, therefore, that we will be capable of understanding all natural phenomena. Extending her argument somewhat, one might argue that we are similarly limited so as to be unable to prove that matters of faith are false, and thus, that exercises of reason that attempt to show that matters of faith are false are epistemically irresponsible. Note that one can hold this view while at the same time holding that the matters of Christian faith *are* false (i.e., secular truth incompatibilism).

patibilism is Colossians 2:8: "Beware lest any man spoil you through philosophy and vain deceit, after the tradition of men, after the rudiments of the world, and not after Christ." A Christian moral compatibilist could try to explain away scriptural passages such as this that are appealed to in support of the incompatibility of faith and reason, or alternatively, could use competing scriptural passages to diminish support for the incompatibilist position, such as this one from Romans 1:20: "For the invisible things of him from the creation of the world are clearly seen, being understood by the things that are made, even his eternal power and Godhead...." In a similar vein, one could argue that reason does not in fact lead to heresy nor to behavior that diminishes trust in God. Arguments in support of these positions could be philosophical, theological, even historical: one might show that all the arguments that yield heresies are actually fallacious; one might argue theologically that reasoning in fact *promotes* or at least does not diminish Christian virtue; one might argue historically that good philosophers in the past were, in fact, not drawn away from virtue as a result of their practices of philosophy. What these approaches all have in common is that they argue that the products of reason do not, in fact, yield morally problematic conclusions or behavior. Christians, therefore, needn't be moral incompatibilists. On the other hand, non-Christians could, in principle, accept a form of Christian moral incompatibilism. Non-Christians, despite believing that the articles of Christian faith are false, might accept nonetheless that Christians, in believing them (and perhaps also by living in accordance with them), are behaving morally. One might also further claim that non-Christians, lacking the moral structure that accompanies Christian belief, behave badly, or at least are at risk of doing so.

Truth compatibilism is slightly more complicated to explicate, for it is not immediately obvious how to hold that the claims of faith and of reason are both true, particularly when science or philosophy often draw conclusions that seem clearly to contradict matters of faith. Truth compatibilism holds that there is no tension about the truths discernible by faith and by reason because faith (when real) discovers the truth, and reason (when correct) does so as well. Apparent contradictions between the conclusions of reason and matters of faith then need to be explained away somehow. Consider the theory of evolution—a product of reason that seems to contradict a number of beliefs of faith, including, in particular, the story of the creation of humans in Genesis. One approach is to impugn the reasoning involved that produced results incompatible with faith. Creation scientists, for instance, argue that other scientists made errors in reasoning (namely in interpreting data, e.g., the fossil record) when they concluded that humans evolved from other species. The creation scientists argue that proper scientific reasoning would not yield the theory of evolution, and hence would not result in a contradiction with faith. A second approach is to interpret Scripture in such a way that apparently categorical faith claims that contradict scientific findings are not interpreted literally. The Christian tradition has left room to interpret Scripture both literally and figuratively. Even so-called "literal" interpretations of Scripture, as, for instance, can be found in Augustine's *De genesi ad litteram*, contain interpretations that do not at all seem to be particularly literal (i.e., "upholding the exact or primary meaning of a word")—for instance, in Genesis 1:1 ("In the beginning God created the heaven and the earth."), Augustine holds that the use of the term "earth" is not meant to refer either to dirt or to our planet, but to unformed matter (the use of "earth" in this passage helps suggest a pliable substance analogous to unformed matter).

With each of these approaches to truth compatibilism, one assumes that *all* the products of reason and of faith are compatible, as long as the reasoning is sound and the matters of faith are properly interpreted. It may be possible, under this view, for any matter of faith to be proved by reason, and any apparent incompatibility would be due to a particular failure of reasoning or of scriptural interpretation.

A different, and perhaps more radical, approach to truth compatibilism would be to hold that faith and reason cannot contradict each other because certain truths of faith are *in principle* unattainable by reason. The Christian Mysteries are commonly held to be of this sort. Thus, *any* attempt to reason about the nature of the Trinity, and *any* scientific or philosophical conclusion that would appear to contradict claims about the Trinity, must be wrong. Truth compatibilism is achieved by restricting the scope of what can properly be known by reason so that reason can never be found to yield (correctly drawn) conclusions incompatible with matters of faith. Under this approach some matters of faith could still be known by reason[16]—so even though the Mysteries would be beyond the scope of reason, the existence of God might not, and could perhaps be knowable by a successful proof (e.g., by one of Aquinas's Five Ways).[17]

---

[16] At this point I would like to resolve potential ambiguity in the expression "matters of faith." This could refer to those propositions that are held on faith, or alternatively those propositions that are typically constitutive of a system of religious beliefs. I use the expression "matters of faith" in this latter sense, so something can be a matter of faith even if no one actually believed it on faith. For example, if God's existence were proven to all, none would believe it on faith, but such a proposition would be part of a religious belief system, and so I call it a "matter of faith."

[17] As with the previous approach to truth compatibilism, errors of reasoning or errors of scriptural interpretation could be grounds for some apparent contradictions between faith and reason. Unlike the previous approach, which holds that once the errors are corrected, both reason and

In this book, I want to focus on the epistemological problem of faith and reason and on Aquinas's solution to that problem, and so I am not particularly interested in resolutions to the problem of faith and reason mentioned thus far (viz., those that rely on embracing some form of moral or truth incompatibilism/compatibilism). The Kierkegaardian solution to the problem that embraces secular epistemic incompatibilism, seems, to me, to be primarily theological in nature, and not particularly philosophical. Similarly, it seems to me that solutions that depend on moral compatibilism, though they do resolve at least some of the tension between faith and reason, are solutions that ultimately require determinations of moral value that are not *primarily* concerned with issues of reason, rationality, justification, and other epistemological concerns. On the other hand, solutions that rely, at least in part, on truth compatibilism do appear to be somewhat epistemological. Approaches taken by creation scientists and nonliteral interpreters of Scripture are not particularly philosophical, and so I am not concerned with them here. On the other hand, much has been written of philosophical interest about whether the articles of faith are in fact, true, and whether or not they have been proven by reason. This is a centuries-long discussion, and much has been written about proofs or disproofs of matters of faith, and I have little to add in the attempt to answer this question. I shall not be particularly concerned with whether or not the beliefs of the Christian faith are true. That said, I have indicated that my interest in writing this book is to examine Aquinas's epistemological solution to the problem of faith and reason. One aspect of the solution of truth compatibilism is relevant to this interest, namely, the approach that limits the scope

---

faith can yield correct and compatible answers, this approach holds that for some matters of faith, at least, reason can *never* correctly yield the right answer.

of what reason can possibly know about divine matters. Approaches to establishing epistemic compatibilism are, of course, of particular interest. I turn now to these approaches.

1.2. *Epistemological approaches to solving the problem of faith and reason*

Many texts in contemporary philosophy of religion seem to be primarily concerned either with the truth or falsity of religious claims, or of the rationality (or justification, etc.) or irrationality of believing such claims. Both truth and epistemic incompatibilism are explanations of the tension between faith and reason— explanations that are of particular interest to those who study the philosophy of religion. These explanations, though related, are separable: even if religious claims turn out to be false, it is possible that believing those claims can be rational or justified. Since epistemic concerns about belief are separable from truth claims, I will focus primarily on attempts to resolve the tension between faith and reason that try to close the epistemic gap between the two (i.e., on solutions that argue for epistemic compatibilism). Meanwhile, for the most part, I shall disregard arguments that attempt to prove some matters of faith to be false and their apologetic counterparts that refute them or attempt to prove matters of faith to be true. Instead, I want to examine whether or not a particular solution—that offered by Aquinas—is one of epistemic compatibilism, and further, I will examine how adequate such a solution is for resolving the tension between faith and reason. In order to understand *any* solution of epistemic compatibilism, however, we must understand what it means to say that having faith in some proposition is epistemically *responsible* or *irresponsible*. Alvin Plantinga, in his *Warranted Christian Belief*, provides a nice survey of a number of possible accounts for what I have described as epistemic responsibility. In trying to develop an account of epistemic responsibility, I shall largely follow Plantinga's lead.[18]

1.2.1. Being epistemically responsible = having rational justification

As we saw earlier, William Clifford made the rather strong assertion that "it is wrong always, everywhere, and for anyone, to believe anything upon insufficient evidence." Let us interpret the claim epistemically rather than morally (though I am not claiming that Clifford himself had this in mind) and understand "wrong" as "epistemically irresponsible" so that to believe on insufficient evidence is to fail to live up to an intellectual or epistemic duty.[19] This seems to provide us an apparently simple criterion for evaluating the epistemic responsibility or irresponsibility of any given belief. Following philosophical tradition, I shall call this view Evidentialism.[20] In short, the Evidentialist position can be characterized as follows:

---

[18] Note, however, that there are approaches to the supposed epistemic failure of faith both in Plantinga's book and elsewhere that I do not survey below. What I discuss below is intended to be an initial and informal survey into various ways in which faith is (I believe) commonly thought to fail to be epistemically responsible. The explanations I discuss below cover enough possibilities that they provide us with a useful vocabulary and conceptual schema for understanding Aquinas's particular resolution of the problem of faith and reason. Note also that while I survey several explanations for the possible epistemic irresponsibility attached to faith, Plantinga thinks that the only correct explanation for the perceived epistemic irresponsibility of faith is that related to faith failing to have warrant. He may well be right; however, this does not change the fact that a number of philosophers and others have identified (and still identify) each of the failures alone as the root cause of the epistemic irresponsibility of faith.

[19] This attenuated sense of "duty" is akin to the responsibilities one has as part of one's job description. These are not moral obligations, in the ordinary sense; they are obligations of a competent worker. Similarly, epistemic duties are those obligations of a competent thinker.

[20] Locke is frequently identified as the progenitor of this view. cf. Plantinga, *Warranted Christian Belief*, 82.

(E) For any belief P held by S: S's belief that P is epistemically *responsible* if and only if there is sufficient evidence for P.[21]

Epistemic responsibility is acquired by means of having sufficient evidence, and when understood this way, philosophers will often say that such propositions are *rationally justified*, or, simply, *justified*. Many philosophers hold the Evidentialist thesis to be incomplete, for it seems to be insensitive to the difference between two very different sorts of "evidence." My beliefs that Paris is the capital of France and that (to borrow an example from Plantinga) 32 x 94 = 3,008 are justified because I have sufficient evidence for each belief. This evidence depends on other beliefs that I have, so for example, I believe 32 x 94 = 3,008 because I also believe that 4 x 2 = 8, 4 x 3 = 12, 8 + 2 = 10, etc. But these latter beliefs are themselves not believed on the basis of further evidential beliefs, they are "basic" or foundational. Foundational beliefs do not seem to require evidence in the ways that nonbasic beliefs do; they seem to be justified as soon as I apprehend them. They must, of course, be apprehended in the right way to count as *properly* basic, that is, as proper justificatory grounds for other beliefs. This division, of beliefs into basic and nonbasic, then, constitutes what Plantinga calls Classic Foundationalism. I have slightly modified Plantinga's formulation of the view to match the

---

[21] I have tried to leave thesis (E) ambiguous between two senses. Each sense has its advocates for what properly counts as justification—I do not wish to try to choose one here. Rather, I will simply identify them:

Internalist Evidentialism holds that S's belief that P is justified if and only if S has (is aware of, etc.) sufficient evidence for P.

Externalist Evidentialism holds that S's belief that P is justified if and only if there is sufficient evidence for P, whether or not S is aware of such evidence. (Stephen Wykstra, "Toward a Sensible Evidentialism: On the Notion of 'Needing Evidence,'" in *Philosophy of Religion: Selected Readings*, ed. Rowe and Wainwright [1989], seems to argue for a version of this view.)

terminology I have been using, but in essence, the formulation is his:[22]

> (CF) S's belief that P is epistemically *responsible* if and only if there is sufficient evidence for P. There is sufficient evidence for P if and only if either:
> (1) P is properly basic (i.e., P is self-evident, incorrigible, or evident to the senses for S), or
> (2) P is believed on the evidential basis of other beliefs that are epistemically responsible and that support P deductively, inductively, or abductively.[23]

Classic Foundationalism provides several ready solutions to the problem of faith and reason. Philosophers or others who wish to impugn the epistemic responsibility of the faithful (secular epistemic incompatibilists) need merely to argue that there is not sufficient evidence for any given matter of faith—that is, that these beliefs are neither properly basic nor evidentially dependent (whether directly or indirectly) on properly basic beliefs. We see such an approach among those who argue against the soundness of proofs for the existence of God, an approach that seeks to eliminate one source of sufficient evidence for faith. Hume takes a similar incompatibilist approach when, for example, he writes on miracles in the *Enquiry* and argues that evidence in favor of miracles is insufficient in light of other evidence against them.[24] Compatibilist solutions under Classic Foundationalism seem to fall into one of two main categories. One approach is to argue that faith does have sufficient evidence so that belief in matters of faith

---

[22] This formulation from Plantinga, *Warranted Christian Belief* (2000) 84-85.

[23] I should also note here that a number of variations on Classical Foundationalism have been proffered. Plantinga surveys them in *Warranted Christian Belief*, 102-103.

[24] Numerous philosophers (including those quoted in the first section of this chapter) have argued that faith lacks sufficient evidence. Plantinga (ibid., 89-90) cites a number of recent philosophers who hold this position.

should count as justified (successful proofs of the existence of God are taken to be one form of this sort of evidence).[25] A second compatibilist approach is to argue that many ordinary claims that we take to be justified (for example, that I have two hands) do not require a great deal of evidence—the bar for sufficiency of evidence is taken to be fairly low. Faith, it is then argued, has sufficient evidence, under this attenuated understanding of sufficient. Plantinga provides just such an argument in his *God and Other Minds* when he argues that though our beliefs in other minds have only a minimal amount of evidence in favor of them, the beliefs are counted as justified, and since faith seems also to meet such minimal standards, it should also be counted as justified.

1.2.2. Being epistemically responsible = being practically rational

A second way in which a believer might be counted as epistemically responsible would be if that person believing a proposition were counted as being practically rational. William Alston, in *Perceiving God*, advances such a position.[26] Alston considers some socially common belief-forming practices that people have—for instance, the practice of forming beliefs on the basis of perception of objects in our environment. (Other common practices include, for instance, forming beliefs by way of reasoning [both deductive and inductive] and forming beliefs on the basis of memory.) Alston believes that these practices cannot be shown to be reliable; however, he argues that a believer can be counted as *practically* rational to engage in them. Alston provides

---

[25] Plantinga (ibid., 90) cites a number of philosophers, including Locke, who hold that there is sufficient evidence for faith (or least might be sufficient evidence).

[26] Plantinga nicely summarizes Alston's views in *Warranted Christian Belief*, 117-34, so I shall continue here with Plantinga's introduction of explanations of epistemic responsibility.

two arguments supporting why beliefs formed according to these sorts of practices should be counted as practically rational:

> According to the first...because (1) those ways do not lead to massive inconsistencies, (2) there is no reason to think them unreliable, (3) we know of no alternative doxastic practices whose reliability we *could* demonstrate in an epistemically noncircular fashion, and (4) changing to some other practice would be massively difficult and disruptive. According to the second argument, any socially and psychologically established doxastic practice that meets certain other plausible conditions is *prima facie* rational (i.e., such that it is *prima facie* rational to engage in it); such a practice will be all-things-considered rational, if, as far as we can see, there is no reason to abandon it.[27]

What makes belief based on these sorts of doxastic practices rational? Let us stipulate that action will count as *practically* rational if I am behaving in the right ways (i.e., behaving rationally) in attempting to bring about the goals for which such action is a means. So, for instance, if I am hungry and my goal is to eat, it would not be practically rational for me to go where I do not believe there is food or where I do not believe I could get food (for example, the bank or a closed supermarket). If, on the other hand, someone were hungry and went to an open restaurant (and had money, etc.), we would say that such an action was quite appropriate for achieving the desired goals, that is, that the person's action was practically rational.

Consider now our social doxastic practices. If we could show that they were reliable (Alston thinks we cannot), then we would know that beliefs formed on the basis of such practices would turn out to be true. If our goal is to believe what is true, then, in order to behave rationally, we ought to believe on the basis of only

---

[27] Plantinga, *Warranted Christian Belief*, 120.

reliable practices. However, if our standard social doxastic practices, for example, the practice of believing on the basis of sense impressions, cannot be shown to be reliable, what then follows from this? According to Alston, and motivated by the two arguments above, believers can still be counted as rational, even if their belief-forming practices cannot be shown to be reliable. Consider again the analogy of someone who is hungry. When I am hungry, I have the practice of going to the kitchen to get food. In the past, this practice has been a very reliable method of achieving the goal of satiating my hunger. However, I cannot *show* that going to the kitchen is a reliable means of ending my hunger, because I cannot be sure my housemate (or rats, etc.) has not eaten all the food (or that the food isn't rotten, or that I haven't forgotten to go shopping, etc.). Despite my inability to show the reliability of going to the kitchen to secure food, we would still count my action of heading to the kitchen as practically rational, as long as: (1) going to the kitchen has typically been successful, (2) I have no reason to think that going to the kitchen would be unreliable, (3) I don't know of any other way to secure food that I can *show* to be reliable, and (4) changing my food-securing routine would be unnecessarily disruptive and difficult. Our social doxastic practices (as well as my food-securing practices) count as practically rational because we have no reason to think that they will fail to yield the desired goal (in this case, securing truth) and because there is no reason to operate under another practice in preference to the current one. Thus, though still susceptible to skeptical worries, believing according to such practices counts as rational, that is, as epistemically responsible.

It is not difficult to see how this account of epistemic responsibility can be employed to advance either the epistemic compatibilist or incompatibilist positions. Epistemic compatibilists (like Alston) will argue that the believing practices associated with faith are rational because faith is one of those doxastic practices for which the two arguments quoted above apply.[28] Though Alston does not take the following position, I suppose one could also try to argue that neither faith nor any other ordinary doxastic practices pass the criteria specified above, and thus no doxastic practices should be counted as rational. In this way, there would be no tension between faith and reason because believing something on faith would be no more *irrational* that believing something on the basis of reason-based doxastic practices. On the other hand, secular epistemic incompatibilists will explain the tension between faith and reason by arguing that though ordinary (secular) social doxastic practices should be counted as practically rational, the practice of faith should not be so counted. Faith might not be counted as practically rational because, for instance, it failed to satisfy condition (1), in that faith leads to massive inconsistencies. Any reader of Christian Scripture quickly finds a number of inconsistencies therein, and church schisms and different denominations also yield significant inconsistencies.[29] Another incompatibilist approach would be to hold that alternative doxastic practices (e.g., those of the natural sciences) might be thought to be more reliable than faith, and thus believing as a result of the practice of faith should not be counted as practically rational.[30]

1.2.3. Being epistemically responsible = having warrant

---

[28] I shall not get into Alston's reasons for why faith *is* such a doxastic practice (this is, after all, a book on Aquinas's reconciliation of faith and reason)—Alston argues for this position in *Perceiving God: The Epistemology of Religious Experience* (1991) chapters 5-7.

[29] Or perhaps there should be a multiplicity of doxastic practices corresponding to the variety of denominations, not simply one Christian doxastic practice? Still, the inconsistencies in Scripture would remain. Alston considers such a worry in *Perceiving God*, 234-38.

[30] Alston considers and responds to such worries in ibid., 238-48.

A third notion of epistemic responsibility is one introduced by Plantinga in his three books on warrant. In *Warranted Christian Belief*, he summarizes his view:

> Put in a nutshell, then, a belief has warrant for a person S only if that belief is produced in S by cognitive faculties functioning properly (subject to no dysfunction) in a cognitive environment that is appropriate to S's kind of cognitive faculties, according to a design plan that is successfully aimed at truth. We must add, furthermore, that when a belief meets these conditions and does enjoy warrant, the *degree* of warrant it enjoys depends on the strength of the belief, the firmness with which S holds it. This is intended as an account of the central *core* of our concept of warrant; there is a penumbral area surrounding the central core where there are many analogical extensions of that central core; and beyond the penumbral area, still another belt of vagueness and imprecision, a host of possible cases and circumstances where there is really no answer to the question whether a given case is or isn't a case of warrant.[31]

Having warrant in what one believes yields epistemically responsible beliefs because the belief-forming process is fundamentally rational—that is, the belief-forming mechanism is functioning properly, and under the proper circumstances, and is the sort of mechanism that is aimed at forming true beliefs. In this sense, to believe rationally is to have a properly functioning belief-forming process. As Plantinga indicates, proper function involves

---

[31] Plantinga, *Warranted Christian Belief*, 156. Readers should note that in light of certain complicating cases, Plantinga adds further conditions (see p. 156ff). Since I am primarily concerned with a rough account of epistemic responsibility that can serve as the grounds for a possible solution (whether compatibilist or not) to the problem of faith and reason and am not particularly concerned with Plantinga's account of warrant *per se*, I shall leave the additional aspects and details of the account to be explored by interested readers individually.

three components: (1) cognitive faculties that function properly in (2) the appropriate environments and (3) aimed at truth. Properly functioning cognitive faculties are essential to any attribution of rationality or epistemic responsibility. If someone formed beliefs on the basis of insane ramblings or imagined voices, we would not consider such beliefs to be rational. Plantinga argues that if our cognitive faculties are functioning properly, that is, if they yield rational beliefs, then the beliefs that are formed will be *internally* *rational*; that is, we will: have coherent beliefs, draw appropriate inferences from our beliefs when the occasion demands, choose the appropriate sorts of actions given our beliefs, and exhibit a preference to believe what is true.[32] So, for instance, we would normally not count someone as rational who believed that she were both flesh and blood and immune to the harmful effects of fire; nor someone who believed that one cannot breathe underwater but did not infer that deep-water diving without oxygen was dangerous; nor someone who would choose to eat something poisonous, while believing that it was deadly; nor someone who never looked for evidence of the truth of one's belief, when such searching was appropriate.

Roughly then, someone counts as being epistemically responsible in forming and holding beliefs when he or she is warranted in holding those beliefs. Those who fail to have warrant fail to function properly in forming his or her beliefs. As with the other notions of epistemic responsibility, the notion of warrant allows three obvious solutions to the problem of faith and reason. The secular incompatibilist solution, similar to the solutions for justification and practical rationality, argues that faith lacks warrant. Plantinga takes the sort of complaint against faith advanced by Marx that was quoted earlier to be a complaint that

---

[32] Plantinga, *Warranted Christian Belief,* 112.

faith lacks warrant.[33] Plantinga interprets Marx as holding that a perversion in the social structure yields the dysfunctional cognition that is faith. Alternatively, one could argue that faith lacks warrant because a capitalist society represents a hostile environment for proper cognitive function (citizens in a capitalist society believe in tales of God as a coping mechanism for the conditions of capitalism), so that second condition of the warrant of faith (appropriate environment for proper cognitive functioning) is not met. Compatibilist solutions could, as before, either argue that faith has warrant, and is thus epistemically responsible,[34] or that we never (or nearly never) have warrant, and thus that faith is no more epistemically irresponsible than any other manner of belief.[35]

1.3. Why Aquinas?

Those who are even slightly familiar with the work of Thomas Aquinas may wonder why I would need to produce a new and lengthy exposition on his views on the tension between faith and reason. Aquinas's solution seems easy to characterize and very straightforward. Pope John Paul II describes Aquinas's view in his encyclical *Fides et Ratio*: "Both the light of reason and the light of faith come from God, he argued; hence there can be no contradiction between them."[36] This seems to be a straightforward declaration of Christian truth compatibilism—both reason and faith can lead to truth about divine matters. And reason clearly yields truth concerning the existence of God, as the Five Ways shows.

---

[33] Ibid., 161-63.

[34] Plantinga argues for this position in chapter 6ff.

[35] I am not familiar with any solutions argued along these lines, though varieties of more or less radical skepticism could motivate such a response.

[36] John Paul II (1998) §43.

Though Aquinas's position on *truth* compatibilism may be clear, his position on *epistemic* compatibilism is less so. And until we fully understand what Aquinas meant by faith and by reason, we can't understand what his solution to the epistemic problem was. Some Aquinas scholars interpret him as holding faith to be primarily an act of the intellect, a form of cognitive assent to a proposition; others interpret him as holding faith to be primarily an act of the will.[37] If faith is taken to be a form of assent, what kind of assent does Aquinas hold it to be? Is faith a form of knowledge, as James Ross explicitly interprets in his paper "Aquinas on Belief and Knowledge," or is it a form of belief, as Ralph McInerny argues in "The Contemporary Significance of St. Bonaventure and St. Thomas," [38] or is it something else? And how exactly are we to understand knowledge and belief (not to mention other apparently epistemic states such as *scientia, opinio,* and *intellectus*)? As we shall see, Aquinas has been interpreted in a number of different (and often incompatible) ways. One project this book will undertake will be to carefully examine Aquinas's views on these subjects in order to form a comprehensive and comprehensible presentation of his solution to the epistemic problem of faith and reason.

---

[37] See chapter 3.1.2: Faith as belief, for a survey of these positions and some scholars who hold them.

[38] See Ross, "Aquinas on Belief and Knowledge," in *Essays Honoring Allan B. Wolter,* ed. Frank and Etzkorn (1985) 245-69, and McInerny, "The Contemporary Significance of St. Bonaventure and St. Thomas" (1974) 11-26.

But why should we be interested in the epistemic solution of a 750-year old theologian? This question becomes particularly salient when we realize that Aquinas did not seem to be explicitly concerned with problems of epistemic justification, nor with worries about skepticism. Aquinas seems perfectly confident in his Aristotelian reasoning faculties (whose reliability he rarely challenges) coupled with God's grace (a God whose existence is never seriously questioned). At first glance, then, it would seem that Aquinas would not be a particularly interesting figure to look towards for an epistemic solution of the problem of faith and reason. Further, Aquinas endorses an Aristotelian logical and scientific framework (with their attendant accounts of cognition and epistemology), each of which has, for the most part, been replaced with Modern versions (and with different accounts of cognition and epistemology).

Attending to Aquinas's position on the problem of faith and reason is worthwhile for a number of reasons. First, Aquinas is a doctor of the Catholic Church and remains an influential Christian theologian: his views (or neo-Thomist approximations) are still endorsed by many. For instance, consider Pope John Paul II's encyclical letter *Fides et ratio*. In this work, the following Thomistic positions are endorsed: a first-principles approach to philosophy and reason (§4), the distinction of faith from other sorts of knowledge (§9), that objects of faith are known only by revelation (§9), that faith involves obedience of the will and is a form of assent (§13), that what is known by faith remains a mystery (§13), that faith is gratuitous (§15,33), and further, Aquinas's views on faith and reason are specifically praised as a model of the right way to do theology (§43-44). That Aquinas reconciled faith and reason is well known; exactly *how* he did it is not. Thus, a careful philosophical examination of Aquinas's views can help illuminate philosophical and theological positions still held by many.

Second, Aquinas was a scholar from the mid-thirteenth century, a period when Aristotle was just beginning to be widely read by theologians. Aquinas's reputation and influence, conjoined with his being one of the first Christian theologians to fully confront Aristotle, makes his account of particular historic interest. As I later argue, Aquinas's accounts of faith and reason are what one might call "Christianized Aristotle" or perhaps "Aristotelian Christian theology"—and Aquinas's account represents a very early, thorough, and influential attempt to reconcile Aristotle's philosophical views with Christian theological doctrine: Aquinas is something of a "founding father" of Scholasticism.

Third, the problem of faith and reason remains a thorny issue to this day (consider, for example, the arguments surrounding teaching creationism/evolution in public schools): as I analyze in this book, part of the difficulty with the contemporary approach to faith and reason is that reason and faith are often placed in mutually exclusive and contrastive epistemic categories, making them not only radically different, but also difficult to reconcile. Aquinas's solution to the problem of faith and reason is to find a sort of middle position for faith, in which it counts as stronger than opinion supported by evidence but is strong for different reasons than *scientia*, or the knowledge that results from deductive reasoning, or proof. This "in between" solution, much overlooked today, brings an interesting voice to the discussion; and Aquinas's reputation, quality, and influence make his solution all the more worth considering.

My approach to studying Aquinas falls under the history of philosophy—I am interested in looking closely and carefully at the account Aquinas actually provided, and thus I shall avail myself primarily of his writings rather than of interpretations by

Thomists or other theologians. My approach falls under philosophy in that I am interested in the force of his philosophical arguments, particularly his epistemological solution to the problem of faith and reason. There are many ways in which we can come to better understand Aquinas's views: for instance, by examining his own theological arguments based on scriptural interpretations, or by studying arguments provided by historians that place and understand Aquinas's views in their historical context; however, these approaches will be of only secondary concern. Of primary concern are the philosophical arguments that can largely be understood independently of historical context and theological training. Since I hold Aquinas to have attempted to reconcile faith and reason, I hold him to have been a compatibilist, and here I will closely examine exactly how Aquinas finds faith and reason to be compatible. I believe Aquinas thinks that faith and reason exemplify moral, truth, and epistemic compatibilism—I shall discuss the first two forms only when necessary for exploring his solution to the epistemic compatibility of faith and reason. Most of the book will attend to this solution.

Any examination of historical solutions to the problem of faith and reason runs the risk of being anachronistic. Part of this risk is due to the fact that accounts of faith and reason, and of the loci of the tension between the two, have changed over time. For instance, early Christian theologians were often concerned with Greek philosophy and its tension with Christian faith—both because Greek philosophy drew conclusions that apparently contradicted faith and because Greek philosophy advocated an ideal way of life that could be seen as an incompatible alternative to the Christian way of life. Many contemporary Christians, by contrast, do not commonly find the threat of reason to be situated in the conclusions of philosophy but in those of the natural sciences, and the moral threat not to be in philosophical ethical theories but in the prevalent "secular humanist" lifestyle of post-Enlightenment Western society. It would be a mistake to understand Tertullian's concerns in exactly the same way as those of modern creation science advocates, and similarly the concerns of Richard Dawkins are not exactly the same as those of Celsus. In surveying the problem between faith in reason in the last section, I consider general ways in which reason and faith have been found to be (or not to be) in tension—these can give us an idea of the nature of the general problem and help categorize and understand potential solutions. However, any treatment of an historical solution should carefully examine the nature of faith, reason, and the tension between the two as was understood at the time.

Chapter 2 carefully examines Aquinas's account of reason. The particular problem of faith and reason of the thirteenth century was the result of the introduction of Aristotelian science and philosophy to the Latin West in the twelfth century. Most of the Aristotelian corpus (with the exception of some of the texts on logic) was not translated or available to Latin scholars until the twelfth or thirteenth century.[39] The reception of Aristotle among Christian scholars was uneven and certainly not without controversy. At the University of Paris, for example, in 1215, reading and teaching Aristotle's natural philosophy and metaphysics were explicitly forbidden, though teaching his texts on logic was acceptable.[40] In 1231, philosophy texts were supposed to be purged of errors before being taught, but by 1255 (during Aquinas's first tenure there), uncensored works of Aristotle's natural philosophy and metaphysics were explicitly assigned for

---

[39] For a chronology of Aristotelian texts available in Latin, see Dod, "*Aristoteles Latinus*," in *The Cambridge History of Later Medieval Philosophy*, ed. Kretzmann et al. (1982) 45-79.

[40] Dates and details are taken from original documents from Paris translated in Thorndike, *University Records and Life in the Middle Ages* (1971).

study. By the mid-thirteenth century, the study of Aristotle was widespread among scholars, though many Aristotelian conclusions (particularly those derived from Averroes's commentaries of Aristotle) caused problems for Christian theologians. In 1270 and again in 1277, authorities in Paris condemned those advocating a variety of specific Aristotelian positions (or positions attributed to Aristotle by Averroes). The problem of reason and faith in the thirteenth century, then, was a problem of reconciling the recently discovered Aristotelian philosophy with Christian views of the time. Aquinas, following a widespread trend among Christian scholars, adopted an Aristotelian account of reason, as well as many of Aristotle's philosophical positions. In order to understand Aquinas' solution to the problem of faith and reason, we must first understand Aquinas's account of reason. This is done in chapter 2, which discusses in detail Aquinas's general account of reason and its ideal product *scientia*, as well as the means for achieving it, namely, demonstration.

Understanding Aquinas's account of faith is of particular importance, since, as chapter 3 argues, his account has been commonly misunderstood. Some accounts of Aquinas's reconciliation of faith and reason suffer from anachronism because they understand faith under the common contemporary notion of unevidenced or unjustified belief (where knowledge is commonly taken to be some sort of evidenced or justified belief). Aquinas's account of faith is substantially different from this, as this chapter argues. He provides an account of Christian faith while trying to maintain a consistent spirit with the Aristotelian account of reason described in chapter 2. This account of faith is discussed in some detail, and pays attention to the roles of the will, charity, and grace, aspects of Aquinas's account of faith that are often overlooked.

Chapter 4 begins to build towards Aquinas' solution of the problem of faith and reason. This chapter examines Aquinas's position on the limitations of reason in divine matters, looking in particular detail at his treatment of the eternity of world as a case study. Aquinas holds that reason is incapable of achieving any demonstration about certain matters relevant to faith (for example, whether the world is eternal or finite in duration, also whether God is Triune, etc.); this is one compatibilist approach to the tension between faith and reason, as was surveyed in the last section. This chapter also examines Aquinas's position on divine matters that are accessible to reason, looking in particular at his presentation of the Five Ways, his proofs for existence of God. These proofs have been commonly interpreted as presented in order to show that faith is justified and is thereby epistemically responsible (and that these proofs serve the goal of establishing epistemic compatibilism); however, I argue that these proofs are not intended by Aquinas for this purpose—he achieves his epistemic compatibilism by a different means.

Chapter 5 provides the full account of Aquinas's solution to the problem of faith and reason. It examines Aquinas's solution in the contexts both of other Medieval theologians as well as later Christians and philosophers in order to understand the extent to which Aquinas's solution was considered philosophically sound (or at least plausible). It also examines a number of epistemological consequences and concerns surrounding Aquinas's solution that, though they might not have explicitly been of concern to Aquinas, are of particular interest to contemporary philosophers of religious epistemology. Finally, the chapter considers and responds to a number of objections to Aquinas's solution to the problem of faith and reason.

AQUINAS'S ACCOUNT OF REASON

2.1. Reason in Aquinas

Along with many other Medieval philosophers, Aquinas held that reasoning is what differentiates us from other animals. Humans are, by the Aristotelian definition, rational animals. We are distinct from other rational beings (namely, angels) because we are animals, but we are also distinct from other animals because we are the only animals who have the power to reason. Reason, for Aquinas, "denotes a transition from one thing to another by which the human soul reaches or arrives at cognition (*cognoscendum*)[1] of

---

[1] Translator's note: many translations of Aquinas into English translate terms that blur together epistemic categories I wish to maintain as distinct. For instance, in the translation of Aquinas's commentary on the *Posterior Analytics*, Larcher translates *notus* and related terms (*notitia, nosco*) as "known" or "knowledge" but also often translates *cognitio* and related terms (*cognosco*) in the same way. (See, for instance, Larcher's translation in the PA prologue). Similarly, McGlynn often translates these terms synonymously in his translation of the *Disputed Questions on Truth* (see, for instance, his translation of QDV 15.1). Ross ("Aquinas on Belief and Knowledge," 1985) explicitly interprets Aquinas as speaking of knowledge when he uses the term *cognitio*. In contrast, I will generally translate *cognitio* as "cognition," "apprehension" or "thought," and *cognitio* and related terms are to be translated as neutral with respect to whether or not they are true, except when the context makes it absolutely clear that these terms should be translated as "knowledge." *Notitia*, on the other hand, I will generally translate as "knowledge," for Aquinas does seem to consider it to include truth. *Scientia* I will leave untranslated, for, as we shall see in section 2.2, it is a rather special epistemic category and has no synonymous English term. Rather than provide a justification for these translation choices here, I refer the reader to Jenkins (*Knowledge and Faith in*

something else."[2] In his commentary on the *Posterior Analytics*, Aquinas is a bit more specific, saying that reason "pertains to bringing principles to their conclusions."[3] This "transition" or "bringing" is often described by Aquinas metaphorically as "movement" (*movari*)[4]—reason is the power picked out by the movement from one cognition to another.

A simple transition from one thought to another is not enough to characterize reason uniquely. The two cognitions must be epistemically linked in order to count as an instance of reasoning. Aquinas describes this act of reason as "[advancing] (*discurrere*) from one thing to another in such a way that through that which is known (*notum*) one comes to a cognition (*cognitionem*) of the unknown (*ignoti*)."[5] In order to have an act of reasoning, we must not only move from an initial to a later thought, but the first thought should somehow bring it about that we have a cognition of the second. In the prologue to the commentary on the *Posterior Analytics*, by means of an analogy

---

Thomas Aquinas, 1997, 16-17) and MacDonald ("Theory of Knowledge," 1993, 160-63). When providing an English translation of Aquinas, I will generally supply the translation directly from the sources I use (see the "Abbreviations" section for the translations used); however, when Aquinas uses an epistemically significant term, I will supply both my translation and the Latin used by Aquinas.

[2] "ratio vero discursum quemdam designat, quo ex uno in aliud cognoscendum anima humana pertingit vel pervenit." (QDV 15.1)

[3] "hic autem addit rationem, quae pertinet ad deductionem principiorum in conclusiones." (PA I.44.n11)

[4] See for example, ST I.79.8.

[5] "scilicet discurrere ab uno in aliud, ut per id quod est notum deveniat in cognitionem ignoti." (PA prologue.n4) See also QDV 15.1. Aquinas references two other types of rational acts, which he describes as part of the intellect rather than of reason proper. These acts—one of understanding simples, the other of combining and dividing—describe more the coming to cognize a proposition rather than a transition from one proposition to another and thus are not instances of reasoning in the sense used here.

Aquinas describes the various ways by which an epistemic relation between the two cognitions can be obtained:

It should be noted that the acts of reason are in a certain sense not unlike the acts of nature: hence so far as it can, art imitates nature. Now in the acts of nature we observe a threefold diversity. For in some of them nature acts from necessity, i.e., in such a way that it cannot fail; in others, nature acts so as to succeed for the most part, although now and then it fails in its act. Hence in this latter case there must be a twofold act: one which succeeds in the majority of cases, as when from seed is generated a perfect animal; the other when nature fails in regard to what is appropriate to it, as when from seed something monstrous is generated owing to a defect in some principle.

These three are found also in the acts of the reason. For there is one process of reason which induces necessity, where it is not possible to fall short of the truth; and by such a process of reasoning the certainty of *scientia* is acquired. Again, there is a process of reason in which something true in most cases is concluded but without producing necessity. But the third process of reason is that in which reason fails to reach a truth because some principle which should have been observed in reasoning was defective.[6]

---

[6] "attendendum est autem quod actus rationis similes sunt, quantum ad aliquid, actibus naturae. unde et ars imitatur naturam in quantum potest. in actibus autem naturae invenitur triplex diversitas. in quibusdam enim natura ex necessitate agit, ita quod non potest deficere. in quibusdam vero natura ut frequentius operatur, licet quandoque possit deficere a proprio actu. unde in his necesse est esse duplicem actum; unum, qui sit ut in pluribus, sicut cum ex semine generatur animal perfectum; alium vero quando natura deficit ab eo quod est sibi conveniens, sicut cum ex semine generatur aliquod monstrum propter corruptionem alicuius principii.

et haec etiam tria inveniuntur in actibus rationis. est enim aliquis rationis processus necessitatem inducens, in quo non est possibile esse veritatis defectum; et per huiusmodi rationis processum scientiae certitudo acquiritur. est autem alius rationis processus, in quo ut in pluribus verum concluditur,

How exactly this analogy is supposed to work is, at first glance, not entirely clear. If cases in which nature acts from necessity is deterministic causation, are cases in which nature acts "so as to succeed for the most part" cases of what we today would consider probabilistic causation? In order to understand the analogy, we must first understand the three cases of natural causation Aquinas describes, and then look at what reasonable analogue from causes to reasoning acts we can draw.

In *On the Principles of Nature*, Aquinas explains what he means by cause: "But cause is said only of that prior thing from which the later being follows; hence a cause is defined as that from whose being another follows."[7] Causes do not merely precede their effects, they *generate* them—something counts as a cause just in case it makes its effect come to be. For this reason, the builder of a house is called its cause, and the house the effect—the builder is the cause because he or she brings it about that the effect exists. With this very rough and simple sketch of causation, we can understand the threefold division of natural causation described in the passage from the *Posterior Analytics* above. Aquinas explains that when nature acts from necessity, it acts in such a way that it cannot fail. In this passage, Aquinas does not provide an example of this sort of causation, but examples can be found in his commentaries on the *Physics* and the *Metaphysics*. In *Physics* II, for instance, he gives the example of the alternation of day and night being necessarily caused by the motion of the sun.[8] When the sun is up, it cannot fail to be the case that it is day (for presumably "day" is simply "when the sun is up"), and when the sun is down,

---

non tamen necessitatem habens. tertius vero rationis processus est, in quo ratio a vero deficit propter alicuius principii defectum; quod in ratiocinando erat observandum." (PA prologue.n5)

[7] "sed causa solum dicitur de illo primo ex quo consequitur esse posterioris: unde dicitur quod causa est ex cuius esse sequitur aliud." (DPN 3)

[8] See lect. 15.

it cannot fail to be the case that it is night. The sun's being up causes it to be day, and causes it necessarily. The sort of necessity here is absolute: "Absolute necessity arises from causes prior in the way of generation, namely matter and the agent, just as the necessity of death comes from matter's disposition to join with contraries. This necessity is called absolute because it has no impediment: and it is also called the necessity of matter."[9] When nature acts from necessity, these are cases of causation in which, given the cause, the effect must follow, because nothing can impede the cause from bringing about the effect.

The second type of causation is one in which "nature acts so as to succeed for the most part, although now and then it fails in its act" and Aquinas further divides this into those acts of nature that succeed "in the majority of cases" and those acts "when nature fails in regard to what is appropriate to it." To illustrate these two types of cases, Aquinas gives the example of a seed "succeeding" in producing a perfect animal versus the case of a seed "failing" to do so and instead producing something monstrous. These cases of causation are to be marked off from necessary causation because the cause does not always bring about the effect. So, for instance, though most men grow beards, simply being a man will not necessarily result in growing a beard, and though taking medicine often cures people of what ails them, taking medicine does not necessarily produce health. Aquinas explains:

> [I]t does not follow that because this has taken place, namely, that he has drunk the medicine, that this will be,

---

[9] "necessitas quidem absoluta est quae procedit a causis prioribus in viam generationis, quae sunt materia et efficiens: sicut necessitas mortis quae provenit ex materia et ex dispositione contrariorum componentium; et haec dicitur absoluta quia non habet impedimentum. haec etiam dicitur necessitas materiae." (DPN 4)

namely, that he will be cured. For it has already been established that a cause which necessarily infers its effect is simultaneous with its effect.... Therefore, having posited what is prior, the subsequent does not follow of necessity in those cases in which the effect of causes can be impeded.[10]

In cases of natural necessity, the cause cannot be impeded from bringing about the effect, but, by contrast, there are cases in which causes, though they may sometimes bring about effects, can be impeded from doing so. So, for instance, seeds have within them the ability to generate animals, but in some cases this causal ability is impeded, so that monstrous things are instead generated. In cases like the latter, in which the seed's causal power fails to produce an animal, it is not the seed but some other, impeding cause that produces the monster. Such impeding causes (whatever they may be) Aquinas terms as "fortune" or "chance."[11] Why chance occurs to produce an accident in a particular case is perhaps the purview of empirical study, though Aquinas does identify three general circumstances in which a cause may fail to produce its normal effect:

> First, because of the conjunction of two causes one of which does not come under the causality of the other, as when robbers attack me without my intending this; for this meeting is caused by a twofold motive power, namely, mine and that of the robbers. Second, because of some defect in the agent, who is so weak that he cannot attain the goal at which he aims, for example, when someone falls on the road because of fatigue. Third, because of the indisposition of the matter, which does

---

[10] "non enim sequitur quod quia hoc factum est, scilicet quod iste medicinam bibit, hoc erit, scilicet sanabitur. iam enim supra dictum est quod causa quae ex necessitate infert effectum, est simul cum effectu.... unde posito priori non sequitur ex necessitate posterius in illis in quibus effectus causarum impediri possunt." (PA II.10.n9)

[11] See P II.8-10.

not receive the form intended by the agent but another kind of form. This is what occurs, for example, in the case of the deformed parts of animals.[12]

This second type of causation, in which effects can be impeded and are thus not absolutely necessary, is causation in which the effect is merely contingent. What makes a cause-and-effect relationship necessary or contingent is ultimately a matter of what God wills—He chooses whether or not certain effects will follow from a given cause of necessity or only contingently.[13]

In cases of natural causation, then, we have two main types: causes that necessitate their effects because the cause cannot be prevented from bringing about its effect, and causes that do not necessitate their effects because the cause can be prevented. Of this latter type, things of a kind (e.g., seeds) are considered causes of certain effects (e.g., grown animals) if, as a general rule, those things bring about the specified effects. In a particular case, some particular seed may fail to produce an animal, and instead a monster is generated; in cases such as these, there is no causal connection between the seed and the monster—some other, chance cause is responsible for producing the monster. In cases when the seed does succeed in producing an animal, there is a sort of necessity, though it is not absolute. Aquinas calls this conditional necessity: "Conditional necessity arises from causes

---

[12] "...quarum una sub altera non continetur, sicut cum praeter intentionem occurrunt mihi latrones. (Hic enim concursus causatur ex duplici virtute motiva, scilicet mea et latronum). Tum etiam propter defectum agentis, cui accidit debilitas, ut non possit pervenire ad finem intentum; sicut cum aliquis cadit in via propter lassitudinem. Tum etiam propter indispositionem materiae, quae non recipit formam intentam ab agente, sed alterius modi sicut accidit in monstruosis partibus animalium." (M VI.3.n1210)

[13] See M VI.3.n1220. This position, that God chooses whether or not some effects follow necessarily or contingently is used by Aquinas to help him out of the problem of divine foreknowledge necessitating all future states of affairs.

posterior in generation, namely form and end, as we say that conception is necessary if a man is to be generated. This is conditional because for this woman to conceive is not absolutely necessary, but under a condition: if a child is going to be born. This is called the necessity of end."[14] Seeds are conditionally necessary for animals—if there is to be an effect that is the production of an animal, there must be a seed which causes it.[15]

Reasoning is, like natural causation, a movement from one thing to another. So, analogous to the three types of causal relation between cause and effect, Aquinas identifies three types of epistemic relation between the first cognition and the second. Acts of reason, Aquinas claims, can be divided into three kinds that are analogous to the three kinds of natural causation: the first "induces necessity, where it is not possible to fall short of the truth," in the second "something true in most cases is concluded but without producing necessity," and the third "fails to reach a truth because some principle which should have been observed in reasoning was defective." Perhaps an initial and straightforward interpretation of Aquinas would be to correlate natural necessity, natural contingency and causal failure (causation by chance) with analogues in the movement of reason. Under this interpretation, natural necessity corresponds to a deterministic movement of the reason: necessarily, if A (the first thought) occurs, then B (the second thought) occurs. But this interpretation cannot be right, for

---

[14] "necessitas autem conditionalis procedit a causis posterioribus in generatione, scilicet a forma et fine: sicut dicimus quod necessarium est esse conceptionem, si debeat generari homo; et ista est conditionalis, quia hanc mulierem concipere non est necessarium simpliciter, sed sub conditione, si debeat generari homo. et haec dicitur necessitas finis." (DPN 4)

[15] Of course, if animals can be effected from a cause other than a seed (for instance, from cloning) then seeds will not be conditionally necessary for animals. *This particular seed* that actually produced *this particular animal* ("Bessie") will still be conditionally necessary for Bessie's coming to be, however.

under this interpretation there would be no actual instances of the kind of reasoning that is analogous to natural necessity. For though it may happen often, and even every time, that for any given reasoner, cognition of some particular first thought invariably yields cognition of some particular second thought, it cannot be the case that this movement is absolutely necessary—for it is always possible that, between the instances of the having of the first and second thoughts, the thinker could die. So it seems that reasoning, though a movement, should not be considered a straightaway analogue to other forms of natural movement.

A preferable interpretation of Aquinas's analogy would be to hold that the three cases of reasoning are analogous to the three cases of natural causation because of the nature of the connection between the two thoughts. In the cases of natural causation, the three kinds of causation can be distinguished by the nature of the connection between cause and effect. For natural necessity, the cause absolutely necessitates the effect—they are essentially bound. For for-the-most-part successful causation, the cause is only contingently linked to the effect, and for chance causation, the purported cause (e.g., the seed) is not causally linked to the effect at all. Perhaps then the appropriate analogue for reasoning should not be: necessarily, if A (the first thought) occurs, then B (the second thought) occurs; instead let us connect the content of the thoughts by a simple logical entailment: it is necessarily the case that if A is true then B is true (where A and B are the propositions successively cognized). This latter interpretation shall be symbolized as s ($\Box A \to B$). So just as there is an absolutely necessary connection between cause and effect in natural necessity, so would there be an absolutely necessary connection between the first and second thoughts in reasoning (i.e., $\Box(A \to B)$). The second and third cases of reasoning would also correspond nicely to causation: with for-the-most-part causation the cause is contingently connected to the effect, and the analogue for a reasoning act would be that it is contingent that (A→B); and corresponding to causal failure, in which the event under consideration as cause and the effect are not actually connected, so with reasoning failures. the first thought does not imply the second. So the analogy, under my interpretation, works as follows:

Natural Causation	Movements of Reason
A absolutely necessitates B	A logically entails B
A contingently causes B	A contingently implies B
A does not cause B	A does not imply B

Though the modal connection between cognitions in the movement of reason makes for a neat correspondence with types of natural causation, Aquinas also has a particular interest in the beginning and ending states of reasoning acts. If we look back at the original passage in the beginning of section 2.1, we see that Aquinas alludes to a second component in acts of reason, namely, the epistemic states of reasoners. Aquinas clearly seems to be referring to the epistemic states of reasoners when he talks about how the first kind of act "induces" necessity and the "certainty (*certitudo*) of *scientia*" is "acquired"; of the second kind of act he also refers to "concluding" truths and of the third kind of act he discusses "failing to observe" principles of reason. On the one hand, reasoning acts resemble natural acts in that the modal connections of the propositions that are reasoned about correspond to similar connections between events in natural causation. On the other hand, reasoning acts also include some reference to epistemic states of reasoners. This should not be surprising, for in order to distinguish the movements of reason from other natural movements we must appeal to what makes reasoners different from other causal entities capable of having states—and this would seem (at least in part) to be that our reasoning states are *epistemic* and not simply causal. Part of our task in understanding Aquinas's account of reason is to examine just how these two aspects of reasoning fit together. This we shall pursue both in the remainder of this section and throughout the rest of the chapter.

These three types of reasoning acts produce several different sorts of epistemic states. For simplicity, I shall refer to the three kinds of reasoning acts as follows: those that correspond to natural necessity (i.e., there is a necessary connection between the two thoughts) I shall refer to as *acts of necessity.* Those that correspond to for-the-most-part causation (i.e., there is a contingent connection between the two thoughts) I shall refer to as *acts of contingency.* Those that correspond to causal failure (i.e., there is no logical connection between the two thoughts) I shall refer to as *reasoning failures.* According to Aquinas, Aristotle divided up his logical treatises according to the epistemic states that are related to these three types of reasoning acts.

An act of necessity is called *"judicative*...because it leads to judgments possessed of the certitude (*certitudine*) of *scientia."*[16] Aquinas observes that three sorts of epistemic states are concerned with acts of necessity: *scientia* with conclusions,[17] understanding (*intellectus*) with principles, and wisdom (*sapienta*) with highest causes.[18] The *Analytics* are concerned with judicative reasoning—

---

[16] "pars iudicativa dicitur, eo quod iudicium est cum certitudine scientiae." (PA prologue.n6)

[17] For the remainder of the paper I shall use these terms interchangeably: "conclusion" and "second cognition"/"second thought." Also interchangeable with each other are "first thought(s)"/"first cognition(s)," "premise(s)," and "principle(s)."

[18] "sed tria eorum, scilicet sapientia, scientia et intellectus, important rectitudinem cognitionis circa necessaria: scientia quidem circa conclusiones, intellectus autem circa principia, sapientia autem circa causas altissimas, quae sunt causae divinae." (PA I.44.n11)

the *Prior Analytics* concerns the form of such reasoning, while the *Posterior Analytics* concerns the content.[19]

Acts of contingency are called "investigative" (*inventiva*). From investigative reasoning, one of several epistemic states may result, with diminished certitude in the truth of the conclusion. Investigative reasoning that yields a fairly high degree of certitude in the conclusion produces the epistemic state of *opinion*, an epistemic state in which one believes the truth of the proposition but fears it may be false—the *Topics* is concerned with this sort of reasoning. If the reasoning process fails to produce even belief in the conclusion, one has *suspicion*, which is merely an inclination to believe that the proposition may be true (or false), but not belief as such. The *Rhetoric* is concerned with this epistemic state. As opposed to *suspicion*, if by mere fancy or personal taste (and without any certitude) one is inclined to accept the conclusion, then the *Poetics* is the applicable text.

Finally, reasoning failures are *sophistry*. This is the subject of *On Sophistical Refutations*.

In sum, Aquinas (following Aristotle) holds that reason is a power of the mind. This power is characterized by its ability to effect the transition from the cognition of one proposition to the

---

[19] There are two logical works of Aristotle concerned with acts of necessity—the *Prior* and the *Posterior Analytics*. I believe we can explain the separation of these acts into two works given the epistemological distinctions made thus far. In acts of necessity, the premises entail the conclusions. That premises can entail conclusions is of some general interest, particularly in understanding logic by examining the logical relations involved in inferences—and this is the purview of the *Prior Analytics*. But we also want to pay special attention to those acts of necessity in which we somehow *recognize* that the premises of some particular reasoning act entail the conclusion *in this particular case*. This recognition, that some particular act of necessity *is just such an act*, is of particular epistemological interest and earns its own consideration in the *Posterior Analytics*. Given that this book is primarily interested in epistemology and not logic, the *Prior Analytics* will not be considered here.

cognition of another. Some acts of reason can produce certitude of the conclusion (*scientia*); others produce belief with fear that what is believed is false (*opinion*) or merely an inclination to believe (*suspicion*). Still other acts of reason are mere sophistry in which premises fail to produce knowledge of or belief in the proper conclusion. Though we have not yet considered Aquinas's account of faith (this is done in chapter 3), it seems quite clear that some acts of reason are irrelevant to any problem of faith and reason. One whose reason leads him to accept a proposition on the basis of sophistry or poetry certainly will be in no epistemic bind should she also believe contradictory propositions on the basis of faith. If Mary believes on faith that God is triune and is persuaded by a lovely piece of wordplay that God is not triune, this may lead to a conflict in Mary's determination of what to accept about God, but it does not create the sort of epistemic worry for faith that a proof against a triune God would. Of the remaining epistemic states—*scientia*, opinion, and suspicion—Aquinas devotes most of his attention to *scientia* (he wrote a commentary on the *Posterior Analytics*, which is concerned with this), but relatively little is said about opinion and suspicion (he apparently did not comment on the *Topics* or the *Rhetoric*). The next section and the remainder of the chapter focuses on Aquinas's account of the acts of reason that produce *scientia*. Chapter 3.1 addresses the reasoning act that produces opinion.

2.2. The account of ideal scientia in the Posterior Analytics[20]

Among the epistemic states identified as products of reason-

---

[20] It is commonly held that the views presented by Aquinas in his commentaries on the works of Aristotle are to be understood as views also held by Aquinas himself. I follow in this tradition, though it is by no means entirely clear that it is justified. For a discussion relevant to this issue, see Pasnau's introduction to Aquinas's *Commentary on Aristotle's De Anima* (1999) xviii-xxi, and Chenu, *Toward Understanding Saint Thomas* (1964) ch. 6.

ing, *scientia* is of particular interest if we are to examine Aquinas's reconciliation of faith and reason. With truth incompatibilism, it is the *products* of reasoning that are held to contradict the matters of faith that are to be believed. Among Medieval philosophers, *scientia* was held to be the product of proper philosophical reasoning. Thus, if philosophy were to produce conclusions that contradicted matters of faith, those conclusions would ideally be forms of *scientia*.[21] Thus *scientia*, as a perfection of philosophical reasoning, must be examined in more detail if we are to understand how faith might be reconciled with it.

As we saw at the end of the previous section, *scientia*, the cognition of a conclusion of an act of necessity, is the epistemic state that results from a judicative reasoning act. According to Aquinas, reasoning that produces *scientia* is covered in the *Posterior Analytics* of Aristotle, and it is to this text that we turn to understand both what *scientia* is and how one might come to have it. After the text was translated into Latin in 1159, and the first full commentary was made by Robert Grosseteste sometime around 1225, the account of *scientia* presented in the *Posterior Analytics* was the ground for nearly all Medieval accounts of knowledge of necessary truths. However, Medieval writers varied somewhat in interpreting Aristotle's determination of exactly what constituted *scientia*, though many of these authors presented their unique accounts as faithful to Aristotle's.[22] Throughout his works, Aquinas appears to be concerned with presenting an Aristotelian notion of *scientia*, even though his account of *scientia* in works outside his commentary on the *Posterior Analytics* differs in some

---

[21] See Serene, "Demonstrative Science," in *The Cambridge History of Later Medieval Philosophy*, ed. Kretzmann et al. (1982) 496-517.

[22] For a careful survey of several views on demonstrative science in the thirteenth and early-fourteenth centuries, see Serene, "Demonstrative Science," 496-517.

important ways from the account covered in his commentary.[23] In this section, we shall examine the basic account of *scientia* that Aquinas presents in his commentary on the *Posterior Analytics*.

In book I, lecture 4 of his commentary on the *Posterior Analytics*, Aquinas defines his account of *scientia*:

> [T]o know something scientifically (*scire*) is to cognize (*cognoscere*) it completely, which means to apprehend (*apprehendere*) its truth perfectly. For the principles of a thing's being are the same as those of its truth, as is stated in *Metaphysics* II. Therefore, the scientific knower (*scientem*), if he is to cognize (*cognoscens*) perfectly, must cognize (*cognoscat*) the cause of the thing known scientifically (*scitae*); hence he says, "when we think that we cognize (*cognosceret*) the cause." But if he were to cognize (*cognosceret*) the cause by itself, he would not yet cognize (*cognosceret*) the effect actually—which would be to know (*scire*) it absolutely (*simpliciter*)—but only virtually, which is the same as knowing in a qualified sense (*scire secundum quid*) and incidentally (*quasi*). Consequently, one who knows scientifically (*scientem*) in the full sense (*simpliciter*) must cognize (*cognoscere*) the application of the cause to the effect; hence he adds, "as the cause of that fact."[24]

---

[23] Aquinas presents accounts of *scientia* outside of his Aristotelian commentaries that seem, at least at first, somewhat different than the account presented here. There has been some debate as to whether or not the account of *scientia* in PA is the same and/or consistent with the account employed in Aquinas's theological treatises. I am inclined to interpret Aquinas as employing substantively the same notion of *scientia* throughout his works, but do not have the space to engage a defense of this interpretation here. Instead, I refer the reader to Jenkins, *Knowledge and Faith*, ch. 2, which thoroughly and usefully discusses this interpretive issue.

[24] "...quod scire aliquid est perfecte cognoscere ipsum, hoc autem est perfecte apprehendere veritatem ipsius: eadem enim sunt principia esse rei et veritatis ipsius, ut patet ex ii metaphysicae. oportet igitur scientem, si est perfecte cognoscens, quod cognoscat causam rei scitae. si autem cognosceret causam tantum, nondum cognosceret effectum in actu, quod est scire simpliciter, sed virtute tantum, quod est scire secundum quid et quasi per

To have *scientia* that P is to have a perfect cognition of P (*perfecte cognoscere*), which amounts to having a perfect apprehension of the truth of P (*perfecte apprehendere veritatem*). Following Aristotle in *Metaphysics* II, he goes on to say that a perfect apprehension of the truth of P amounts to the same thing as knowing the ground or cause of the truth of P. That is, a perfect apprehension of the truth of P, if actually perfect, would include apprehension of why P is true, which requires both knowing the cause of the truth of P and knowing that the cause of the truth of P actually did cause P to obtain.[25] After providing this condition, Aquinas adds that *scientia* also involves complete certitude.

---

accidens. et ideo oportet scientem simpliciter cognoscere etiam applicationem causae ad effectum." (PA I.4.n5)

[25] Note that we are referring to propositions here—"the cause of the truth of P." The parallel between premises and causes is a very tight one for Aquinas, and he often shifts from the language of propositions to the language of things. In PA I.3, he is very clear on the close connection: "Now the principles in demonstrative matters are to the conclusion as efficient causes in natural things are to their effects; hence in *Physics* II the propositions of a syllogism are set in the genus of efficient cause." Thus, Aquinas often speaks of *scientia* as if it concerned things, not propositions. For instance, he speaks of the certain cognition of a thing (*res*) rather than a certain cognition of a proposition referring to that thing. When using causal language he often speaks of the content of premises causing the content of conclusions. The two modes of speaking can be reconciled, I believe, by considering Aquinas to hold that the relations between propositions and the truth of propositions will typically reduce to the objects (or their essences) that are specified by their contents. So we can consider the following sorts of expressions to be equivalent, under appropriate contexts: an object caused something, e.g., "the match caused the fire"; an object caused a cognition, e.g., "the match caused the cognition that *there is a fire*"; a cognition led to another cognition, e.g., "the cognition that *there is a match* brought about the cognition that *there is a fire*." In each of these cases we should understand Aquinas to have the following picture in mind: object A causes B, A is the ground for the truth of proposition P, B is the ground for the truth of Q, Q logically follows from P precisely because A causes B; however, A causing B does not necessarily result in someone thinking Q, even if that person has already cognized P. For more on this, see section 2.2.2.

Note that the notion of *scientia* here is stronger than one merely of complete certitude. In segregating reasoning acts into three groups, Aquinas noted that in one type of reasoning act the premises entail the conclusion; further, of these acts, the judicative concerns complete certitude of the necessity of the conclusion. This account of *scientia*, however, adds a second condition, one of perfect apprehension of the truth of a proposition. Let us characterize the account of *scientia* presented here as *perfect scientia*.[26] We can define *perfect scientia* as follows:

> S has *perfect scientia* that P =df (1) S cognizes P; and
> (2) S has complete certitude that P; and
> (3) S has a perfect apprehension of the truth of P.

In order for the first condition to be met, S must have had a thought that P, though cognizing P does not in itself involve any attitude concerning the truth or falsity of P. The following subsections will consider the second and third conditions in detail.

2.2.1. The certitude criterion

In the initial account of judicative acts provided in section 2.1, these were so called because they led to "judgments possessed of the certitude (*certitudine*) of *scientia*." Investigative acts are differentiated from the judicative because "they are not always accompanied by certitude. Hence in order to have certitude a

---

[26] Aquinas calls this notion *scientia simpliciter*. See PA I.4.n5.

judgment must be formed...."[27] Aquinas goes on to say that investigative acts achieve only "more or less perfect certitude," similar to how various for-the-most-part cases of natural causation are closer to or farther from natural necessity. This notion of certitude seems closely bound with the judicative act, appearing to be what distinguishes the judicative act from the investigative. At several points in the *Posterior Analytics*, Aquinas asserts that *scientia* is certain (*certa*) cognition of something.[28] This certitude seems to be key to categorizing an epistemic state as one which involves cognition of necessary truths. Thus, we can reasonably infer that the certitude of a cognition somehow maps onto its necessity.

A natural interpretation of *certitudo* would be to interpret it as synonymous with "necessity"—thus, judicative acts by definition involve cognition of certain, that is, necessary truths. Under this interpretation, judicative acts would be a species of acts of necessity—for all acts of necessity, the first cognition entails the second (i.e., $\Box(A \rightarrow B)$), and judicative acts are those acts of necessity for which the conclusion is also a necessary truth (i.e., $\Box B$). Investigative acts are distinguished from judicative acts both in that they do not involve cognition of necessary (certain) conclusions and that the premises do not entail the conclusions. However, this interpretation of *certitudo* is problematic. In the previous paragraph, we saw that Aquinas allowed that investigative acts result in "more or less" certitude, which is difficult to understand if certitude is simply necessity. Also cited in the previous paragraph, Aquinas says that "in order to have certitude a judgment must be formed" which also does not seem

---

[27] "nam inventio non semper est cum certitudine. unde de his, quae inventa sunt, iudicium requiritur, ad hoc quod certitudo habeatur." (PA prologue.n6)

[28] See PA I.4.n5, I.44.n3.

to fit with the interpretation that certitude just is necessity. Finally, Aquinas seems to hold that the necessity of a proposition is a necessary condition of its certitude, thus that certitude could not simply be the same as necessity: "because *scientia* is also sure and certain cognition of a thing, whereas a thing that could be otherwise cannot be cognized with certitude, it is further required that what is scientifically known could not be otherwise."[29] From these passages, it seems clear that certitude is a property of a cognizing act, not the property of a cognized proposition: (a) certitude can be had in degrees; (b) it requires the forming of a judgment; and (c) certitude requires that its object cannot be otherwise.

Aquinas does not define certitude in his commentary on the *Posterior Analytics*; he does, however provide definitions in his *Commentary on the Sentences of Peter Lombard*:[30]

"...it must be said that certitude is nothing else than the determination of the intellect to one thing."[31]

"...it must be said that the firmness of the adherence of the cognitive power to its knowable object is properly called certitude."[32]

From these passages and the passages from the *Posterior Analytics*, we can arrive at the sense of *certitudo* used in connection with judicative reasoning. From the *Sentences* we see that certitude is a determination to one thing, also a firmness of adherence to an

---

[29] "quia vero scientia est etiam certa cognitio rei; quod autem contingit aliter se habere, non potest aliquis per certitudinem cognoscere" (PA I.4.n5)

[30] See also QDV 14.1.ad 7.

[31] III Sent d. 23, q. 2, a. 2, sol. 3. This translation and the next are by Griffin ("The Interpretation of the Two Thomistic Definitions of Certitude," *Laval Theologique et Philosophique* 10 [1954]: 9-35) who on p. 11 provides a useful and thorough account of Aquinas's use of "certitude."

[32] III Sent d. 26, q. 2, a. 4.

object.[33] From the *Posterior Analytics* we know that certitude results from a judgment. What we seem to have in the case of *scientia* are two propositional attitudes conjoined—first, the cognition, or apprehension of the proposition; second, a judgment that results in a determination concerning that proposition. What does "determination to one thing" mean in this context? Certitude and necessary truth need to be closely connected, since *scientia*, which is the product of judicative reasoning, is both a necessary truth and includes complete certitude. I suggest that what Aquinas has in mind here is that certitude of cognition amounts to a second, conjoined apprehension: that the proposition is necessary. When cognizing a proposition, we can judge whether or not its contradictory is possible. If we judge that we cannot conceive of any possibility but the truth of the proposition (that is, if we cannot conceive that what we cognize could be otherwise), then we have determined and firmly adhered to the one option left— that the proposition is necessarily true.[34] Thus *scientia* is the

---

[33] These two accounts of certitude—as determination to one thing and as firmness of adherence—are not identical. In cases of *scientia*, they are coextensive, but they can separate in certain circumstances. For more on this, see chapter 3.1.2.4.

[34] To help explain this position, here is a definitely non-Thomistic explanation: suppose you cognize some proposition P. You decide to judge whether or not P is necessary, and you do so by "looking" into other possible worlds. If you find some possible world where P has a truth value different than this one, then your attention would be divided between these two options for the truth value of P in any unspecified possible world. Should you find no possible world where the truth value of P is otherwise, then your attention would be fixed on the truth value of P as set—you would consider P to be necessary. This judgment about P is the same as being determined to only one thing—the truth value of P—and your adherence to that truth value for P would be firm.

epistemic state that cognizes a necessarily true conclusion and also includes a determination that the proposition is necessarily true.[35]

At this point the reader may wonder how certitude, if it is a recognition that the conclusion is necessary, could possibly apply to cognitions of contingent propositions, and how so to a "more or less" degree. Here I believe that Aquinas has in mind an analogous sense of certitude—not complete certitude, but certitude-to-a-degree. He sets up the analogy as follows: "But just as in the works of nature which succeed in the majority of cases certain levels are achieved—because the stronger the power of nature the more rarely does it fail to achieve its effect—so too in that process of reason which is not accompanied by compete certitude certain levels are found accordingly as one approaches more or less to complete certitude."[36] In nature, there is a sort of hierarchy concerning natural necessity: some causes necessitate their effects, which means that they bring about those effects 100 percent of the time. But of those causes that do not necessitate their effects, some yield their effects more often than others (ranging, suppose, from 1 percent of the time to 99 percent). Thus, those causes that bring about their effects more often are most similar to necessitating causes. The epistemic analogue here is that some reasoning (namely, acts of necessity) can yield complete

---

[35] Note that the certitude as determination to one thing by judging that the proposition cannot be otherwise does not correspond well to the certitude we have of *conclusions*—presumably, the former sort of certitude corresponds more to self-evident premises rather than conclusions. The certitude of conclusions of deductive reasoning is, for Aquinas, a by-product of the certitude of the premises and of deductive inference. I discuss Aquinas's views on this derived certitude in section 2.4.1.

[36] "sicut autem in rebus naturalibus, in his quae ut in pluribus agunt, gradus quidam attenditur (quia quanto virtus naturae est fortior, tanto rarius deficit a suo effectu) ita et in processu rationis, qui non est cum omnimoda certitudine, gradus aliquis invenitur, secundum quod magis et minus ad perfectam certitudinem acceditur." (PA prologue.n6)

certitude that the conclusion is necessary, but of other sorts of reasoning (acts of contingency), some yield conclusions that seem more likely to be true than others. Those that are most likely to be true seem to have some kind of certitude greater than that of those conclusions much less likely to be true. For more on this, see section 2.3.1.

2.2.2. The perfection criterion

There is a another cognition involved in *perfect scientia*, and that is a perfect apprehension of the truth of the conclusion. As we saw earlier, Aquinas introduces this cognition as a necessary condition of *perfect scientia* as follows:

> [T]o know something scientifically is to cognize it completely, which means to apprehend its truth perfectly. For the principles of a thing's being are the same as those of its truth, as is stated in *Metaphysics* II. Therefore, the scientific knower, if he is to cognize perfectly, must cognize the cause of the thing known scientifically; hence he says, "when we think that we cognize the cause." But if he were to cognize the cause by itself, he would not yet cognize the effect actually—which would be to know it absolutely—but only virtually, which is the same as knowing in a qualified sense and incidentally. Consequently, one who knows scientifically in the full sense must cognize the application of the cause to the effect; hence he adds, "as the cause of that fact."[37]

---

[37] "...quod scire aliquid est perfecte cognoscere ipsum, hoc autem est perfecte apprehendere veritatem ipsius: eadem enim sunt principia esse rei et veritatis ipsius, ut patet ex ii metaphysicae. oportet igitur scientem, si est perfecte cognoscens, quod cognoscat causam rei scitae. si autem cognosceret causam tantum, nondum cognosceret effectum in actu, quod est scire simpliciter, sed virtute tantum, quod est scire secundum quid et quasi per accidens. et ideo oportet scientem simpliciter cognoscere etiam applicationem causae ad effectum." (PA I.4.n5)

From the observation that the principles of a thing's being are the same as those of its truth, Aquinas notes that there are two necessary conditions for perfect apprehension of the truth of a conclusion: first, we must apprehend the cause of it; and second, we must not merely apprehend the cause of the conclusion, but apprehend *how* the cause brings about the conclusion.

Aquinas says that "the principles of a thing's being are the same as those of its truth." In order to understand this, we must take a quick look at the grounds for the truth of a thing (*res*). Though Aquinas talks in terms of the truth of things, which makes it seem that objects can be true, this is just a loose and casual way of speaking (see footnote 25). That truth does not attach (at least properly speaking) to objects is clear from what he says in his commentary on the *Metaphysics* VI:

> [W]hen the intellect forms a concept of mortal rational animal, it has within itself a likeness of man; but it does not for that reason cognize (*cognoscit*) that it has this likeness, since it does not judge that "Man is a mortal rational animal." There is truth and falsity, then, only in this second operation of the intellect, according to which it not only possesses a likeness of the thing understood (*intellectae*) but also reflects on this likeness by cognizing (*cognoscendo*) it and by making a judgment about it. Hence it is evident from this that the truth is not found in things but only in the mind, and that it depends upon combination and separation.[38]

---

[38] "cum enim intellectus concipit hoc quod est animal rationale mortale, apud se similitudinem hominis habet; sed non propter hoc cognoscit se hanc similitudinem habere, quia non iudicat hominem esse animal rationale et mortale: et ideo in hac sola secunda operatione intellectus est veritas et falsitas, secundum quam non solum intellectus habet similitudinem rei intellectae, sed etiam super ipsam similitudinem reflectitur, cognoscendo et diiudicando ipsam. ex his igitur patet, quod veritas non est in rebus, sed solum in mente, et etiam in compositione et divisione." (M VI.4.c1236)

Truth and falsity properly attach to our judgments and not the things (objects) about which we judge. Thus, the object *man* is neither true nor false, but the judgment "man is a mortal rational animal" can be true or false. From this it is clear that for Aquinas the things that are true or false are the judgments themselves, that is, that the propositions about which we form judgments are themselves true or false. We opened with "the principles of a thing's being (*esse*) are the same as those of its truth." But then what are the principles of a thing's being?

What Aquinas has in mind here is that the being of a thing—the object itself—is the ground for the truth of any proposition about that thing. He says that "a thing's being is the cause of any true judgment which the mind makes about a thing...."[39] Briefly, Aquinas's theory of truth is this: a judgment of a proposition can be counted as true only if the content of the proposition resembles the state of affairs that it is purported to represent.[40] Aquinas says:

> Now it must be noted that any kind of cognition (*cognitio*) attains its completion (*perficatur*) as a result of the likeness of the thing cognized (*cognitae*) existing in the cognizing subject (*cognoscente*). Therefore, just as the completion (*perfectio*) of the thing cognized (*cognitae*) depends upon this thing having the

---

[39] "et hoc ideo, quia esse rei est causa verae existimationis quam mens habet de re. verum enim et falsum non est in rebus, sed in mente, ut dicetur in sexto huius." (M II.2.c299)

[40] The examples used here concern propositions that represent material particulars, and thus it is natural to refer to the "state of affairs" represented by the propositions. This is not meant to suggest that propositions only represent states of affairs of material particulars—Aquinas holds that propositions about nonmaterial objects (e.g., mathematical objects) can also be true. For the sake of brevity, I will continue to refer to states of affairs as the referents of propositions, but we should understand this expression to refer not only to states of material objects but also to non-material ones. Some readers may prefer something like "relation of ideas" in cases like these, to "states of affairs." I mean for "states of affairs" to be metaphysically broad enough to cover all such cases, both sensible and intelligible.

kind of form which makes it to be such and such a thing, in a similar fashion the completion (*perfectio*) of the act of cognition (*cognitionis*) depends upon the cognizing subject having the likeness of this form. ...truth and falsity designate perfections of cognition (*cognitionum*).[41]

What we conceive when we form and judge propositions are likenesses of objects—we don't have a man in the mind when we judge that "man is a mortal rational animal"; instead, we have a likeness of a man, and when we judge that man is a mortal rational animal, we judge that our likeness of man is such that it contains mortality, rationality and animality. This proposition counts as true if the state of affairs represented by the likenesses in the mind correspond to the state of affairs of actual men. So though truth and falsity are properties of propositions, the ground of the truth or falsity of a proposition are the objects (or perhaps the state of affairs) that the propositions represent.

We're now prepared to understand what Aquinas meant when he said that "the principles of a thing's being are the same as those of its truth." The principles of a thing's being are those causes (principles) that bring about the state of affairs in which the thing exists. These principles, since they cause the state of affairs, also serve as the epistemic ground (or cause) of the truth of any proposition that represents that state of affairs. We now turn to how this observation yields the two necessary conditions specified by Aquinas for perfect apprehension of the truth of a conclusion: first, that we must know the cause of it; and second, that we must not merely know the cause of the conclusion but *how* the cause brings it about that the conclusion obtains.

---

[41] "sciendum est autem, quod cum quaelibet cognitio perficiatur per hoc quod similitudo rei cognitae est in cognoscente; sicut perfectio rei cognitae consistit in hoc quod habet talem formam per quam est res talis, ita perfectio cognitionis consistit in hoc, quod habet similitudinem formae praedictae.... ita verum et falsum designant perfectiones cognitionum." (M VI.4.c1234)

As observed above, the truth of a proposition depends on its resembling that state of affairs to which it refers. The cause of that state of affairs is thus the cause of that by which a proposition can be counted as true. In his commentary on *Metaphysics* V, Aquinas holds "perfect" and "whole" (*totum*) to be synonymous[42]—perfect apprehension of the truth of a proposition amounts to apprehending the whole truth, which involves apprehending not only the state of affairs but its cause. Thus, apprehending the cause of a thing is a necessary condition for having a perfect apprehension of its truth. However, simply apprehending the cause of the conclusion is not sufficient for perfect apprehension of its truth. One also needs to apprehend that the cause does indeed bring about the effect. For instance, we can't know why a car crashed simply by knowing that the brake cable was cut—it is only when we know that it was *because* the brake cable was cut and *how* this resulted in a crash that we start to have a more perfect apprehension of the truth concerning the car crash. Thus, in order to have a perfect apprehension of the truth of a conclusion, we must apprehend three things: (1) the grounds for the truth of the conclusion (i.e., the state of affairs referred to by the conclusion), (2) the cause of those grounds (i.e., the principles), and (3) that (and more importantly, how) the principles caused the state of affairs referred to by the conclusion.

---

[42] In M V.18.c1033. See also P III.11.c385.

2.2.3. Perfect scientia — *summary*

Aquinas defines *perfect scientia* as follows.

<u>S has *perfect scientia* that P</u> =df (1) S cognizes P; and
(2) S has complete certitude that P; and
(3) S has a perfect apprehension of the truth of P.

In order for the first condition to be met, S must have a thought that P, though cognizing P does not in itself involve any attitude concerning the truth or falsity of P. In order for the second condition to be met, P must be necessary and S must have determined that P is necessary. In order for the third condition to be met, S must know the grounds for the truth of P, and that and how such grounds actually result in the truth of P. Aquinas does note that there are various kinds of *scientia,* differing in both the degree of certitude and the presence or absence of perfect apprehension of the truth of P, but that the *scientia* that satisfies the conditions above is the "proper and perfect" form (*proprius et perfectus*).[43] In addition to this notion of *scientia,* Aquinas also considers less perfect or complete notions of *scientia,* as well as a very different but related notion of *scientia*—that of a field of study. I turn now to these accounts.

2.3. *Other varieties of* scientia *in the* Posterior Analytics

The *Posterior Analytics* gives three criteria for what I have dubbed *perfect scientia,* and the easiest way to create weaker versions of *scientia* would be to vary the extent to which the

---

[43] See PA I.4.n8.

certitude and perfect apprehension criteria obtain. (Presumably, the first criterion, that the subject cognizes the proposition, cannot be weakened for Aquinas, since it seems that one either cognizes P or does not.) Aquinas considers both sorts of variations on *perfect scientia*.

2.3.1. Scientia *obtained by weakening the certitude criterion*

As originally considered (in 2.1 and 2.2), *scientia* resulted from the cognition of a necessary conclusion. When the definition of *perfect scientia* was presented, this cognition of necessity was cashed out as certitude of absolute necessity; however, we can easily speak of certitude of the truth of a proposition without having to appeal to its being absolutely necessary. In lectures 37-41 of book I of his commentary on the *Posterior Analytics*, Aquinas concerns himself with comparisons between different sorts of demonstrations and different sorts of *scientia*. In lecture 41, he observes that one way in which some sciences can be considered to have more certitude than others is by examining how closely tied to sensible matter the subject matter of the science is. The propositions of some sciences depend on mutable, contingent matter, and thus would come with less certitude (less assuredness of necessity) than the propositions of, for instance, a purely mathematical (and *a priori*) science. Arithmetic, Aquinas points out, has more certitude than music, for "lack of certitude arises from matter's changes. Hence the closer one gets to matter, the less certain the science."[44] Aquinas clearly is prepared to grant that there are sciences that deal with matter, and that the propositions of that science cannot be known with complete certitude; thus we

---

[44] "quia incertitudo causatur propter transmutabilitatem materiae sensibilis; unde quanto magis acceditur ad eam, tanto scientia est minus certa." (PA I.41.n3)

can infer that there must be a form of *scientia* that involves a certitude less than complete.

In book I, lecture 42 of his commentary on the *Posterior Analytics*, we see that Aquinas has a notion of certitude different from complete certitude in mind: "It should be noted, however, that there happens to be demonstration of things which occur, as it were, for the most part, insofar as there is in them something of necessity. But the necessary, as it is stated in *Physics* II, is not the same in natural things (which are true for the most part and fail to be true in a few cases) as in the disciplines, i.e. in mathematical things, which are always true."[45] The certitude that he has in mind here derives from some sort of natural regularity that occurs for the most part. He gives the example of an olive being generated from an olive seed: "…if a demonstration is formed from that which is prior in generation, it does not conclude with necessity, unless perhaps we take as necessary the fact that an olive seed is frequently generated of an olive, because it does this according to a property of its nature, unless it is impeded."[46] Aquinas seems to be referring to the powers of natural causes—though effects of these causes cannot be deduced with absolute certainty (the causes don't necessitate their typical effects). He holds that the efficacy of these sorts of causes is sufficiently regular to grant that a weak variety of *scientia* results. In book II, lecture 12 of his commentary on the *Posterior Analytics*, he says, "Yet such demonstrations do

---

[45] "est autem considerandum quod de his quidem quae sunt sicut frequenter, contingit esse demonstrationem, in quantum in eis est aliquid necessitatis. necessarium autem, ut dicitur in ii physicorum, aliter est in naturalibus, quae sunt vera ut frequenter, et deficiunt in minori parte; et aliter in disciplinis, idest in mathematicis, quae sunt semper vera." (PA I.42.n3)

[46] "unde si fiat demonstratio ex eo quod est prius in generatione, non concludet ex necessitate; nisi forte accipiamus hoc ipsum esse necessarium, semen olivae ut frequenter esse generativum olivae, quia hoc facit secundum proprietatem suae naturae, nisi impediatur." (PA.I.42.n3)

not enable one to know that what is concluded is true absolutely but only in a qualified sense, namely, that it is true in the majority of cases. Hence sciences of this kind fall short of sciences which deal with things absolutely necessary, so far as the certitude of demonstration is concerned."[47]

2.3.2. Scientia *obtained by weakening the perfection criterion*

A second variety of *scientia* can be had by weakening the perfection criterion. A subject that has perfect apprehension of the truth of P knows the cause of P. In book I, lecture 23 of his commentary on the *Posterior Analytics*, Aquinas tells us that this knowledge of the cause of P gives us knowledge of *why* (*propter quid*) P is true. We might have a weaker sort of knowledge than this: we could know *that* (*quia*) P is true, but not know *why* P is true. In this case, one could have cognition with complete

---

[47] "huiusmodi tamen demonstrationes non faciunt simpliciter scire verum esse quod concluditur, sed secundum quid, scilicet quod sit verum ut in pluribus; et sic etiam principia quae assumuntur, veritatem habent. unde huiusmodi scientiae deficiunt a scientiis, quae sunt de necessariis absolute, quantum ad certitudinem demonstrationis." (PA II.12.n5) At this point I would like to raise a red flag: this certitude-weakened form of *scientia* does not allow one to know conclusions as absolutely necessary but only "that it is true in the majority of cases." But the reader will recall that acts of contingency are those kinds of reasoning in which the cognitions are connected not necessarily but only contingently. This sort of certitude-weakened *scientia* would thus seem to be an act of contingency, not an act of necessity. But as we saw in section 2.1, acts of contingency yield opinion (or suspicion) and acts of necessity yield *scientia*. So how are we to understand this certitude-weakened *scientia*? Is it actually a form of *scientia* or is it opinion? Or do the two shade into each other? It is not entirely clear how Aquinas would resolve these questions. However, in chapter 3.1.1, I argue that Aquinas intends each of faith, opinion and *scientia* to be quite distinct from the others. Allowing a certitude-weakened *scientia* that counts both as *scientia* and as contingent causes problems for Aquinas's account of faith as I present it in chapter 3, and for his solution to the problem of faith and reason as I present it in chapter 5. This is a thorny problem not easily resolved, and unfortunately it must be put off because there is not enough space to engage it here.

certitude *that* P, and thus a sort of *scientia, scientia quia*, but not *perfect scientia* or *scientia propter quid*. In lecture 23, Aquinas provides an example of the difference between the two kinds of *scientia*. With *scientia quia*, we know *that* the conclusion is true but not *why*—this often occurs when we know that some effect obtains but do not know its cause. He provides as an example the following demonstration *quia*:

(a)   Whatever does not twinkle is near.
(b)   The planets do not twinkle.
∴ (c)   The planets are near.

Setting aside how we know the premises (a) and (b), we may come to know that the conclusion (c), which follows from (a) and (b), is true, but we do not have *scientia propter quid* of the conclusion. That the planets are near follows from the premises, but the truth of the premises does not explain *why* the planets are near. In fact, it is the nearness of the planets that explains why they do not twinkle, as in the following demonstration *propter quid* given by Aquinas:

(d)   Every planet is near.
(e)   Any planet which is near does not twinkle.
∴ (f)   No planet twinkles.

We could have *scientia propter quid* about the conclusion (f) because the non-twinkling of the planets is explained by their nearness. The premises (d) and (e) explain *why* (f) is true, whereas (a) and (b) do not explain *why* (c) is true; thus we may have *scientia propter quid* about (f) but only *scientia quia* about (c).[48]

---

[48] Other ways one can have *scientia quia* but not *scientia propter quid* are considered in PA I.24-25. I will not cover them here, because it serves my

2.3.3. *A different notion of* scientia

We've seen that Aquinas employs variations in the notion of *scientia* both in the degree of certitude about a proposition and in the degree of perfection of the apprehension of it. In addition to these senses of *scientia*, Aquinas introduces a completely different, though dependent, sense of *scientia*, one I shall translate as "science." Roughly speaking, sciences in the commentary on the *Posterior Analytics* are similar to our modern sciences in that they are fields of knowledge or inquiry unified by subject matter. The account of science follows from the definition of reason set out earlier in this chapter:

> [A] science is said to be one from the fact that it is concerned with one generic subject. The reason for this is that the process of science of any given thing is, as it were, a movement of reason. Now the unity of any motion is judged principally from its terminus, as is clear in *Physics* V. Consequently, the unity of any science must be judged from its end or terminus. But the end or terminus of a science is the genus concerning which the science treats: because in speculative sciences nothing else is sought except a knowledge of some generic subject; in practical sciences what is intended as the end is the construction of its subject.[49]

---

purpose to point out the distinction between knowledge *that* and knowledge *why*, but does not serve my purposes to go into detail describing all the various ways we can have *scientia quia.*

[49] "dicit ergo primo quod scientia dicitur una, ex hoc quod est unius generis subiecti. cuius ratio est, quia processus scientiae cuiuslibet est quasi quidam motus rationis. cuiuslibet autem motus unitas ex termino principaliter consideratur, ut patet in v physicorum, et ideo oportet quod unitas scientiae consideretur ex fine sive ex termino scientiae. est autem cuiuslibet scientiae finis sive terminus, genus circa quod est scientia: quia in speculativis scientiis nihil aliud quaeritur quam cognitio generis subiecti; in practicis autem scientiis intenditur quasi finis constructio ipsius subiecti." (PA I.41.n7)

Reason is a movement from one thought to another, and *scientia* is a species of reason. Various movements that lead to *scientia* can be unified by identifying the end for which those acts are performed. Certain kinds of reasoning to *scientia*, namely the speculative, are defined as having no other end than attaining knowledge of some "generic subject"—that is, a subject matter falling under some particular genus. Thus, acts of speculative reasoning that share the same subject will fall under the same science. If, suppose, we come to have *scientia* whose subject is magnitude (for instance, *scientia* that *the interior angles of a triangle equal two right angles*) we have thus come to knowledge of geometry, whose specific genus is magnitude.[50]

Scientia-producing reasoning acts are united into a science by having the same genus as subject matter. What still needs to be determined is how the genus of one science will be differentiated from the genus of another. To this Aquinas says, "...since something scientifically knowable is the proper object of a science, the sciences will not be diversified according to a material diversity of their scientifically knowable objects, but according to their formal diversity."[51] By a "material diversity" Aquinas means something akin to what we might describe as the objects themselves. One way to divide the sciences into subjects according to material diversity would be according to natural kinds of objects; thus we might have a science of man, another of birds (or perhaps of falcons, eagles, etc.), fish, rocks, trees, etc. Or perhaps a division of subjects according to material diversity might be according to functional parts: we might split the sciences into the science of legs, arms, stomachs, etc. Dividing sciences according to

---

[50] See PA I.41.n7.

[51] "cum ergo scibile sit proprium obiectum scientiae, non diversificabuntur scientiae secundum diversitatem materialem scibilium, sed secundum diversitatem eorum formalem." (PA I.41.n11)

material diversity looks unpromising for its arbitrariness. Aquinas, in addition, has a principled reason to prefer formal diversity as grounds for division: sciences are constituted *by* things in virtue of the fact that we have *scientia about* them. At root, therefore, sciences are epistemological constructions, not metaphysical ones, and how sciences should be divided is not by the material objects with which they are concerned but by the ways in which the *scientia* of its subject matter is obtained. That is, we gain *scientia* of a proposition by means of a form of reasoning (demonstration) that starts from principles that are better known, prior to, and cause the conclusions of which we have *scientia* (see section 2.4.1 below). Differences in principles are, at root, what distinguish differences in our *scientia*, and thus sciences should be distinguished on this basis. Here is Aquinas's argument:

> Now just as the formality of visible is taken from light, through which color is seen, so the formal aspect of a scientifically knowable object is taken according to the principles from which something is scientifically known. Therefore, no matter how diverse certain scientifically knowable objects may be in their nature, so long as they are known through the same principles, they pertain to one science, because they will not differ precisely as scientifically knowable. For they are scientifically knowable in virtue of their own principles.[52]

Support for this position is given by several examples:

> This is made clear by an example, namely, that human voices differ a great deal according to their nature from the

---

[52] "sicut autem formalis ratio visibilis sumitur ex lumine, per quod color videtur, ita formalis ratio scibilis accipitur secundum principia, ex quibus aliquid scitur. et ideo quantumcunque sint aliqua diversa scibilia secundum suam naturam, dummodo per eadem principia sciantur, pertinent ad unam scientiam; quia non erunt iam diversa in quantum sunt scibilia. sunt enim per sua principia scibilia." (PA I.41.n11)

sounds of inanimate bodies; but because the consonance of human voices and the sounds of inanimate bodies is considered according to the same principles, the science of music, which considers both, is one science. On the other hand, if there are things which have the same nature but are considered according to diverse principles, it is obvious that they pertain to diverse sciences. Thus, the mathematical body is never really distinct from a natural body; yet because the mathematical body is known through the principles of quantity, but a natural body through the principles of motion, the science of geometry and the science of nature are not the same.[53]

The distinction between sciences clearly depends on the distinction between their first principles, a distinction that results in different *ways* in which the propositions are known. Different first principles bring about different sorts of *scientia*, and the unity of any given science results from the subject matter of that science belonging to a particular genus.[54]

---

[53] "sicut patet quod voces humanae multum differunt secundum suam naturam a sonis inanimatorum corporum; sed tamen, quia secundum eadem principia attenditur consonantia in vocibus humanis et sonis inanimatorum corporum, eadem est scientia musicae, quae de utrisque considerat. si vero aliqua sint eadem secundum naturam, et tamen per diversa principia considerentur, manifestum est quod ad diversas scientias pertinent. sicut corpus mathematicum non est separatum subiecto a corpore naturali; quia tamen corpus mathematicum cognoscitur per principia quantitatis, corpus autem naturale per principia motus, non est eadem scientia geometria et naturalis." (PA I.41.n11)

[54] The principles of a science serve as the grounds for the truth of the conclusion, that is, they cause the conclusion to be true. This statement can be interpreted in two ways: it can be taken as an observation about epistemology (earlier thoughts bring about later thoughts) or about metaphysics (A, which makes the first thought true, causes B, which in turn causes the later thought). The account of science just given seems to allow the ambiguity to remain. Are the sciences divided as they are because we distinguish their first principles on purely epistemological grounds (by their various modes of apprehension) or are the sciences divided on metaphysical grounds first, and for this reason

2.4. The epistemology of reason and scientia

Thus far I have tried to develop an exegesis of Aquinas's account of reason and his account of its principal product, *scientia*. What remains to be discussed are the consequences for epistemology that result from this account. The account of reasoning supplied by Aquinas does not, at root, have much in the way of epistemological consequences. Since reason, simply understood, is a movement from one cognition to another, a movement that can produce a variety of epistemic states in the thinker (*scientia*, opinion, suspicion, etc.), reason itself is not a particularly interesting epistemic category. This should not be surprising, since reason, according to Aquinas, is simply a natural power of the mind, and reasoning *simpliciter* is simply an exercise of that power. Reasoning acts can be divided into various epistemic categories, however, and from these a more interesting epistemology can be constructed. Aquinas divides reasoning acts into three broad categories: those in which premises and conclusions are necessarily connected, those in which premises and conclusions are contingently connected, and those in which premises are not connected to conclusions. The remainder of this chapter is concerned primarily with the first kind of reasoning act, acts of necessity; the second kind of reasoning act will be considered when we discuss faith in chapter 3, and in section 2.4.2 we will consider some cases of the third kind (demonstrative errors that produce falsehoods). The paradigm case of acts of necessity is the reasoning act that results in *scientia*, so we will first turn to the epistemology of *perfect scientia*.

---

we make subsequent epistemic divisions? Aquinas scholars are divided on this issue. For a metaphysical division of the sciences, see, for instance, MacDonald, "Theory of Knowledge" (1993) 170. For the opposing view, see Jenkins, *Knowledge and Faith in Thomas Aquinas* (1997) 258 fn 5.

If you reason to *perfect scientia*, you not only have cognition of a necessary truth, but also cognition *that* the proposition is necessary and *why* it is true. As a basis for anti-skeptical epistemology, *perfect scientia* appears to be a good starting point, since someone who has it should be immune from skeptical worries. If we can have *perfect scientia* about divine matters, and the propositions about which we have such *scientia* contradict matters of faith, then it would appear that no epistemic reconciliation between faith and reason would be possible. However, we must first address two immediate epistemological worries about *perfect scientia*: "How do we get *perfect scientia*?" and "How do we know we have *perfect scientia*?" Without knowing the circumstances under which we obtain *perfect scientia* or when we have it, we would be unable to test whether or not faith and reason were epistemically compatible.[55] We shall consider each of these questions in turn.

2.4.1. Demonstration: Reasoning that produces scientia

After providing a definition of *perfect scientia* in lecture 4 of his commentary on the *Posterior Analytics*, Aquinas then provides a definition of demonstration. Demonstration is a syllogism that produces *perfect scientia*. Thus "demonstration" is the name of that reasoning act that starts with some proposition(s) and ends with *perfect scientia* of another. In the remainder of lecture 4, Aquinas discusses exactly what qualities a syllogism must satisfy in order count as demonstration. The proposed definition is as follows:

---

[55] I should note here that Aquinas does not seem particularly struck by these epistemic worries. In considering them, I am making a purely dialectical move—by considering the worries concerning how we get *scientia* and how we know that we have it, we can better understand Aquinas's account of *scientia*.

<u>X is a demonstration</u> =df   (1) X is a syllogism that proceeds
from principles that are:
(a) true, (b) first, and
(c) immediate, and
(d) better known than, (e) prior
to, and (f) causes of:
(2) a conclusion that is known
with *perfect scientia.*

I will leave the in-depth analysis of Aquinas's definition of demonstration to those who have already provided one[56] and instead give only a few brief comments on this definition that suit my immediate purposes.

This definition of demonstration is provided in order to satisfy the jointly necessary and sufficient conditions that establish *perfect scientia.* In the course of his defense of the definition, Aquinas does not start with some common conception of demonstration that happens to be something that produces *perfect scientia*; rather, the definition is provided and defended precisely *because* it produces *perfect scientia.* In other words, in developing this notion of demonstration, Aquinas is seeking out a reasoning act that results in *perfect scientia.*[57] In order for a reasoning act to result in *perfect scientia*, it must produce a cognition of the proposition, a cognition of its certitude, and a perfect apprehension of the truth of the proposition. Perfect apprehension of the truth of a proposition, as we saw before, entails that we know the causes or grounds for the truth of that proposition. The conditions specified in this definition of demonstration are

---

[56] See MacDonald, "Theory of Knowledge," and Jenkins, *Knowledge and Faith.* For a thorough account of an interpretation of how Aristotle understood these conditions, see McKirahan (*Principles and Proofs: Aristotle's Theory of Demonstrative Science*, 1992).

[57] Aquinas does seem to hold that other acts of the reason can produce *scientia* that is less than perfect—for example, *scientia quia.*

necessary for perfect apprehension of the truth of a conclusion for the following reasons.

(a) The premises must be *true*. Though true conclusions may follow from false premises in ordinary syllogisms, the premises in a demonstration must be true. For if the premises were not true, then we would have no basis for cognizing the truth of the conclusion (that is, we would have no basis for *knowing* that the conclusion is true). Aquinas says, "Now what is not true does not exist, for *to be* and *to be true* are convertible. Therefore, anything scientifically knowable (*scitur*) must be true. Consequently, the conclusion of a demonstration which does beget scientific knowing (*facit scire*) must be true, and *a fortiori* its premises."[58] If some proposition is not true, then its ground does not exist (that is, it has no ground for its truth). Thus, if one of the premises in a syllogism is false, it could not serve as an epistemic ground for the truth of the conclusion. And if one does not apprehend the grounds of the truth of the conclusion (that is, have perfect apprehension of its truth), then one cannot have *perfect scientia* of the conclusion.

(b) & (c) The premises must be *first* and *immediate*. Though one might be able to have cognition of a true conclusion if one came to the truth of it by accident, one would not have perfect apprehension of the truth of the conclusion. And if premises in a syllogism are not immediate, then they do not serve as grounds for the truth of the conclusion. What Aquinas has in mind here is that immediate premises are known in themselves, but mediate premises are known in virtue of some intermediary. Self-evident propositions, for instance, can be known immediately, but theorems are known as a result of proof, and thus are known only

---

[58] "nam esse et esse verum convertuntur. oportet ergo id quod scitur esse verum. et sic conclusionem demonstrationis, quae facit scire, oportet esse veram, et per consequens eius propositiones." (PA I.4.n.13)

mediately. Mediate premises cannot serve as epistemic grounds for conclusions of which we have perfect apprehension of its truth, since the grounds for the truth of these mediate premises rest in some other premises from which they were derived. Aquinas says, "Suppose, therefore, that a demonstrator syllogizes from demonstrable, i.e. mediate, premises. Now he either possesses a demonstration of those premises or he does not. If he does not, then he does not know the premises in a scientific way; nor consequently, the conclusion because of the premises. But if he does possess their demonstration, then, since one may not proceed to infinity in demonstrations, principles immediate and indemonstrable must be reached."[59] Either the truth of a conclusion of a demonstration is grounded in immediate premises, which need no proof, or are mediate, which must first be proven in order for there to be perfect apprehension of the truth of the conclusion. Thus, a demonstration that produces perfect apprehension of the truth of the conclusion must come either from immediate premises or from mediate premises that are first resolved into immediate ones. "First" is taken as synonymous to "immediate," though their senses differ slightly—"first" identifies premises as having no prior, "immediate" simply to the fact that they are not mediately known (which would also entail that they are "first" principles for us).[60]

---

[59] "detur ergo quod aliquis demonstrator syllogizet ex demonstrabilibus, sive mediatis: aut ergo habet illorum demonstrationem, aut non habet: si non habet, ergo non scit praemissa, et ita nec conclusionem propter praemissa; si autem habet, cum in demonstrationibus non sit abire in infinitum, ut infra ostendet, tandem erit devenire ad aliqua immediata et indemonstrabilia." (PA I.4.n.14)

[60] There is another sense of "immediate" beyond the meaning "indemonstrable" used here. "Immediate" is also used to pick out the result of an act of *intellectus*, or understanding, in which we intellectually "see" the truth of a proposition. For more on this, see chapter 3.1.2.4.

That premises must be first also seems to be necessary for satisfying the certitude condition of *perfect scientia*. Aquinas holds that the certitude in *scientia* comes from the premises: "However, the case is otherwise in regard to first things, which do not have a cause. For these are understood in virtue of themselves; and such cognition (*cognitio*) of these things is more certain than any *scientia*, because it is from such understanding (*intelligentia*) that *scientia* acquires its certitude."[61]

(d) & (e) & (f) The premises must be *better known, prior to,* and *causes of* the conclusion. With perfect apprehension of the truth of the conclusion, the grounds for the truth of the conclusion are apprehended. In order for us to be able to apprehend these grounds, the premises must be the cause of the truth of the conclusion—if we did not know the cause of the truth of a proposition, we could not perfectly know the grounds for its truth. Similarly, the premises must be better known and prior to the conclusion: prior, because in order for the premises to serve as grounds, they must be known *before*; and better known, because if the premises are grounds *by which* the conclusion becomes known, they must have been initially better known than the conclusion.

This definition of demonstration may adequately cover all the jointly necessary and sufficient conditions needed to bring about *perfect scientia*; what they leave unclear, however, is whether we demonstrate often, if at all. The certitude of the necessity of *perfect scientia* would seem to rule out any contingent premises, which would rule out most propositions about the natural world. Further, it is not clear how often we know the causes of the truth of a proposition. Aside from analytic or *a priori* connections between propositions, we may never actually have *perfect*

---

[61] "sed de primis, quae non habent causam, est alia ratio. illa enim per se intelliguntur; et talis eorum cognitio est certior omni scientia, quia ex tali intelligentia scientia certitudinem habet." (PA I.42.n.8)

apprehension of the truth of any proposition. Thus demonstration, as defined above, though perhaps applicable to logic and geometry, may be too stringent to serve as an example of reasoning to be contrasted with faith.[62] For, if the standard of reason were held to be demonstration, instances of faith along with many other cases of reasoning fail to meet that standard. Rather than typical exemplar, demonstration seems more like an idealization of reason. However, other weaker notions of *scientia* and demonstration are considered in the *Posterior Analytics*. Though we shall not consider them here (they will be considered in chapter 4), the weaker notions of *scientia* considered earlier in this chapter have correspondingly weaker varieties of demonstration.

The answer to the epistemic worry "How do we get *perfect scientia*?" seems to be "by demonstration." But this answer seems quite unsatisfactory. Since demonstration is defined as that act of discursive reason that produces *perfect scientia*, its introduction seems a rather empty response to the worry about how we get it— we get it by the act that satisfies the necessary and sufficient conditions for producing it. On the other hand, this response is perfectly straightforward—we do, in fact, syllogize to conclusions. Some of these syllogisms are of such a nature that when we perform them, the result is *perfect scientia* of the conclusion. Let us set aside, for the time being, worries that demonstration inadequately answers *how* we get *perfect scientia*, and turn now to

---

[62] Aquinas seems to recognize the limitations of the applicability of demonstration. In M II.5.c336, he says that demonstration should be used "only in the case of those things which have no matter," for these things have certitude in virtue of being unchangeable. Mathematics, because it is abstracted from matter, is demonstrable, as is the science of celestial bodies, because they are unchanging. Since natural philosophy is concerned with changeable matter, according to Aquinas "[demonstration] does not belong to natural philosophy."

the more pressing epistemological concern of how do we know that we have it.

2.4.2. How do we know that we have perfect scientia?

Though demonstration guarantees *scientia*, Aquinas admits that we can be wrong in thinking that we have demonstrated a conclusion. In the case of the eternity of the world, for instance (which we will cover in more detail in chapter 4), Aquinas considers whether it is an article of faith or a demonstrable conclusion that the world began[63]—and given that he does not think it is demonstrable, it follows that others have mistakenly thought so (and mistakenly thought their arguments to be demonstrations).[64] In the commentary on the *Posterior Analytics*, lectures 27-30, Aquinas is explicitly concerned with demonstrative error. In these chapters, he covers in some detail a large number of fallacies that yield false premises, false conclusions, or syllogistic failures (failures that result in an argument form that is not a syllogism). It is clear from these chapters that we can (and probably do) often fail to demonstrate some conclusions, despite the fact that we believe we have demonstrated adequately. In these cases, we do not have *perfect scientia* of the conclusion, because we have not provided a demonstration. As it is with any fallacy, we can avoid demonstrative error by carefully checking our reasoning.

Perfect scientia involves three cognitions—cognition of the conclusion, perfect apprehension of its truth, and certitude. We can mistake some syllogisms (or nonsyllogistic argument forms) for demonstrations, but it would seem that we cannot be mistaken

---

[63] In ST I.46.1.prol.

[64] In ST I.1.1, Aquinas states that truths about God that are investigated by reason come only to a few and are mixed with many errors. From the context of the article, I think it is clear that the reasoning Aquinas has in mind here is merely purported demonstration, that is, paralogism.

about having *perfect scientia*—for either we have the cognitions that constitute it or we do not. Perhaps a more efficient way of checking to see if one falsely claimed to have *perfect scientia* would be to assess whether one had all the proper cognitions, rather than to try to determine how one got to one's current epistemic state (i.e., whether one properly demonstrated or not). But what about these other cognitions? Is it possible to be mistaken about having a perfect apprehension of the truth of some proposition, or about having a certitude in its necessity? It would seem that Aquinas does hold that there can be some error here, for after he defines *perfect scientia* (as involving certitude and perfect apprehension of the truth), he says: "…both those who know scientifically and those who do not know in that way but believe that they do, take scientific knowing to be as above described. For those who do not know in a scientific manner but believe that they do, are convinced in the manner described, whereas those who know in a scientific manner do know in the manner described."[65] If we can be mistaken about having *perfect scientia*, then we should examine exactly how such mistakes can arise. We shall consider the possible sources of error first in certitude, then in perfect apprehension of the truth.

2.4.2.1. *Failure of certitude*

As mentioned above (in section 2.2.1), certitude is the result of a judgment, one that determines the intellect to one thing. If we are mistaken about having certitude with respect to some proposition, the source of the error resides in some erroneous judgment, namely, that the intellect is determined to only one

---

[65] "…quod tam scientes, quam non scientes, existimantes tamen se scire, hoc modo accipiunt scire sicut dictum est: non scientes enim qui existimant se scire, opinantur sic se habere in cognoscendo, sicut dictum est; scientes autem vere sic se habent." (PA I.4.n6)

thing, when it should not be. In the *Disputed Questions on Truth*, Aquinas gives a rough account of how the intellect comes to be determined to one thing:

> Sometimes, again, the possible intellect is so determined that it adheres to one member without reservation. This happens sometimes because of the intelligible object and sometimes because of the will. Furthermore, the intelligible object sometimes acts mediately, sometimes immediately. It acts immediately when the truth of the propositions is unmistakably clear immediately to the intellect from the intelligible objects themselves. This is the state of one who understands principles, which are cognized (*cognoscuntur*) as soon as the terms are known (*notis*), as the Philosopher says. Here, the very nature of the thing itself immediately determines the intellect to propositions of this sort. The intelligible object acts mediately, however, when the understanding, once it cognizes (*cognitis*) the definitions of the terms, is determined to one member of the contradictory proposition in virtue of first principles. This is the state of one who has *scientia*.
>
> Sometimes, however, the understanding can be determined to one side of a contradictory proposition neither immediately through the definitions of the terms, as is the case with principles, nor yet in virtue of principles, as is the case with conclusions from a demonstration. And in this situation our understanding is determined by the will, which chooses to assent to one side definitely and precisely because of something which is enough to move the will, though not enough to move the understanding, namely, since it seems good or fitting to assent to this side. And this is the state of one who believes (*credentis*). This may happen when someone

believes what another says because it seems fitting or useful to do so.[66]

According to Aquinas, the intellect is determined to one thing either by the object (what is being cognized) or by the will, and either of these can determine the intellect to one thing when it "moves" it (*movendum*). Again, we see the metaphor of motion bringing about cognition. With reason, we "move" from one cognition to another, that is, from premises to conclusion. In the case of certitude, however, our intellect is moved to considering only one possible truth value for some cognized proposition. When the intelligible object itself moves the intellect, the process is automatic—in virtue of our understanding the object we cannot help but consider it to be true (or false). Take, for instance, the principle of non-contradiction. When we understand the meaning of the terms that constitute the principle, we cannot help but hold that it is true.[67] The principle of non-contradiction itself is such

---

[66] "quandoque vero intellectus possibilis determinatur ad hoc quod totaliter adhaereat uni parti; sed hoc est quandoque ab intelligibili, quandoque a voluntate. ab intelligibili quidem quandoque quidem mediate, quandoque autem immediate. immediate quidem quando ex ipsis intelligibilibus statim veritas propositionum intellectui infallibiliter apparet. et haec est dispositio intelligentis principia, quae statim cognoscuntur notis terminis, ut philosophus dicit. et sic ex ipso quod quid est, immediate intellectus determinatur ad huiusmodi propositiones. mediate vero, quando cognitis definitionibus terminorum, intellectus determinatur ad alteram partem contradictionis, virtute primorum principiorum. et ista est dispositio scientis.

quandoque vero intellectus non potest determinari ad alteram partem contradictionis neque statim per ipsas definitiones terminorum, sicut in principiis, nec etiam virtute principiorum, sicut est in conclusionibus demonstrationis; determinatur autem per voluntatem, quae eligit assentire uni parti determinate et praecise propter aliquid, quod est sufficiens ad movendum voluntatem, non autem ad movendum intellectum, utpote quia videtur bonum vel conveniens huic parti assentire. et ista est dispositio credentis, ut cum aliquis credit dictis alicuius hominis, quia videtur ei decens vel utile." (QDV 14.1)

[67] These are principles that are known *per se*. See, for example, PA I.10.

that we must believe that it is true—it moves or determines our intellect to its truth—and this Aquinas has defined as certitude. In cases of *scientia*, the certitude comes not from the object directly, but mediately—when we understand the premises, it is in virtue of these that we are determined to the truth (or falsity) of the conclusion. Our cognitive ability to perform deductive inferences moves us to see that the conclusion must be true (or false), given the truth of the premises.[68] If the intelligible object itself moves the intellect to certitude, then we cannot be mistaken about having certitude, unless we can be mistaken about the truth of self-evident propositions or unless our deductive faculties fail. Aquinas holds that we cannot be mistaken in cases of self-evident propositions, and as far as I have been able to determine, he never considers the possibility that our deductive faculties might not be reliable.[69]

There are two ways in which we can come to have certitude—either when the intelligible object determines the intellect to one thing, or when the will does. Though I have claimed that no error is introduced in the first manner, the second certainly leaves room for deception. If the will can cause a cognition of certitude, how can we be sure that our certitude in some proposition is not the result of some unjustified act of will? I will leave this skeptical worry unanswered for the time being, but

---

[68] Using contemporary terms, we might say that when we have certitude about a principle, it is in virtue of its being analytic (which, for Aquinas, is that the notion of the predicate is contained in the notion of the subject—cf. M XI.4.c2210, M IV.5.c595); when we have certitude about a conclusion, it is in virtue of self-evident premises employed in a deductive inference.

[69] Aquinas holds that we cannot err in understanding first principles. See ST I.85.6, DA III.15.n826. I will not relate Aquinas's account of the reliability of our intellect here, but see Kretzmann, "Infallibility, Error and Ignorance" (1991) for a thorough treatment on error according to Aquinas.

shall return to it in chapter 3 when I consider Aquinas's account of faith and the role played by the will.

2.4.2.2. Failure of perfect apprehension of the truth

Given the account of perfect apprehension of the truth of a proposition, we can fail to have perfect apprehension in one of three ways: (1) we could judge falsely about a state of affairs (we judge that some proposition is true even though it does not resemble the state of affairs to which it refers), (2) we could fail to apprehend the principles that actually caused the conclusion, or (3) we could fail to apprehend how the principles bring about the conclusion (by, for instance, drawing a false causal inference). It seems that we would rarely succeed in having a perfect apprehension of the truth concerning the effects of natural causation, for we will frequently fail to understand precisely how causes brought about their effects. Our ability to understand nature, and consequently to perform adequate causal reasoning about natural processes, is something Aquinas is quite skeptical about: "...our cognition (*cognitio*) is weak to such a point that no philosopher would be able to investigate perfectly the nature of a single fly. Thus one reads that one philosopher spent thirty years in solitude that he might know (*cognosceret*) the nature of a bee."[70] Depending on the subject matter, then, failure to have a perfect apprehension of the truth of some proposition can be quite common, for it would be easy for someone to judge mistakenly something to be a cause of the truth of some proposition or to misapprehend how the cause brings it about that the conclusion is true.

---

[70] "Sed cognitio nostra adeo debilis est quod nullus philosophus potuit perfecte inuestigare naturam unius musce; unde legitur quod unus philosophus fuit triginta annis in solitudine ut cognosceret naturam apis." (*The Sermon-Conferences of St. Thomas Aquinas on the Apostles' Creed*, I.4.)

2.5. Conclusions

Aquinas holds that reasoning is a movement in the intellect from one cognition to another. This movement can be characterized in two different ways. First, reasoning acts can be divided by the logical relations between the two cognitions: the two cognitions can be necessarily connected (the first entails the second), and these are *acts of necessity*; the two cognitions can be only contingently connected (the first merely contingently implies the second), and these are *acts of contingency*; or the two cognitions may turn out not to be logically connected at all (the first neither entails nor contingently implies the second). Second, reasoning acts can be divided by the epistemic states that initiate or result from reasoning. Of particular interest are the following epistemic states: understanding (*intellectus*), which is concerned with grasping the initial cognitions (i.e., the first principles) of acts of necessity; *scientia*, which is concerned with grasping the final cognition (i.e., the conclusion) of acts of necessity; and opinion, which is concerned with grasping the conclusion of acts of contingency. This chapter is concerned primarily with *scientia*; the next discusses understanding and opinion in more detail.

Perfect scientia is an ideal form of *scientia*, involving not only certitude in the necessity of the conclusion, but a perfect apprehension of its truth. Since *perfect scientia* provides an apprehension that the conclusion is necessary, one can only come to such a cognition as a result of an act of necessity. With *perfect scientia*, one discerns both the necessity of the conclusion and the necessary connection between premises and conclusion (the latter is a necessary condition of perfect apprehension of the truth of the conclusion). Demonstration is the name of that kind of reasoning act that produces *perfect scientia* and provides a thorough knowledge both of the conclusion and of the reasons for its truth.

Though demonstration guarantees *perfect scientia*, we often fail to demonstrate and can even be fooled into thinking that we have demonstrated some conclusion when we have not done so (and also been fooled into thinking that we have *perfect scientia*, when we do not have it). There is a danger of demonstrative failure in three ways. First, we can fail to demonstrate when we commit demonstrative fallacies by employing false premises, false conclusions, or invalid arguments. These sorts of errors we generally know how to look for, and thus do not threaten the in-principle reliability of our ability to obtain (and know that we have) *perfect scientia*. Second, we can fail to have certitude about the conclusion, and thus fail to have *perfect scientia* about it. Certitude, which results when an intelligible object moves the intellect to accept the truth of the conclusion, is reliable, according to Aquinas. However, in cases when we assent to a conclusion as the result of an act of will rather than demonstration, there is a risk of error. Assent by willing introduces the possibility that certitude in the conclusion is misplaced, and that we can mistakenly hold ourselves to have certitude and *perfect scientia* of the conclusion. This epistemic worry is considered in chapters 3 and 4. Third, though demonstration guarantees perfect apprehension of the truth of the conclusion, we can fail to demonstrate by not satisfying the necessary conditions for perfect apprehension of its truth. We would fail to have perfect apprehension of the truth of a conclusion were we to employ false premises (in which case we would fail to apprehend the principles that cause the conclusion), or to draw a false conclusion (where we judge falsely about the state of affairs that results from some cause), but we can also fail to judge properly *how* or *that* the principles cause the conclusion. Though not a logical fallacy, such a failure in causal explanations would prevent a perfect apprehension of the truth of the conclusion, and thus prevent one from having *perfect scientia*.

The epistemological promise of *perfect scientia* is great—it provides not only knowledge of the conclusion, but knowledge that it is necessary and *why* it is true; when we have it, it is infallible. However, the conditions for obtaining *perfect scientia* are severe and extremely difficult to obtain, and we can be mistaken in attributing it to ourselves. These concerns will be taken up again in chapter 4, when we consider the limitations of reason in matters of faith.

AQUINAS'S ACCOUNT OF FAITH

3.1. *The movement of reason revisited*

The last chapter presented Aquinas's account of reason generically as a movement from one cognition to another. The *Posterior Analytics* is primarily concerned with one such movement, demonstration, which involves a movement from cognition of necessarily true premises to a cognition of a necessarily true conclusion. The ideal epistemic state resulting from demonstration is *perfect scientia*, which is comprised of three different cognitions: a cognition of the conclusion, a cognition that the conclusion is necessarily true (certitude), and a perfect cognition of the truth of the conclusion (which amounts to an apprehension of what makes the conclusion true and why it makes it true). When we have *perfect scientia* of a proposition, we have what amounts to a perfect form of knowledge of that proposition. However, as we observed in the last chapter, the occasions for *perfect scientia* are rather limited: in order for us to have complete certitude in the conclusion, the conclusion itself must be necessary, which rules out many truths of natural science;[1] and the conditions for perfect apprehension of the truth of a conclusion would seem to limit demonstration and *perfect scientia* to analytic or *a priori* truths.

---

[1] Certain truths concerning the natural world can fall under the domain of demonstration if they exemplify some sort of necessity. For instance, some conclusions about celestial bodies can be demonstrated because the bodies themselves are unchanging and thus they have a sort of physical necessity.

Complementing *perfect scientia* (and its weakened variants) is the epistemic state opinion. Though Aquinas did not comment on Aristotle's *Topics*, a text devoted to the treatment of opinion, he does discuss it briefly in his last lecture from his commentary on book I of the *Posterior Analytics*. In this lecture, Aquinas describes opinion as being parallel in structure to *scientia* and understanding.[2] Just as demonstration is a movement from premises immediately held (by understanding) to *scientia* of the conclusion, the dialectical syllogism is a movement from premises immediately held (by opinion) to opinion of the conclusion.[3] The

---

[2] Recall that understanding is the epistemic state involving a cognition of the premises of a demonstration. See section 2.4.1.

[3] "In order to elucidate what opinion is, he adds that opinion is the acceptance, i.e., the grasping, of a proposition that is immediate and not necessary. And this can be understood in two ways: in one way, so that the immediate proposition in itself is indeed necessary, but it is accepted by opinion as non-necessary; in another way, so that it is in itself contingent. For an immediate proposition is one that cannot be proved through a middle, whether it be a necessary proposition or not. For it has been shown above that there is no process to infinity in predications, neither on the part of the middles nor on the part of the extremes. And this was shown not only analytically in demonstrations, but also logically in general as to syllogisms.

"...Hence what remains is that some contingent propositions are immediate and some mediate. Thus, 'the man does not run,' is mediate, for it can be proved through this middle, 'the man is not in motion,' which is also contingent, albeit immediate. This acceptance of such immediate contingent propositions is opinion. Yet this does not mean that the accepting of a mediate contingent proposition is not opinion. For opinion is related to contingent things, as science and understanding to necessary things."

"et ad exponendum quid sit opinio, subiungit quod opinio est acceptio, idest existimatio quaedam, immediatae propositionis, et non necessariae. quod potest duobus modis intelligi: uno modo sic quod propositio immediata in se quidem sit necessaria, sed ab opinante accipiatur ut non necessaria; alio modo, ut in se sit contingens. dicitur enim immediata propositio, quaecunque per aliquod medium probari non potest, sive sit necessaria sive non necessaria. ostensum est enim supra quod non proceditur in infinitum in praedicationibus, neque quantum ad media neque quantum ad extrema; et

dialectician starts from some immediately held premises. These are premises that are themselves unproven,[4] and from them he proves his conclusion. Though Aquinas differentiates two states involved in demonstration—understanding is the state of cognizing premises, *scientia* of conclusions—he does not distinguish two separate states involved in the dialectical syllogism, though the opinion of premises is distinguished from the opinion of the conclusion by the former being unproven, and the latter being reached as the conclusion of a syllogism. What differentiates opinion from *scientia* or understanding is that the

---

hoc non solum analytice in demonstrationibus, sed etiam logice communiter quantum ad omnes syllogismos.

...unde relinquitur quod sit aliqua propositio immediata contingens. sicut, homo non currit, est mediata; potest enim probari per hoc medium, homo non movetur, quae etiam est contingens, sed immediata. existimatio ergo talium propositionum contingentium immediatarum est opinio: sed per hoc non excluditur quin etiam acceptio propositionis contingentis mediatae sit opinio. sic enim se habet circa contingentia, sicut intellectus et scientia circa necessaria." (PA I.44.n5)

[4] "For since [a dialectical syllogism] aims at producing opinion, the sole intent of a dialectician is to proceed from things that are most probable, and these are things that appear to the majority or to the very wise. Hence if a dialectician in syllogizing happens upon a proposition which really has a middle through which it could be proved, but it seems not to have a middle because it appears to be *per se* known on account of its probability, this is enough for the dialectician: he does not search for a middle, even though the proposition is mediate. Rather he syllogizes from it and completes the dialectical syllogism satisfactorily."

"quia enim syllogismus dialecticus ad hoc tendit, ut opinionem faciat, hoc solum est de intentione dialectici, ut procedat ex his, quae sunt maxime opinabilia, et haec sunt ea, quae videntur vel pluribus, vel maxime sapientibus. et ideo si dialectico in syllogizando occurrat aliqua propositio, quae secundum rei veritatem habeat medium, per quod possit probari, sed tamen non videatur habere medium, sed propter sui probabilitatem videatur esse per se nota; hoc sufficit dialectico, nec inquirit aliud medium, licet propositio sit mediata, et, ex ea syllogizans, sufficienter perficit dialecticum syllogismum." (PA I.31.n4)

objects of opinion are contingent propositions instead of necessary ones. Aquinas says:

> [I]if every truth belongs to either understanding or *scientia* or opinion, and there are some contingent truths, and they belong neither to *scientia* nor understanding, what is left is that opinion is concerned with them, whether they be actually true or actually false, provided that they could be other than they are.
>
> ...For opinion is not exclusively about things contingent in their very nature, because then a man could not have opinion about everything he knows. Rather opinion is about that which is accepted as possible to be otherwise, whether it is that or not.[5]

Opinion fundamentally differs from *scientia* and understanding in that it is concerned with what could be otherwise; however, "could be otherwise" is not to be taken as "not necessary," but rather, "conceived as not-necessary." He says that one can have opinion of premises "so that the immediate proposition in itself is indeed necessary, but it is accepted by opinion as non-necessary."[6] When one cognizes that it is possible for the truth value of a proposition to be otherwise than what it is, one fails to have certitude of that proposition (which, recall, is a determination to only one possible truth value for a proposition). Thus, the primary distinction between opinion and *scientia* is that

---

[5] "...si ergo cuiuslibet veri vel est intellectus, vel scientia, vel opinio, et sunt quaedam vera contingentia, quorum non est neque scientia neque intellectus; relinquitur quod circa huiusmodi sit opinio, sive sint actu vera sive sint actu falsa, dummodo possint aliter se habere." (PA I.44.n4)

"...non enim opinio est solum de his quae sunt contingentia in sui natura; quia secundum hoc, non omne quod quis novit, contingeret opinari. sed opinio est de his quae accipiuntur ut contingentia aliter se habere, sive sint talia sive non." (PA I.44.n8)

[6] "...quod propositio immediata in se quidem sit necessaria, sed ab opinante accipiatur ut non necessaria...." (PA I.44.n5)

the former lacks certitude.[7] That a proposition is only contingently true is not essential to opinion, but what is essential to opinion, namely, the lack of certitude, can result from a proposition's being contingent.

The movement of reason from one opinion to another (the dialectical syllogism) parallels the movement of reason from understanding to *scientia* (the demonstrative syllogism), with the essential difference being that the latter epistemic states include a cognition of certitude whereas the former does not. What we seem to have at the end of the *Posterior Analytics* is a fairly detailed account describing the mechanisms of reason that produce *scientia*, and had Aquinas commented on the *Topics*, we could expect a similar account behind the mechanisms of reason that produce opinion.[8] We have the acts of reason carved at the joints in two different ways: acts of reason can be divided by the logical connection between propositions (either a necessary or contingent connection, or no connection between the propositions[9]), and they can be divided by the epistemic states that result from the movement of reason (either including certitude or failing to include it). What we do not yet have is Aquinas's account of faith. We turn now to this.

---

[7] "...if someone proceeds through middles to immediates in such a way that the middles are not considered capable of being otherwise, but are considered to behave as definitions which are the middles through which demonstrations proceed, there will not be opinion but science."

"...quod si aliquis per media procedat ad immediata, ita quod illa media non arbitretur ut contingentia aliter se habere, sed arbitretur ea sic se habere sicut definitiones, quae sunt media per quae demonstrationes procedunt, non erit opinio, sed scientia." (PA I.44.n9)

[8] Potts ("Aquinas on Belief and Faith," 1971) starts with the account of belief and opinion from QDV 14 rather than the account from PA, which leads him to identify some problems for Aquinas's account of opinion.

[9] Recall that this division was discussed in section 2.1.

3.1.1. Faith, scientia, and opinion compared and contrasted

Aquinas does not give an account of faith (*fides*) in his commentary on the *Posterior Analytics*, so for this we must turn to his other works.[10] In his treatise on faith from the *Summa theologiae*, Aquinas provides a characterization of the difference between *scientia*, opinion, and faith:

> *Scientia* cannot simultaneously be together with opinion about the same thing simply speaking, since it is part of the account of *scientia* that what is known by *scientia* cannot possibly be otherwise. It is part of the account of opinion that what someone opines, he recognizes as possibly being in another way. But what is had by faith, because of the certitude of faith, is also recognized as not possibly being otherwise. One thing in one respect cannot simultaneously be known by *scientia* and believed, for the reason that the known is seen (*visum*) and the believed is not seen....[11]

As we saw in the last section, *scientia* is distinguished from opinion in that the former has certitude but the latter lacks it. Faith, on the other hand, appears to have certitude. The difference, according to Aquinas, is that *scientia* is of something "seen" (*visum*) whereas faith is of the "unseen" (*non visum*). In order to understand what it means for faith to be of something "unseen," we must first examine what Aquinas means for something to be "seen."

---

[10] Aquinas only uses the term *fides* a handful of times in his PA commentary, and how the term is to be understood is not made entirely clear from the contexts in which he uses it.

[11] "scientia enim cum opinione simul esse non potest simpliciter de eodem, quia de ratione scientiae est quod id quod scitur existimetur esse impossibile aliter se habere; de ratione autem opinionis est quod id quod quis existimat, existimet possibile aliter se habere. sed id quod fide tenetur, propter fidei certitudinem, existimatur etiam impossibile aliter se habere, sed ea ratione non potest simul idem et secundum idem esse scitum et creditum, quia scitum est visum et creditum est non visum, ut dictum est." (ST II-II.1.5 ad 4)

"Seeing" a proposition, or alternatively, having "vision" of it, is a metaphorical way of referring to understanding things with the intellect. Just as the eye sees things in the world, the mind's "eye" "sees" things in the mind. Aquinas explains:

> By likeness to bodily sense, there is also said to be a sense about intelligence…. This sense that is about intelligence does not perceive its object through a medium of bodily distance, but by some other medium, just as it perceives the essence of a thing through its property, and perceives a cause through its effect. He is said to be sharp in sense about intelligence who comprehends at once the nature of the thing when he has apprehended its property or even its effect, and so far as he attains to the smallest conditions of the thing to be considered. He is said to be dull about intelligence who cannot attain to apprehending the truth of the thing except by much exposure to it, and even then cannot attain to considering completely all that belongs to the account of the thing.[12]

Understanding is the epistemic state that results when we have intellectual vision of the sort described in the passage above. We understand the proposition "man is a rational animal" when we *see* that manhood includes rationality and animality. From this

---

[12] "ad similitudinem autem corporalis sensus dicitur etiam circa intelligentiam esse aliquis sensus, qui est aliquorum primorum extremorum, ut dicitur in vi ethic., sicut etiam sensus est cognoscitivus sensibilium quasi quorundam principiorum cognitionis. hic autem sensus qui est circa intelligentiam non percipit suum obiectum per medium distantiae corporalis, sed per quaedam alia media, sicut cum per proprietatem rei percipit eius essentiam, et per effectus percipit causam. ille ergo dicitur esse acuti sensus circa intelligentiam qui statim ad apprehensionem proprietatis rei, vel etiam effectus, naturam rei comprehendit, et inquantum usque ad minimas conditiones rei considerandas pertingit. ille autem dicitur esse hebes circa intelligentiam qui ad cognoscendam veritatem rei pertingere non potest nisi per multa ei exposita, et tunc etiam non potest pertingere ad perfecte considerandum omnia quae pertinent ad rei rationem." (ST II-II.15.2)

vision, or understanding of principles, we can then derivatively *see* that certain conclusions are true as a result of the truth of the principles. So, for instance, from our understanding or seeing that "man is a rational animal" we can construct a demonstration yielding the conclusion that "horses are not men." If we see the truth of all the premises that yield this conclusion, and see that these premises yield the conclusion, then we can also say that we see the truth of the conclusion. But this intellectual vision of the conclusion satisfies exactly the same conditions as perfect apprehension of the truth of the conclusion. With the latter, we understand both that the premises lead to the truth of the conclusion and why they do—this amounts to seeing why the conclusion is true. Thus, we can take Aquinas's account of intellectual vision to be equivalent to a perfect apprehension of the truth of a proposition.

From our definition of the previous chapter, *perfect scientia* that P involves three cognitions: cognition of P, certitude of P, and perfect apprehension of the truth of P. Opinion, according to Aquinas, lacks the last two cognitions, and faith has the first two but not the last. The three epistemic states *perfect scientia*, opinion, and faith are mutually exclusive: one cannot have both *perfect scientia* that P and opinion that P, nor faith that P and opinion that P, because it is impossible that one both have certitude that P and not have it (one cannot simultaneously hold P to be necessary and non-necessary). One cannot have both *perfect scientia* that P and faith that P because it is impossible that one both have a perfect apprehension of the truth that P and lack it (one cannot simultaneously apprehend why P is true and not apprehend it).[13] As we saw in the previous chapter, *perfect scientia* is had by means of a demonstration from principles that are understood (i.e., are

---

[13] Aquinas argues that one cannot simultaneously have *scientia* and faith about the same object in ST II-II.1.5 ad 4.

seen) to conclusions that are seen. Opinion is had by means of a dialectical syllogism from principles that are accepted as true (but are not seen to be true, nor are seen to be necessary) to conclusions that follow from those principles (but likewise are not seen to be true, nor are seen to be necessary). But what exactly is the movement involved in faith? And how does faith have certitude while lacking vision? To address these questions, we turn now to Aquinas's account of faith.

3.1.2. Faith as belief

As opposed to the relative scarcity of recent work on Aquinas's account of reason and *scientia*, quite a bit has been written recently on his account of faith. Interpreters of Aquinas roughly tend to fall into one of two broad categories: Intellectualists or Voluntarists. Intellectualist interpreters of Aquinas tend to stress the intellectual component of his account of faith. For these interpreters, faith is primarily a cognitive state, involving cognition of and assent to propositions (e.g., that God exists, that He is triune, etc.). Under an Intellectualist interpretation, the question of how faith acquires its certitude is frequently understood as a question of how belief acquires its justification (or its warrant)—and thus many Intellectualist interpreters look for places where Aquinas seems to provide or appeal to evidence that grounds belief and certitude.[14] The Intellectualist stance is well expressed by Anthony Kenny in his book *The Five Ways*:

> To me it seems that if belief in the existence of God cannot be rationally justified, there can be no good reason for adopting any of the traditional monotheistic religions. A

---

[14] Some who seem to hold this Intellectualist position include Hick (*Faith and Knowledge*, 1966) Penelhum ("The Analysis of Faith in St. Thomas Aquinas," 1977) Plantinga ("Reason and Belief in God," 1983) and Pojman (*Religious Belief and the Will*, 1986).

philosophical proof of God's existence from the nature of the world would not be the only form such a rational justification might take: a man might, for instance, come to accept the existence of God through believing something in the world to be a revelation from God...Those philosophers and theologians who still consider belief in God to need rational justification frequently offer the arguments of Aquinas as such a justification.[15]

Many critics find the Intellectualist interpretation to be unsatisfactory because it seems to provide an account of faith that is not characteristically Christian. Eleonore Stump raises some important questions about faith that Intellectualist interpretations seem unable to answer:

> First, if there is an omniscient and omnipotent God, why would he want human relationships with him to be based on faith? Why wouldn't he make his existence and nature as obvious and uncontroversial to all human beings as the existence of their physical surroundings is? Second, why should having faith be meritorious, as Christian doctrine maintains it is? And why should faith be supposed to make acceptable to God a person whom God would otherwise reject? Finally, why is it that epistemological considerations seem to play so little role in adult conversions?[16]

Often, critics of the Intellectualist interpretation will focus instead on the role of the will in Aquinas's account of faith, finding in it the locus of the merit and salvation that is more typical of Christian faith. These Voluntarist interpreters tend to

---

[15] Kenny, *The Five Ways: St. Thomas Aquinas' Proofs of God's Existence* (1969) 4.

[16] Stump, "Aquinas on Faith and Goodness," in *Being and Goodness*, ed. MacDonald (1991) 179-80.

place more emphasis on the will and its movement to produce a characteristically Christian faith.[17]

Because Aquinas reserves a role for both the will and the intellect in faith,[18] it is not immediately clear whether an Intellectualist or Voluntarist interpretation (or something else) should be advanced. That faith involves both a cognitive and a voluntary component also makes it not entirely clear what Aquinas understands faith to be. In the remainder of this section and the rest of the chapter, we shall examine closely what Aquinas does say about faith, keeping in mind two questions: What exactly is the movement involved in faith? And how does faith have certitude while lacking vision? The first question is of fundamental importance for understanding how any Voluntarist interpretation of faith is supposed to work; similarly, the second is fundamental for any Intellectualist interpretation.

That we do not have a perfect apprehension of the truth of matters of faith seems quite appropriate. Perfect apprehension of the truth of faith requires understanding what made the matters of faith true as well as why they made the matters of faith true. Now matters of faith, for instance, that God is triune or that He is incarnate, are supposed to be mysteries—we are not supposed to understand why they are true. Aquinas says, "The most important thing we can know (*scire*) about the first cause is that it surpasses all our knowledge (*scientiam*) and power of expression. For that one apprehends (*cognoscit*) God most perfectly who holds that whatever one can think or say about Him is less than what God is.... [Dionysius] presents this proposition: *The first cause*

---

[17] See, for example, Stump, "Aquinas on Faith and Goodness" (1991) and Ross, "Aquinas on Belief and Knowledge," in *Essays Honoring Allan B. Wolter*, ed. Frank and Etzkorn (1985).

[18] "...this act [of faith] proceeds from both the will and the intellect...." (ST II-II.4.2)

transcends description."[19] Thus, excluding perfect apprehension of the truth from the epistemic state of faith seems correct. However, many have objected that if faith does not provide vision, then it could not provide certitude.[20] This objection has at least an initial plausibility, for it would seem that if you cannot see why a proposition is true (i.e., you lack perfect apprehension of its truth), you would not be determined to hold it as necessary (you would have no reason for ruling out other possible truth values).

In order to see why faith could include certitude, we need to return to Aquinas's discussion of the motion that leads to certitude that we covered in the last chapter (in 2.4.2.1). From that section I include again a passage from the *Disputed Questions on Truth*:

> Sometimes, however, the understanding can be determined to one side of a contradictory proposition neither immediately through the definitions of the terms, as is the case with principles, nor yet in virtue of principles, as is the case with conclusions from a demonstration. And in this situation our understanding is determined by the will, which chooses to assent to one side definitely and precisely because of something which is enough to move the will, though not enough to move the understanding, namely, since it seems good or fitting to assent to this side. And this is the state of one

---

[19] "de causa autem prima hoc est quod potissime scire possumus quod omnem scientiam et locutionem nostram excedit; ille enim perfectissime deum cognoscit qui hoc de ipso tenet quod, quidquid cogitari vel dici de eo potest, minus est eo quod deus est. unde dionysius dicit i capitulo mysticae theologiae, quod homo secundum melius suae cognitionis unitur deo sicut omnino ignoto, eo quod nihil de eo cognoscit, cognoscens ipsum esse supra omnem mentem. et ad hoc ostendendum inducitur haec propositio: causa prima superior est narratione." (LC prop. 6, n. 43)

[20] Aquinas considers and responds to this sort of objection. See, for instance, ST II-II.4.8 ob 2.

who believes. This may happen when someone believes what another says because it seems fitting or useful to do so.[21]

Certitude is the result of a judgment, one that moves the intellect to consider only one side of a contradiction as possibly true. This movement of the intellect can be brought about either by the intelligible object (as we examined in the last chapter) or by the will. In the former case, we have vision—we see that the proposition is true, and in seeing this we cannot help but hold that it is necessarily true; our certitude follows from the intellectual vision of the truth. In the latter case, we have what Aquinas calls 'belief' (*credere*)—something moves the will, but not the intellect (we lack vision), and as a result of this movement of the will we are determined to one side of a contradiction, and thus to certitude. Faith (*fides*), for Aquinas, is a species of belief (*credere*)—it lacks the vision that comes with understanding, and thus lacks perfect apprehension of the truth, but it has certitude in the truth of the object of belief, though the certitude comes to the believer as a result of an act of will rather than a result of vision. Under this account, there are two sources of certitude: vision and will. The former source provides certitude of understanding; the latter provides certitude of belief. This account does not yet fully explain how the will generates certitude, nor does it yet offer a satisfactory answer to the objection raised earlier that certitude requires vision.

---

[21] "quandoque vero intellectus non potest determinari ad alteram partem contradictionis neque statim per ipsas definitiones terminorum, sicut in principiis, nec etiam virtute principiorum, sicut est in conclusionibus demonstrationis; determinatur autem per voluntatem, quae eligit assentire uni parti determinate et praecise propter aliquid, quod est sufficiens ad movendum voluntatem, non autem ad movendum intellectum, utpote quia videtur bonum vel conveniens huic parti assentire. et ista est dispositio credentis, ut cum aliquis credit dictis alicuius hominis, quia videtur ei decens vel utile." (QDV 14.1)

3.1.2.1. Aquinas's account of belief

According to Aquinas, the will is a "rational appetite" (*appetitus rationalis*).[22] An appetite is "an inclination of a person desirous of a thing towards that thing."[23] What makes this appetite rational is that the thing we desire is presented to us in an apprehension. Rational appetites differ from other appetites in that what is desired is *apprehended* as desirable—natural and sensitive appetites, though they also incline persons and things towards desirable states, do not present to the intellect the desired object *as* desirable. In short, the will is that power by which something we apprehend as good is desired. Whether or not we desire something by the will does not depend on whether or not the object itself is actually good for us, but only whether we apprehend it as good for us. All goods except happiness are capable of being apprehended by us as not good, as Aquinas explains:

> Wherefore if the will be offered an object which is good universally and from every point of view, the will tends to it of necessity, if it wills anything at all; since it cannot will the opposite. If, on the other hand, the will is offered an object that is not good from every point of view, it will not tend to it of necessity. And since lack of any good whatever, is a non-good, consequently that good alone which is perfect and lacking in nothing is such a good that the will cannot not-will it; and this is Happiness. But any other particular goods, in so far as they are lacking in some good, can be regarded as non-goods, and from this point of view, they can be set aside or approved by

---

[22] What immediately follows is a rather quick and rudimentary account of the will in Aquinas. For a more detailed account, see Barad, *Consent: The Means to an Active Faith According to St Thomas Aquinas* (1992) ch. 2, and Stump, "Aquinas on Faith and Goodness," (1991) 180-83.

[23] "cuius ratio est quia appetitus nihil aliud est quam inclinatio appetentis in aliquid." (ST I-II.8.1)

the will, which can tend to one and the same thing from various points of view.[24]

Once something is apprehended as good and desired, one is then able to initiate a course of action in order to obtain this desired good. So, for instance, should one apprehend that eating lunch now would be good and develops a desire for lunch, in this way one will have willed to have lunch. From this a person may initiate a deliberation as to how to achieve this goal, which ultimately can lead to choosing and pursuing some course of action aimed at getting lunch.[25]

The initial movement of the will, or simple willing,[26] proceeds from apprehension of something as good for it to desire. In the passage from the previous section (from QDV 14.1), Aquinas characterizes belief as the state resulting from the will "which chooses to assent to one side definitely and precisely because of something which is enough to move the will, though not enough to move the understanding, namely, since it seems good or fitting to assent to this side." We can see that belief is more than simple willing—though it does involve an apprehension of something as good ("it seems good…") and involves desire ("is enough to move

---

[24] "unde si proponatur aliquod obiectum voluntati quod sit universaliter bonum et secundum omnem considerationem, ex necessitate voluntas in illud tendet, si aliquid velit, non enim poterit velle oppositum. si autem proponatur sibi aliquod obiectum quod non secundum quamlibet considerationem sit bonum, non ex necessitate voluntas feretur in illud. et quia defectus cuiuscumque boni habet rationem non boni, ideo illud solum bonum quod est perfectum et cui nihil deficit, est tale bonum quod voluntas non potest non velle, quod est beatitudo. alia autem quaelibet particularia bona, inquantum deficiunt ab aliquo bono, possunt accipi ut non bona, et secundum hanc considerationem, possunt repudiari vel approbari a voluntate, quae potest in idem ferri secundum diversas considerationes." (ST I-II.10.2)

[25] For more on the process that leads to action, see Barad, *Consent*, ch. 1.

[26] Following Barad, *Consent*, 10, I shall refer to this initial movement of the will (from apprehension to desire) as "simple willing."

97

the will…"); it also results in an action, namely assent to a proposition. That belief is more than simple willing is clear from the following: "…the understanding assents to something, not because it is sufficiently moved by the proper object, but by a choice of the will tending to one alternative rather than another."[27] We can thus define belief in P as follows:

S has *belief* that P =df (1) S apprehends P,
(2) S apprehends that assenting to P would be good for S,
(3) this leads to a desire in S to assent to P,
(4) this leads to a choice by S to assent to P, and
(5) this leads S to assent to P.[28]

For Aquinas, faith (*fides*) is simply a species of *belief* (*credere*). We see that the assent to matters of faith follows the same model as that of *belief* from this response that Aquinas gives to the question What is faith? in the *Disputed Questions on Truth*:

---

[27] "alio modo intellectus assentit alicui non quia sufficienter moveatur ab obiecto proprio, sed per quandam electionem voluntarie declinans in unam partem magis quam in aliam." (ST II-II.1.4)

[28] Note to the reader: this definition of "belief" used by Aquinas is a technical term that does not match the common definition of belief frequently held by contemporary philosophers. In order to avoid confusion, when I refer to Aquinas's account of belief I will italicize the term in order to distinguish it from ordinary usage. The reader may also find it curious that an epistemic *state* has been defined partially in terms of a sequential process. Aquinas, I believe, holds that *belief* is the epistemic state constituted by assent—however, it is difficult to characterize exactly what that state is, without describing the process by which it was generated. Thus, the definition, though picking out an epistemic state, appeals to the process by which that state was generated, in order to identify it uniquely and more easily.

For the state of the believer...is such that the intellect is determined to something through the will, and the will does nothing except in so far as it is moved by its object, which is the good to be sought for and its end. In view of this, faith needs a twofold principle, a first which is the good that moves the will, and a second which is that to which the understanding gives assent under the influence of the will.

...But the will, under the movement of this good, proposes as worthy of assent something which is not evident to the natural understanding. In this way it gives the understanding a determination to that which is not evident, the determination, namely, to assent to it. Therefore, just as the intelligible thing which is seen by the understanding determines the understanding, and for this reason is said to give conclusive evidence to the mind; so also, something which is not evident to the understanding determines it and convinces the mind because the will has accepted it as something to which assent should be given.[29]

In faith, as with other acts of *belief*, there is a "twofold principle": the first that generates a simple willing to assent to some matter of faith, and the second in which the will chooses to

---

[29] "cum enim dispositio credentis, ut supra dictum est, talis sit, quod intellectus determinetur ad aliquid per voluntatem; voluntas autem nihil facit nisi secundum quod est mota per suum obiectum, quod est bonum appetibile, et finis; requiritur ad finem duplex principium: unum primum quod est bonum movens voluntatem; et secundo id cui intellectus assentit voluntate faciente.

voluntas autem mota a bono praedicto proponit aliquid intellectui naturali non apparens, ut dignum cui assentiatur; et sic determinat ipsum ad illud non apparens, ut scilicet ei assentiat. sicut igitur intelligibile quod est visum ab intellectu, determinat intellectum, et ex hoc dicitur mentem arguere; ita etiam et aliquid non apparens intellectui determinat ipsum, et arguit mentem ex hoc ipso quod est a voluntate acceptatum, ut cui assentiatur. unde secundum aliam litteram dicitur convictio, quia convincit intellectum modo praedicto; et ita in hoc quod dicitur argumentum non apparentium, tangitur comparatio fidei ad id cui assentit intellectus." (QDV 14.2)

pursue the desired good and influences the intellect to assent. For Aquinas, faith counts as a species of *belief* because it satisfies the five conditions given in the definition of *belief*. I have not yet provided the criteria by which faith differs from other acts of *belief*, nor have we examined how Aquinas explains how Christian faith does, in fact, satisfy the five conditions given above. I turn to the latter issue in the next section (the former will be visited in section 3.1.3).

3.1.2.2. Belief *and the will*

Conditions (1) through (3) of the definition of *belief* yield a simple willing to assent to some proposition—one apprehends that it would be good to assent to the proposition and subsequently desires to do so. What we need to examine is how one might come to have a simple willing to assent to some matter of faith first by looking at how one might come to apprehend that assenting to some matter of faith would be good. Aquinas repeatedly and tersely identifies what grounds this apprehension:

> [F]aith is called "the substance of things hoped for," inasmuch as it is for us an initial participation of the eternal life for which we hope by reason of the divine promise. And in this way mention is made of the relation between faith and the good which moves the will in its determination of the intellect.[30]

Thus, too, we are moved to believe what God says because we are promised eternal life as a reward if we believe. And this

---

[30] "et sic fides, in quantum est in nobis inchoatio quaedam vitae aeternae, quam ex divina repromissione speramus, dicitur substantia rerum sperandarum: et sic in hoc tangitur comparatio fidei ad bonum quod movet voluntatem determinantem intellectum." (QDV 14.2)

reward moves the will to assent to what is said, although the intellect is not moved by anything which it understands.[31]

Aquinas also characterizes this good in terms of an evil to be avoided: "Faith produces in us an apprehension of certain punitive evils that are assigned because of divine judgment. And in this way faith is the cause of the fear by which someone fears to be punished by God, which is servile fear."[32]

We can apprehend that assenting to matters of faith would be good for us because we apprehend that if we accept them, we will be rewarded with eternal life.[33] (A second, related motivation appears to be that if we reject them, we will be punished by God.) Once we apprehend that accepting matters of faith yields eternal life (and also apprehend that having eternal life is good), it becomes understandable why we would desire to accept matters of faith. These motivations will generate in us a simple willing to assent to matters of faith.

In order to understand how a simple willing to assent can lead to a choosing to assent (condition [4]) and finally to assenting to matters of faith (condition [5]), we must first take a look at what Aquinas means by "assent." For Aquinas, the assent in faith is not simply accepting the proposition to be true, for opinion includes such acceptance but lacks assent:

---

[31] "et sic etiam movemur ad credendum dictis dei, inquantum nobis repromittitur, si crediderimus, praemium aeternae vitae: et hoc praemio movetur voluntas ad assentiendum his quae dicuntur, quamvis intellectus non moveatur per aliquid intellectum." (QDV 14.1)

[32] "per fidem autem fit in nobis quaedam apprehensio de quibusdam malis poenalibus quae secundum divinum iudicium inferuntur, et per hunc modum fides est causa timoris quo quis timet a deo puniri, qui est timor servilis." (ST II-II.7.1)

[33] Implicit in such an apprehension is the assumption that God exists and rewards those who have faith. This assumption is a thorny one and is considered in the first objection raised in chapter 5.5.2.

Sometimes, however, the understanding tends more to one side than the other; still, that which causes the inclination does not move the understanding enough to determine it fully to one of the members. Under this influence, it accepts (*accipit*) one member, but always has doubts about the other. This is the state of one holding an opinion, who accepts (*accipit*) one member of the contradictory proposition with some fear that the other is true.

...Thus, also, one who has an opinion does not give assent, because his acceptance (*acceptio*) of the one side is not firm. The Latin word *sententia*, as Isaac and Avicenna say, is a clear or very certain (*certissima*) comprehension of one member of a contradictory proposition. And *assentire* is derived from *sententia*.[34]

Aquinas links assent with firm acceptance and certain (*certissima*) comprehension, in other words, certitude.[35] Here he explicitly links certitude and assent:

In a second way, the understanding assents to something, not because it is sufficiently moved by the proper object, but by a choice of the will tending to one alternative rather than another. And if this occurs with doubt and hesitation about the

---

[34] "quandoque vero intellectus inclinatur magis ad unum quam ad alterum; sed tamen illud inclinans non sufficienter movet intellectum ad hoc quod determinet ipsum in unam partium totaliter; unde accipit quidem unam partem, semper tamen dubitat de opposita. et haec est dispositio opinantis, qui accipit unam partem contradictionis cum formidine alterius....similiter etiam nec opinans, cum non firmetur eius acceptio circa alteram partem. sententia autem, ut dicit isaac et avicenna, est conceptio distincta vel certissima alterius partis contradictionis; assentire autem a sententia dicitur." (QDV 14.1)

[35] Other passages in which Aquinas holds that opinion lacks the firmness of certitude are: ST II-II.2.9 ad 2; II-II.2.1; QDV 14.2.

other alternative, there is opinion. If it occurs with certitude and without any such hesitation, there is faith.[36]

Opinion and faith differ generically because faith involves firm assent, which includes certitude, whereas opinion lacks both. The assent of faith differs, as we have seen, from the assent of understanding or *scientia* because the former is a result of the will inducing certitude, whereas the latter two are a result of vision determining certitude. Assent, then, is simply the act by which the intellect is brought to certitude about a proposition. If the cause of the assent is vision, then the assent yields understanding. We are now brought back to the concern raised at the end of section 3.1.1: how can the will (without vision) generate certitude? The answer to this question is that the will (in producing *belief*) generates assent and assent yields certitude. But this answer is simply analytic: *belief* is defined as producing assent and assent is defined as producing certitude. What we still need to understand is how a simple willing can result in assent, and how this assent induces certitude in a *believer*. We turn now to these issues, considering in the next section how the will produces assent, and in section 3.1.2.4 how this assent induces certitude.

3.1.2.3. *The will and assent*

That one might have a simple willing to assent to a proposition of faith seems quite understandable—once someone recognizes that assent to these matters can lead to eternal life, a desire to assent follows fairly naturally. How one proceeds from a simple desire to assent to assent itself is a bit more complicated. Aquinas

---

[36] "alio modo intellectus assentit alicui non quia sufficienter moveatur ab obiecto proprio, sed per quandam electionem voluntarie declinans in unam partem magis quam in aliam. et si quidem hoc fit cum dubitatione et formidine alterius partis, erit opinio, si autem fit cum certitudine absque tali formidine, erit fides." (ST II-II.1.4)

identifies two causes by which one proceeds from a desire to assent to actually assenting:

> The will can move the intellect in two ways. First, from the ordering of the will to the good; in this way believing is a praiseworthy act. In another way, because the intellect is convinced in judging that there is something to be believed in what is said, even if it is not convinced by the evidence of the thing. Just so some prophet might predict some future thing with the word of the Lord, and add to it the sign of raising the dead, and might convince by this sign the understanding of an observer, so that the observer might clearly apprehend that the things said were said by God, who does not lie. Even so the predicted future thing would not be evident in itself, so that the account of faith would not be taken away.[37]

The second sort of cause mentioned in the above passage suggests that we can have some sort of evidence that what someone tells us is true if that person accurately prophesies or performs miracles. In these sorts of cases, we are supposed to infer that God is speaking through this messenger, and thus that what the messenger says is true. Notice that this does not give us vision (i.e., perfect apprehension) of the truth of what the messenger says—even if we know that everything he says is true, we do not see *why* those things are true; however, we may see why we might be justified in *believing* them. This sort of evidence, evidence that P is true on the basis of what someone asserts, would count (as

---

[37] "quod autem voluntas moveat intellectum ad assentiendum potest contingere ex duobus. uno modo, ex ordine voluntatis ad bonum, et sic credere est actus laudabilis. alio modo, quia intellectus convincitur ad hoc quod iudicet esse credendum his quae dicuntur, licet non convincatur per evidentiam rei. sicut si aliquis propheta praenuntiaret in sermone domini aliquid futurum, et adhiberet signum mortuum suscitando, ex hoc signo convinceretur intellectus videntis ut cognosceret manifeste hoc dici a deo, qui non mentitur; licet illud futurum quod praedicitur in se evidens non esset, unde ratio fidei non tolleretur." (ST II-II.5.2)

Kenny admits above) towards the justification of belief of matters of faith. If faith were based on such evidence, this would seem to support an Intellectualist interpretation of Aquinas.

Suppose we witness John performing miracles, then uttering some statement P about God (perhaps that God is triune). We might think that this constitutes conclusive evidence for P, along the lines of the following argument, which I shall call the *veracity argument*:[38]

(a)   John performs miracles and utters P.

(b)   If someone performs a miracle, then that person is a messenger of God.

(c)   If someone is a messenger of God, then any assertion uttered by that person comes from God.

(d)   If an assertion comes from God, then that assertion is true.

∴ (e)   P is true.

Though we do not have *perfect scientia* of the conclusion (this argument does not show us why P is true), one might plausibly hold that the argument constitutes a demonstration *quia* and hence that we have *scientia quia* of the conclusion, that is, knowledge *that* the conclusion is true (recall the account of *scientia quia* from section 2.3.2). *Scientia quia* lacks the perfect apprehension that is part of *perfect scientia* but does have certitude, which is also the case for faith. As we saw in section 3.1.1 above, faith lacks the vision of *perfect scientia*, but so does *scientia quia*. Thus, one might be inclined to interpret faith as a species of *scientia*, one that lacks vision because the faithful do not understand why matters of faith

---

[38] Jenkins, *Knowledge and Faith in Thomas Aquinas* (1997) 163ff, calls this sort of argument from the evidence of the credibility of the speaker "credibility arguments".

are true but do understand why they are to be *believed*. Faith, under this interpretation, would be a species of knowledge, which would very quickly resolve the epistemic tension between faith and reason.

This interpretation, though tempting, cannot accurately capture what Aquinas means by faith, and this is for several reasons.[39] First, from the passage above, Aquinas identifies a second and separate cause of faith and that is "the will being directed to the good," and faith that comes from this cause is that of the "faithful of Christ," whereas the faith from evidence of the veracity argument is that of the demons (for more on this see section 3.2.2 below). This other cause of faith, one that does not rely on evidence, seems to be more in line with the conception of *belief* and the will that has been developed thus far. Second, though evidence without vision can be a cause of faith, this evidence alone is not sufficient for faith, according to Aquinas. He says that external inducement (e.g., by evidence of miracles) is not "a sufficient cause. Among those seeing one and the same miracle, and those hearing the same preaching, some believe and some do not believe. And so another inward cause must be recognized, which moves man inwardly to assent to the things that are of faith."[40] If this external evidence is not sufficient, then faith cannot be some sort of *scientia quia*, for a demonstration *quia* is sufficient

---

[39] That Aquinas rejects this position is where he makes a mistake about faith, according to Penelhum, "Analysis of Faith in St. Thomas Aquinas," (1977) 152. For more on conclusive evidence for faith see the section on the Five Ways in chapter 4.

[40] "quantum vero ad secundum, scilicet ad assensum hominis in ea quae sunt fidei, potest considerari duplex causa. una quidem exterius inducens, sicut miraculum visum, vel persuasio hominis inducentis ad fidem. quorum neutrum est sufficiens causa, videntium enim unum et idem miraculum, et audientium eandem praedicationem, quidam credunt et quidam non credunt. et ideo oportet ponere aliam causam interiorem, quae movet hominem interius ad assentiendum his quae sunt fidei." (ST II-II.6.1)

for this form of *scientia*; but, as Aquinas claims, it is not sufficient for faith. Finally, Aquinas explicitly rejects this interpretation. He says that the act of *believing* is distinguished from all other acts of the intellect (including *scientia*).[41]

This first rejected interpretation for faith was that it was assent brought about by conclusive evidence for the veracity of testimony—one who has faith has proof (and from this, certitude) that matters of faith are true. Aquinas tells us that this sort of conclusive evidence is not sufficient for faith, and that Christian faith is caused by the will being directed toward the good. He also tells us that assent comes from some internal cause, which moves man inwardly to assent. What is this internal cause, and how does it lead one from a simple willing to assent? In short, this cause is God's *grace*:

> [B]elieving does lie in the will of the believer. But it is required that the will of man be prepared by God through grace in order to be elevated to the things that are above nature, as was said above.[42]

> And so as regards assent, which is the principal act of faith, faith is from God moving inwardly by grace.[43]

> Nicodemus, having an imperfect opinion about Christ, affirmed that he was a teacher and performed these signs [i.e., miracles] as a mere man. And so the Lord wishes to show Nicodemus how he might arrive at a deeper understanding (*cognitionem*) of him. And as a matter of fact, the Lord might

---

[41] See ST II-II.2.1.

[42] "ad tertium dicendum quod credere quidem in voluntate credentium consistit, sed oportet quod voluntas hominis praeparetur a deo per gratiam ad hoc quod elevetur in ea quae sunt supra naturam, ut supra dictum est." (ST II-II.6.1 ad 3)

[43] "et ideo fides quantum ad assensum, qui est principalis actus fidei, est a deo interius movente per gratiam." (ST II-II.6.1)

have done so with an argument, but because this might have resulted in a quarrel—the opposite of which was prophesied about him: "He will not quarrel" (Is 42:2)—he wished to lead him to a true understanding (*cognitionem*) with gentleness. As if to say: It is not strange that you regard me as a mere man, because one cannot know (*scire*) these secrets of the divinity unless he has achieved a spiritual regeneration. And this is what he says: *unless one is born again, he cannot see the kingdom of God.*[44]

Though miracles would seem to provide evidence for the truths of matters of faith, this evidence alone is not sufficient for instilling faith in a person. Nicodemus, according to the Gospel of John (3:5), explicitly acknowledged Jesus as a divine messenger, and seemed to accept the veracity argument. Yet Nicodemus did not yet have faith. In the passages above it is God's grace that is necessary for faith, not the evidence of the veracity of the messenger.

In coming to *believe* one first apprehends a proposition, and then apprehends it as good (conditions [1] & [2]). The awareness of the proposition comes from the testimony of another—someone tells us about it. Once we hear the proposition and hear that assenting to it can give us eternal life, we apprehend that it would be good to assent to it, and we desire to assent to it (condition [3]).

---

[44] "Sed notandum, sicut iam dictum est, quod Nicodemus imperfectam opinionem habens de Christo, confitebatur eum magistrum et haec signa facere tamquam hominem purum. Vult ergo ei dominus ostendere, quomodo ad altiorem cognitionem de ipso posset pervenire. Et quidem poterat de hoc dominus disputare; sed quia hoc fuisset versum in contentionem, cuius contrarium de eo scriptum est Is. XLII, 2: *non contendet*, ideo cum mansuetudine voluit eum ad veram cognitionem perducere, quasi diceret: non mirum si me purum hominem credis, quia illa secreta divinitatis non potest aliquis scire, nisi adeptus fuerit spiritualem regenerationem. Et hoc est quod dicit *nisi quis natus fuerit denuo, non potest videre regnum Dei.*" (*Commentary on the Gospel of John*, III, lect. 1)

Aquinas says that for faith, we do not choose to assent to the proposition (condition [4]) on the basis of conclusive evidence for the veracity of the testimony of the person we heard it from— instead, we choose to assent to it because of an inward cause, namely, the grace of God. Scripture (e.g., John 3:5) tells us that grace is necessary for eternal life, and Aquinas construes grace as also necessary for faith.[45] We move from a desire to assent to matters of faith to a choice to assent not by mere wishful thinking, and not by evidence, but by grace. The grace of God moves (or helps move) the will from simple willing to choice. For our purposes, I shall merely observe here that, for Aquinas, one proceeds from conditions (3) to (4) in the definition of *belief* by means of grace.[46] I wish now to examine the last stage of *belief*: how we proceed from a choice to assent to assent itself, and how that assent yields certitude.

3.1.2.4. *Assent and certitude*

Assent is the act that brings about certitude—one assents to P only when it yields certitude that P. In the last chapter (section 2.2.1), we presented Aquinas's definition of certitude as determination of the intellect to one thing, or, as firmness of adherence of the intellect. That the intelligible object (e.g., a self-evident proposition) moves the intellect to assent in cases of understanding seems fairly straightforward: we simply see that some proposition is true, and in seeing it to be true, we cannot

---

[45] It would seem that a natural psychological tendency would be for a person who desires to assent to something (condition 3) to then choose to assent to it (condition 4). This is the phenomena that we see with wishful thinking—someone's mere desire to believe leads them to so believe. This is a form of belief, but it is not faith. Aquinas holds that faith requires that the move from condition (3) to condition (4) to be by grace.

[46] Exactly *how* Aquinas holds that grace moves the will in such a way that the will still freely assents to faith is not easily understood. Unfortuntely, there is not room here to engage in this topic.

help but assent to it, and we cannot help but firmly adhere to its being true, and we cannot help but think that it must be true (that it could not be otherwise). Taking some propositions that we understand, that is, that we see to be true, and from them demonstrating other propositions, it is also clear how we cannot help but assent to these conclusions as well, even though in this case the assent is a result of a movement of reason rather than an immediate intellectual vision as with self-evident propositions. Of the assent in faith, Aquinas says the following:

> But, in faith, the assent and the discursive thought are more or less parallel. For the assent is not caused by the thought, but by the will, as has just been said. However, since the understanding does not in this way have its action terminated at one thing so that it is conducted to its proper term, which is the sight of some intelligible object, it follows that its movement is not yet brought to rest. Rather, it still thinks discursively and inquires about the things which it believes, even though its assent to them is unwavering. For, in so far as it depends on itself alone, the understanding is not satisfied and is not limited to one thing; instead, its action is terminated only from without. Because of this the understanding of the believer is said to be "held captive," since, in place of its own proper determinations, those of something else are imposed on it...Due to this, also, a movement directly opposite to what the believer holds most firmly can arise in him, although this cannot happen to one who understands or has scientific knowledge.[47]

---

[47] "sed in fide est assensus et cogitatio quasi ex aequo. non enim assensus ex cogitatione causatur, sed ex voluntate, ut dictum est. sed quia intellectus non hoc modo terminatur ad unum ut ad proprium terminum perducatur, qui est visio alicuius intelligibilis; inde est quod eius motus nondum est quietatus, sed adhuc habet cogitationem et inquisitionem de his quae credit, quamvis eis firmissime assentiat. quantum enim est ex seipso, non est ei satisfactum, nec est terminatus ad unum; sed terminatur tantum ex extrinseco. et inde est quod

The assent of faith is caused by the will, not by the intelligible object. Since the intellect is not moved to determine one thing or moved to adhere firmly to the truth of the object by the object itself, in a way, the intellect has not stopped moving. We can explain this situation as follows. Suppose John is considering whether or not P is true. He does not see that it is true, so both truth values for P are still possible options as far as John is concerned. His attention *moves* back and forth between the two possibilities. Should John see the evident truth of P, or have it demonstrated for him, he would then no longer consider the falsehood of P as a possible option—he would be determined to the truth of P, and the movement of his attention would cease and settle only on the truth of P. In the case of faith, John does not see why P is true, and thus his attention can still move between possible truth values for P, and yet, at the same time, the will pushes the intellect to assent to P. There can be, somehow, simultaneously motion and determination (non-motion) involved in the assent of faith. Aquinas acknowledges that faith has exactly this characteristic:

> In faith there is some perfection and some imperfection. The firmness which pertains to the assent is a perfection, but the lack of sight, because of which the movement of discursive thought still remains in the mind of one who believes, is an imperfection. The perfection, namely, the assent, is caused by the simple light which is faith. But, since the participation in this light is not perfect, the imperfection of the understanding

---

intellectus credentis dicitur esse captivatus, quia tenetur terminis alienis, et non propriis. ii corinth. x, 5: in captivitatem redigentes omnem intellectum etc.. inde est etiam quod in credente potest insurgere motus de contrario eius quod firmissime tenet, quamvis non in intelligente vel sciente." (QDV 14.1)

is not completely removed. For this reason the movement of discursive thought in it stays restless.[48]

What we have with faith, according to Aquinas, is certitude that derives from some sort of firmness of assent, yet this firmness does not derive from intellectual vision, because the intellect can still entertain the possibility that the proposition assented to is false. Somehow this assent of faith comes from the will, and in the passage above, Aquinas tells us that the assent is "caused by the simple light which is faith." Under this account of faith, then, it seems that the Intellectualist interpretation of Aquinas cannot be right—for if the certitude of faith stems from some sort of rational justification for believing that P, we would seem to have reached an answer regarding the truth of P, one that results from the termination of discursive thought. Since discursive reasoning does not terminate in cases of faith, faith does not seem to involve this sort of rational justification.[49]

Just as there is a metaphorical light of natural reason, by which we "see" the truth of propositions, Aquinas holds that there is also a light of faith.

---

[48] "ad quintum dicendum, quod fides habet aliquid perfectionis, et aliquid imperfectionis. perfectionis quidem est ipsa firmitas, quae pertinet ad assensum; sed imperfectionis est carentia visionis, ex qua remanet adhuc motus cogitationis in mente credentis. ex lumine igitur simplici, quod est fides, causatur id quod perfectionis est, scilicet assentire; sed in quantum illud lumen non perfecte participatur, non totaliter tollitur imperfectio intellectus: et sic motus cogitationis in ipso remanet inquietus." (QDV 14.1 ad 5)

[49] Penelhum, "Analysis of Faith in St. Thomas Aquinas," (1977) 151-53, holds that if faith is based on inconclusive evidence (i.e., that the evidence does not determine the intellect) then this would be a weakness of the account. He holds this, I believe, because he does not see how one can have certitude without evidence that at least *seems* conclusive to ground the certitude. As I discuss next, Aquinas does provide an account of faith that yields certitude without having conclusive evidence.

And thus the human understanding has a form, namely, intelligible light itself, which of itself is sufficient for knowing certain intelligible things, namely, those we can come to know through the senses. Higher intelligible things the human intellect cannot know, unless it be perfected by a stronger light, namely, the light of faith or prophecy which is called the light of grace, since it is added to nature.[50]

[T]he light of faith makes one see the things that are believed. Just as by other habits of virtues a man sees what is appropriate for him according to that habit, so also by the habit of faith the mind of man is inclined to assent to the things that are appropriate to right faith and not to others.[51]

The light of faith allows us to "see" what it is we are supposed to *believe*. In a way, propositions that are potential candidates for Christian *belief* are "lit up" so that we can "see" that they are supposed to be *believed*. Aquinas has here introduced another notion of vision, seeing by the light of faith, which I shall refer to as *faith-* or *f-seeing*. One *f-sees* a proposition P when the light of faith reveals to one that P is to be *believed*. In contrast, one may see by the light of natural reason in such a way that one has a perfect apprehension of the truth of P—this I shall refer to as *perfect-* or *p-seeing*. Finally, I will refer to someone as *quia-* or *q-seeing* P for whom the light of natural reason provides knowledge

---

[50] "sic igitur intellectus humanus habet aliquam formam, scilicet ipsum intelligibile lumen, quod est de se sufficiens ad quaedam intelligibilia cognoscenda, ad ea scilicet in quorum notitiam per sensibilia possumus devenire. altiora vero intelligibilia intellectus humanus cognoscere non potest nisi fortiori lumine perficiatur, sicut lumine fidei vel prophetiae; quod dicitur lumen gratiae, inquantum est naturae superadditum." (ST I-II.109.1)

[51] "ad tertium dicendum quod lumen fidei facit videre ea quae creduntur. sicut enim per alios habitus virtutum homo videt illud quod est sibi conveniens secundum habitum illum, ita etiam per habitum fidei inclinatur mens hominis ad assentiendum his quae conveniunt rectae fidei et non aliis." (ST II-II.1.4 ad 3)

that P is true (*scientia quia*) but for whom it does not provide perfect apprehension of why P is true.[52]

When we *p-see* that P is true, we cannot help but assent to it, and we have certitude about the truth of P, for we simply cannot entertain the possibility of its being false—our determination to the truth of P and the firmness of adherence is absolute. When we *q-see* that P is true, we cannot help but assent to it, and we have certitude about the truth of P, though the certitude seems to be less strong. Even were we persuaded by the veracity argument to accept some proposition P, it seems we could at least clearly *entertain* the possibility that P is false, even though we might adhere firmly to its truth. This is probably why Aquinas characterizes the knowledge from *q-seeing* (i.e., *scientia quia*) as having less certitude than the knowledge from *p-seeing* (i.e., *scientia propter quid*).[53] On the other hand, when we *f-see* that P is to be *believed*, it is up to our free choice whether or not we want to assent to it.[54] When we *f-see*, we do not see *why* the proposition is true (we do not *p-see* it), and thus we are not compelled by the proposition itself to assent to it; we also do not see *that* the proposition is true (we do not *q-see* it), and also for this reason are not compelled to assent to it. Instead, we see that the proposition is to be *believed* as part of faith. As a Christian, one already desires to assent to certain propositions, the assenting to which promises eternal life. Grace helps the faithful move from a simple *desire* to assent to a *choice* to assent, and this *infused* light of faith (which is also a result of grace)[55] allows the faithful to *f-see* what propositions are worthy of assent. Confident that the light of faith

---

[52] Aquinas does not say much about *q-seeing*. Generally, his discussion of intellectual vision is limited to cases of *p-seeing*. I have introduced this notion here because it helps illustrate the differences between *p-seeing* and *f-seeing*.

[53] In PA I.41.

[54] See, for instance, ST II-II.2.9.

[55] See, for instance, ST II-II.2.3 ad 2; see also III Sent. 23, ii.l ad 4.

correctly picks out the propositions to be *believed*, that God is not a deceiver, and that *believing* matters of faith will help bring one eternal life, the Christian believer willingly and confidently assents to matters of faith, and derived from this confidence, the believer will have a very firm adherence to the truth of these propositions—and this satisfies Aquinas's definition of certitude.

Aquinas is sensitive to the worry that the certitude of faith does differ in important respects from the certitude of understanding, and on numerous occasions he points out that "certitude" can have multiples senses, as he does in the *Disputed Questions on Truth*:

> Certitude can mean two things. The first is firmness of adherence, and with reference to this, faith is more certain than any understanding [of principles] and *scientia*. For the first truth, which causes the assent of faith, is a more powerful cause than the light of reason, which causes the assent of understanding or *scientia*. The second is the evidence of that to which assent is given. Here, faith does not have certainty, but *scientia* and understanding do. It is because of this, too, that understanding has no discursive thought.[56]

Understanding and *perfect scientia* have both the certitude of firmness of adherence and the certitude of evidence, and faith only has the former. What is striking is Aquinas's claim that faith has *more* firmness of adherence than understanding—it would seem that assent that is subject to a free choice of the will would be less firm than assent that results from the intellect being

---

[56] "ad septimum dicendum, quod certitudo duo potest importare: scilicet firmitatem adhaesionis; et quantum ad hoc fides est certior etiam omni intellectu et scientia, quia prima veritas, quae causat fidei assensum, est fortior causa quam lumen rationis, quae causat assensum intellectus vel scientiae. importat etiam evidentiam eius cui assentitur; et sic fides non habet certitudinem, sed scientia et intellectus: et exinde est quod intellectus cogitationem non habet." (QDV 14.1 ad 7)

completely unable to entertain other possible truth values for a proposition. We shall return to this worry in section 3.3 when we consider the epistemological consequences of Aquinas's account of faith.

3.1.3. Faith as habit and virtue

We have thus far been concerned with the act of faith (as a species of act of *belief*), that is, the particular movements of the intellect and the will that result in assenting to matters of faith. However, for Aquinas, faith is properly a habit, not an act.[57] Aquinas takes his definition of faith from Scripture: "Faith is the substance of things to be hoped for, the evidence of things that appear not" (Heb 11:1). In the *Summa theologiae*, Aquinas explains how this passage is to be interpreted. From it, he extracts the following definition for faith: "If therefore someone wanted to reduce words of this kind to the form of a definition, it could be said that 'faith is a habit of mind, by which eternal life begins in us, making the understanding assent to what does not appear'."[58]

Since faith is a habit, that is, a settled state of mind, by examining this habit more closely we can better understand its principal act: the act of faith that we have been considering thus far. What is this habit of faith? A habit is defined as "a disposition to do well in those powers of the soul that stand in relation to opposites."[59] There are two powers involved in the act of faith: first, a power to *choose* to assent or not to assent (condition [4] in the definition of the act of *belief*), and this is a power of the will;

---

[57] There are also habits of *scientia* and understanding. See, for example, ST I-II.57.

[58] "si quis ergo in formam definitionis huiusmodi verba reducere velit, potest dicere quod fides est habitus mentis, qua inchoatur vita aeterna in nobis, faciens intellectum assentire non apparentibus." (ST II-II.4.1)

[59] "dispositio autem ad bene agendum in illis potentiis animae quae se habent ad opposita est habitus, ut supra dictum est." (ST II-II.4.2)

second, a power to assent or not to assent (condition [5]), and this is a power of the intellect.[60] The habit of the will that disposes one to *choose to assent* Aquinas identifies as the habit of charity, and the habit of the intellect that disposes one to *assent* to matters of faith is the habit of faith.[61]

As we saw in the account of the act of faith, assent to matters of faith are provoked by *f-seeing* them by the light of faith. The habit of faith is simply a disposition to assent to propositions that one *f-sees*. Here Aquinas identifies the disposition to assent: "The habit of faith helps our minds in two ways: it makes us easy and assured about what should be believed, and discerning about what should be rejected."[62] And, as we saw before, by *f-seeing* we can tell which propositions should be *believed* and which should not. Because *f-seeing* by the light of faith is available to us only by the grace of God, so too the habit of faith (which is a disposition to assent to what one *f-sees*) comes from the grace of God—it is an infused habit.

The act of faith satisfies the necessary and sufficient conditions specified in the definition of *belief*, but not every act of *belief* need be an act of faith. *Beliefs* are formed when one assents to a proposition after forming a desire to assent. There are a number of circumstances in which this can occur without God's grace—for instance, a heretic might assent to the proposition "Jesus was not divine" not from a habit of faith but because he perceives that assenting to the proposition will result in the good of his membership in a heretical group (membership he could, for instance, perceive as good because it yielded him more sensual

---

[60] See ST II-II.4.2 ad 2.

[61] See ST II-II.4.5.

[62] "...qui quidem in duobus nos adjuvat: in hoc scilicet quod intellectum facit facilem ad credendum credenda, contra duritiem, et discretum ad refutandum non credenda, contra errorem." (III Sent 23.iii.2, trans. Gilby—see Aquinas (1955) 198).

pleasures). What distinguishes acts of faith from other acts of *belief* is that the assent from faith stems from the infused habit of faith: a settled state of character in which one is disposed to assent to propositions revealed by the light of faith. Even if a heretic *believes* most of the matters of faith, he does not have faith if he does not have the habit. Aquinas explains:

> A heretic does not have the habit of faith even if it is only one article of faith which he refuses to believe. For infused habits are lost through one contrary act. And the habit of faith has this power, that through it the understanding of the believer is withheld from giving assent to things contrary to faith, just as chastity restrains us from acts opposed to chastity. Now, when a heretic believes something which is beyond the scope of natural knowledge, he does this not by reason of an infused habit, for such a habit would direct him equally to all objects of belief, but by reason of some human judgment, as happens also with pagans who believe certain things surpassing nature about God.[63]

Take some matter of faith that "is beyond the scope of natural knowledge," that is, not knowable by natural human reason—for instance, that God is triune—and suppose someone (a heretic) *believes* that God is triune but does not assent to some other matter of faith (e.g., that Christ was resurrected). Aquinas argues that this person cannot have the habit of faith—for if he did have the habit, it would direct him to assent to every object of faith equally—that

---

[63] "ad decimum dicendum, quod haereticus non habet habitum fidei, etiamsi unum solum articulum discredat; habitus enim infusi per unum actum contrarium tolluntur. fidei etiam habitus hanc efficaciam habet, ut per ipsum intellectus fidelis detineatur ne contrariis fidei assentiat; sicut et castitas refrenat a contrariis castitati. quod autem haereticus aliqua credat quae sunt supra naturalem cognitionem, non est ex aliquo habitu infuso, quia ille habitus dirigeret eum in omnia credibilia aequaliter; sed est ex quadam aestimatione humana, sicut etiam pagani aliqua supra naturam credunt de deo." (QDV 14.10 ad 10)

is, someone who has the habit of faith would assent to any matter of faith, once it is proposed to him. That the heretic *believes* some matter of faith (that God is triune) does not show that he has the habit of faith, but that someone denies some matter of faith shows that he does not have it. When the heretic assents to or denies a proposition he does so not on the basis of an infused habit, but rather on the basis of his own reasoning and his own judgment on the matter—the heretic judges that he should assent to the triune nature of God, while judging that he should not assent to the resurrection of Christ. Instead of assenting as a result of *f-seeing*, heretics assent on the basis of their own determinations. But there can even be some who *believe* all the matters of faith and still lack the habit:

> [J]ust as one who remembers the conclusions of geometry does not have the science of geometry if he does not assent to these conclusions because of the reasons of geometry, but he holds these conclusions only as opinion; so also one who holds those things which are of faith but does not assent to them because of the authority of Catholic teaching, does not have the habit of faith. For, he who assents to anything because of Catholic teaching assents to all those things which that teaching contains. Otherwise, he would believe himself more than the teaching of the Church. From this it is clear that he who obstinately denies an article of faith does not have faith in the other articles—that faith, I say, which is an infused habit— for he holds the conclusions of faith as opinion.[64]

---

[64] "et ideo, sicut aliquis memorialiter tenens conclusiones geometricas, non habet geometriae scientiam, si non propter media geometriae eis assentiatur, sed habebit conclusiones illas tamquam opinatas: ita, qui tenet ea quae sunt fidei, et non assentit eis propter auctoritatem Catholicae doctrinae, non habet habitum fidei. Qui autem propter doctrinam Catholicam alicui assentit, omnibus assentit quae doctrina Catholica habet: alioquin magis credit sibi quam Ecclesiae doctrinae. Ex quo patet, quod qui deficit in uno articulo pertinaciter, non habet fidem de aliis articulis: illam dico fidem quae est

In the passage above, Aquinas refers to the "virtue of faith." According to Aquinas, "Virtue denotes a certain perfection of a power. Now a thing's perfection is considered chiefly in relation to its end. But the end of power is act. Therefore power is said to be perfect, according as it is determined to its act."[65] In order for the habit of faith to be perfected, and thus be a virtue, the acts that result from the habit must themselves be perfect. Aquinas explains how the act of faith can be perfected:

> [T]wo things are required for completing this act. One is that the understanding infallibly tends to its good, which is the truth; the other is that it infallibly be ordered to the last end, because of which the will assents. And both of these are found in the act of formed faith. It is part of the very account of faith that it always carry the understanding to the truth, since the false cannot come under faith, as was had above. From charity, which forms faith, the soul has it that it is infallibly ordered to the good end. And so all formed faith is a virtue.[66]

The act of faith is perfected if one always assents only to true propositions, and further, that the choice to assent is motivated by a will that seeks something that is truly good, namely, the "last

---

habitus infusus; sed oportet quod teneat ea quae sunt fidei, quasi opinata." (QDC 13 ad 6)

[65] "respondeo dicendum quod virtus nominat quandam potentiae perfectionem. uniuscuiusque autem perfectio praecipue consideratur in ordine ad suum finem. finis autem potentiae actus est. unde potentia dicitur esse perfecta, secundum quod determinatur ad suum actum." (ST I-II.55.1)

[66] "cum enim credere sit actus intellectus assentientis vero ex imperio voluntatis, ad hoc quod iste actus sit perfectus duo requiruntur. quorum unum est ut infallibiliter intellectus tendat in suum bonum, quod est verum, aliud autem est ut infallibiliter ordinetur ad ultimum finem, propter quem voluntas assentit vero. et utrumque invenitur in actu fidei formatae. nam ex ratione ipsius fidei est quod intellectus semper feratur in verum, quia fidei non potest subesse falsum, ut supra habitum est, ex caritate autem, quae format fidem, habet anima quod infallibiliter voluntas ordinetur in bonum finem. et ideo fides formata est virtus." (ST II-II.4.5)

end" which is union with God in an eternal afterlife. If one assents only because one *f-sees* that the proposition should be assented to, then one will not assent to anything false[67]—and this is the case of the person who has the habit of faith. In order for the will to identify properly the ultimate good to be desired, and to choose to assent on this basis, the will must be perfected by the habit of charity. When one chooses to assent with a will perfected by charity, that person is assured that he or she is willing the ultimate good (rather than some lesser good misperceived as the ultimate good).

One has the virtue of faith, then, when one has two habits that have been perfected: faith and charity. Having perfect habits of faith and charity ensures that when one forms *beliefs* about matters of faith, the proposition is true, and the desired goal is the ultimate good. As we saw above, it is possible for someone to *believe* matters of faith while lacking the habit of faith. In the section 3.2.1 below, we shall examine how it is possible for someone to have faith that P without having the virtue of faith.

3.2. Issues related to Aquinas's account of faith

In the account of faith given thus far, we see that the act of faith is a species of an act of *belief*. The act of faith involves God's grace at two points: one in which grace helps someone move from a simple desire to assent to a decision to assent, and another in which grace allows one to *f-see* that matters of faith are to be assented to, thus allowing one to assent with the firmness of adherence that constitutes certitude. In the next two sections, we shall consider some issues that arise from this account: first, in section 3.2.1, we will examine how one might assent to matters of

---

[67] For a discussion of why assenting to matters of faith from the virtue of faith is truth-preserving, see section 3.3.

faith without having the virtue of faith; then, in section 3.2.2, we will examine the faith attributed to demons.

3.2.1. Lifeless faith—faith without charity

There is a sort of faith that one can have without having the habit of charity; this is called "lifeless" or "unformed" faith. Lifeless faith, because it lacks charity, is not a virtue because the habit of the will has not been perfected,[68] though it does count as faith because it includes the habit of faith. The virtue of charity, which lifeless faith lacks, involves a special relationship with God:

> Accordingly, since there is a communication between man and God, in so far as He communicates His happiness to us, there must be some kind of friendship based on this same communication, of which it is written (1 Cor. 1:9): "God is faithful: by Whom you are called unto the fellowship of His Son." The love which is based on this communication, is charity. And so it is evident that charity is the friendship of man for God.[69]

Charity is an infused habit that arises within us by means of communication with God. If we have charity, we form a special friendship or union with God, a particular bond. As a result of this bond, we properly see God to be the ultimate good that our wills always desire—for the blessed, because they have charity and union with God, "it entirely fills the potentiality of the rational mind, since every actual movement of that mind is directed to

---

[68] See ST II-II.4.5.

[69] "cum igitur sit aliqua communicatio hominis ad deum secundum quod nobis suam beatitudinem communicat, super hac communicatione oportet aliquam amicitiam fundari. de qua quidem communicatione dicitur i ad cor. i, fidelis deus, per quem vocati estis in societatem filii eius. amor autem super hac communicatione fundatus est caritas. unde manifestum est quod caritas amicitia quaedam est hominis ad deum." (ST II-II.23.1)

God."[70] For ordinary men, the will can tend toward other perceived goods, and those infused with less-than-perfect charity sometimes may desire something other than God:

> For at first it is incumbent on man to occupy himself chiefly with avoiding sin and resisting his concupiscences, which move him in opposition to charity; and this concerns beginners, in whom charity has to be fed or fostered lest it be destroyed. In the second place man's chief pursuit is to aim at progress in good, and this is the pursuit of the proficient, whose chief aim is to strengthen their charity by adding to it. Man's third pursuit is to aim chiefly at union with and enjoyment of God, and this pertains to the perfect who "desire to be dissolved and to be with Christ."[71]

For our purposes, we can conceive of charity as a habit of the will in desiring better goods. Beginners, who do not have a close communion with God, try to develop a habit to avoid sinful desires. Those further along try to develop a habit to pursue only goods, and those approaching perfection of charity desire only the best good—union with and enjoyment of God; no other goods are desired over God. We lose charity when we desire inordinately— by desiring sin over goodness, or by desiring some lesser good

---

[70] "sic igitur caritas patriae, quia replet totam potentialitatem rationalis mentis, inquantum scilicet omnis actualis motus eius fertur in deum, inamissibiliter habetur. caritas autem viae non sic replet potentialitatem sui subiecti, quia non semper actu fertur in deum. unde quando actu in deum non fertur, potest aliquid occurrere per quod caritas amittatur." (ST II-II.24.11)

[71] "nam primo quidem incumbit homini studium principale ad recedendum a peccato et resistendum concupiscentiis eius, quae in contrarium caritatis movent. et hoc pertinet ad incipientes, in quibus caritas est nutrienda vel fovenda ne corrumpatur. secundum autem studium succedit, ut homo principaliter intendat ad hoc quod in bono proficiat. et hoc studium pertinet ad proficientes, qui ad hoc principaliter intendunt ut in eis caritas per augmentum roboretur. tertium autem studium est ut homo ad hoc principaliter intendat ut deo inhaereat et eo fruatur. et hoc pertinet ad perfectos, qui cupiunt dissolvi et esse cum christo." (ST II-II.24.9)

when we should desire God; we withdraw from our friendship with God, and thereby lose the charity that results from such a closeness.

Charity perfects faith because it orients the will to desire the proper goods. One who has the virtue of faith not only *f-sees* that matters of faith are to be *believed*, but also has charity and desires them easily and without struggle. One clear difference between lifeless faith and the faith formed by charity is that one who has the latter is subject to filial fear, which is a fear of being separated from God, and in response to such a fear one desires eagerly and easily to assent to matters of faith, such assent being necessary for union with God in heaven. With lifeless faith, on the other hand, there is merely servile fear, in which one desires to assent to matters of faith merely to avoid punishment by God.[72] Faith formed by charity easily and, so to speak, naturally assents to matters of faith, whereas lifeless faith does so uneasily. Finally, unformed faith, though it involves assent to matters of faith, is not sufficient for salvation because the heart has not been purified:

> This impurity happens when the human understanding inordinately inheres in things below it, namely, when it wills to measure divine things according to the accounts of sensible things. But when it is formed by charity, it admits no impurity within itself, since "charity covers all faults," as it is said in Proverbs 10.[73]

---

[72] See ST II-II.7.1.

[73] "ad secundum dicendum quod fides etiam informis excludit quandam impuritatem sibi oppositam, scilicet impuritatem erroris, quae contingit ex hoc quod intellectus humanus inordinate inhaeret rebus se inferioribus, dum scilicet vult secundum rationes rerum sensibilium metiri divina. sed quando per caritatem formatur, tunc nullam impuritatem secum compatitur, quia universa delicta operit caritas, ut dicitur prov. x." (ST II-II.7.2 ad 2)

3.2.2. Faith of the demons

A source of controversy in interpreting Aquinas's account of faith surrounds the claim he seems to make that demons also have faith. Motivated by a passage from James 2:19, "The devils believe, and tremble," Aquinas seems to attribute faith to demons—he says that they cannot perceive certain truths about Christ "except through faith,"[74] he adds that "the first sort of faith exists in demons,"[75] and he also refers to "the faith which the demons have."[76] Attributing faith to demons is problematic because the idea that demons have faith seems inconsistent with the account of faith we have presented thus far. Unlike the virtue of faith, demonic faith lacks charity,[77] assent is not a result of grace,[78] and belief results from the evidence of miracles and other signs rather than by a will being directed to the good.[79] Aquinas holds that the demons do not assent on the basis of their wills at all; rather, their intellects are compelled by the evidence of miracles: "It is not their wills which bring demons to assent to what they are said to believe. Rather, they are forced by the evidence of signs which convince them that what the faithful believe is true."[80] The case of the demons seems to present a problem for Aquinas's account of faith: according to the account of faith provided thus far, faith depends essentially on the will and is *not* compelled by evidence,

---

[74] ST III.76.7

[75] III Sent. 23.iii.3.ii, sol. I

[76] ST II-II.5.2 ad 2. See also the *responsio* of this article.

[77] See ST I.25.11 ad 1.

[78] See ST I.64.1 ad 5; see also ST II-II.5.2 ad 2.

[79] See ST II-II.5.2. Refer back to section 3.1.2.3, where I presented the *veracity argument* based on belief caused by evidence of miracles. Aquinas holds that this sort of belief is the kind the demons have. See also ST II-II.5.2 ad 1.

[80] "…quod daemones non voluntate assentiunt his quae credere dicuntur, sed coacti evidentia signorum, ex quibus convincitur verum esse quod fideles credunt…." (QDV 14.9 ad 4). See also ST III.76.7.

but the demons seem to have faith, and their assent appears to be compelled by evidence. This apparent inconsistency in allowing for demonic faith has motivated various complaints against Aquinas: John Hick believes that Aquinas should jettison demons from his theology (thus solving the problem by denying that there are any demons that have faith);[81] Terence Penelhum suggests that the human faithful have access to the same conclusive evidence that the demons have (which would render our account of faith as not involving *q-seeing* incorrect);[82] James Ross denies that the demons are really *compelled* to believe and thus can be said to have faith;[83] and Eleonore Stump seems to hold a position similar to Ross's that demons and humans have the same sort of faith, that the faith of the demons is lifeless, and that the evidence motivates (rather than compels) demons to assent.[84]

These responses suffer from one of two problems: they seem either to correct or change Aquinas's position (Hick, Ross, Stump) or to advocate an account of faith that differs from the one presented here (Penelhum, Ross). I wish to present an explanation of demonic faith that does not undermine the account of faith provided thus far and does take Aquinas seriously and literally. Given that Aquinas clearly holds that the demons' assent is compelled, unformed, and lacking grace, demonic faith does not seem to be the same as human faith. Aquinas does hold explicitly that demonic faith is not exactly the same as human faith; he asserts that "faith" is equivocal for demons and for humans: "...belief is predicated equivocally of men who believe and of the demons. And faith does not result in them from any infused light

---

[81] Hick, *Faith and Knowledge*, 21.
[82] Penelhum, "Analysis of Faith in St. Thomas Aquinas," 146.
[83] Ross, "Aquinas on Belief and Knowledge," 264.
[84] Stump, "Aquinas on Faith and Goodness," 190-91.

of grace as it does in the faithful."[85] If demonic faith is not the same as human faith, then what is it, and why does Aquinas call it "faith"?

When we examined the veracity argument in section 3.1.2.3 above, in which the truth of some proposition is proven by evidence for the veracity of the person uttering it, we considered the possibility that *belief* might be a form of *scientia quia*: knowledge that the proposition is true, but not why it is true. This interpretation was rejected for Christian faith, but Aquinas tells us that the demons, unlike humans, do seem to believe on the basis of the veracity argument: "Demons see many clear indications from which they perceive that the doctrine of the Church is from God, even if they do not see things that the Church teaches, for example, that God is three and one or something else of this kind."[86] Aquinas seems to think that assent of this sort still should be called "faith," since the proposition believed "would not be evident in itself, so that the account of faith would not be taken away."[87] Aquinas seems to construe an essential characteristic of faith as lacking *p-vision* of the truth of propositions—recall his definition of faith: "faith is a habit of the mind, whereby eternal life is begun in us, making the intellect assent to what is nonapparent." Demons can be said to have faith because they assent to what is nonapparent, though they have a different sort of faith from that of the Christian faithful since their faith is not motivated by eternal life with God.

---

[85] "unde et credere quasi aequivoce dicitur de hominibus fidelibus et daemonibus: nec est in eis fides ex aliquo lumine gratiae infuso sicut est in fidelibus." (QDV 14.9 ad 4)

[86] "vident enim multa manifesta indicia ex quibus percipiunt doctrinam ecclesiae esse a deo; quamvis ipsi res ipsas quas ecclesia docet non videant, puta deum esse trinum et unum, vel aliquid huiusmodi." (ST II-II.5.2)

[87] "…licet illud futurum quod praedicitur in se evidens non esset, unde ratio fidei non tolleretur." (ST II-II.5.2)

Though the demons have a sort of faith, demonic faith cannot be a species of *belief* as was defined above: the demons do not apprehend that assenting to matters of faith would be good for them (condition [2]),[88] and thus do not desire to assent (condition [3]), and because they are compelled by the evidence, they also do not freely choose to assent to matters of faith (condition [4]).

Rather than *belief* or faith, I think what Aquinas has in mind as primary is the assent itself, and there are two kinds: assent with *p-vision* and assent without *p-vision*. In the former kind of assent, one has *p-vision* of the truth of the proposition because the intelligible object forces the intellect to assent. This form of assent yields the epistemic states of *perfect scientia* and understanding. The latter kind of assent lacks *p-vision* because the assenter does not see why the proposition is true. There are two kinds of assent that lack *p-vision*: in the first, the assenter, on the basis of some sort of veracity argument, *q-sees* that the proposition is true, which yields something merely resembling *belief* that results from a demonstration *quia*; in the second kind, one assents on the basis of the will, which yields *belief* proper. Demonic faith is a species of the former kind of assent without *p-vision*,[89] human faith a species of the latter. When Aquinas says that the demons believe, or that they have faith, he is calling attention to the similarity between demonic assent from evidence (*q-seeing*) and human assent from faith proper (*f-seeing*). These are similar to each other because

---

[88] "...that the demons are compelled to believe, is displeasing to them..."

"ad tertium dicendum quod hoc ipsum daemonibus displicet quod signa fidei sunt tam evidentia ut per ea credere compellantur. et ideo in nullo malitia eorum minuitur per hoc quod credunt." (ST II-II.5.2 ad 3)

[89] The reader here should note that demonic belief is not the only case that involves this sort of assent. Demonstrations *quia* that prove causes from their effects (see section 4.4.1 in the next chapter on the Five Ways) as well as demonstrations of subaltern sciences (see PA I.25) also yield this form of assent.

neither of them has vision (*p-seeing*) though both involve assent, and neither results in the sort of complete certitude of evidence (i.e., the contradictory of what is assented to is conceivable), though they both involve the certitude that is firmness of assent. When compared with understanding or *perfect scientia*, demonic and human faith appear to be more similar to each other than different, and this is why Aquinas says that the demons have faith. But when he contrasts human and demonic faith (as he does in the passage quoted in section 3.1.2.3 above, in which he discusses two different causes of faith), we see that two different acts are being described—one that results from *f-seeing*, one from *q-seeing*. So, unlike the solutions presented by Hick et al., my proposed solution to the problem of demonic faith is this: the demons, unlike humans, have assent compelled by evidence, and for this reason do not have the same sort of faith that humans have. But what demons have is similar enough to be called "faith," and thus we can do so, at least in some contexts.[90]

3.3. The epistemology of faith

According to Aquinas, the act of faith is a species of *belief*. Recall the definition for *belief* presented earlier:

S has *belief* that P =df   (1) S apprehends P,

(2) S apprehends that assenting
to P would be good for S,

(3) this leads to a desire in S
to assent to P,

(4) this leads to a choice by S

---

[90] A second reason to think that Aquinas holds demonic and human faith as equivocal is that the demons, as fallen angels, have the same kind of intellect as angels and, in particular, do not reason discursively. They can syllogize, in a way, by seeing conclusions in the premises, but there is not "movement" of the intellect towards *belief* as there is with humans. See, for instance, ST I.58.3 including replies, and ST I.58.5.

to assent to P, and
(5) this leads S to assent to P.

For matters of faith, the first condition is brought about by testimony: we are either told directly by someone that P is true, for instance, in a sermon or by someone who is presented to us as a messenger of God; or indirectly, for instance, by reading about the truth of P from Scripture. In conjunction with learning about the proposition, we learn that assenting to the proposition is necessary for and promotes eternal life. This leads to the satisfaction of the second and third conditions. In order to *believe*, one must proceed from desire to choice—there are many things we may desire, but presumably we decide to pursue only a very limited number of them. In the paradigmatic case of faith, faith formed by charity, one is motivated to choose to assent to P because one strives to maintain or promote the union with and love of God that is charity. In cases of lifeless faith, the motivation to assent is not from charity, and so it is not love of God but something else that motivates one to choose to assent. Aquinas identifies one motivation, fear of punishment, so that one chooses to assent to P because one is afraid of the punishment that will accrue if one fails to do so. There are likely other motivations beyond servile fear that could lead one to choose to assent. Regardless of motivation, what is key to faith is that God moves one to choose by grace. If one has faith (whether lifeless or not), then the act of faith follows from an established habit of faith. This habit moves the faithful actually to assent to the matters of faith. The will moves the intellect to assent in faith by a process analogous to other movements of the intellect to assent. For self-evident propositions, for example, one "sees" that the proposition is true because it is "illuminated" by the light of reason (one has *p-vision*) and this "seeing" moves the intellect to assent. Similarly, those who have the habit of faith have an infused light of faith, and by this light they "see" that the proposition is to be *believed* (they have *f-vision*); the habit of faith disposes one who "sees" in this way to move the intellect to assent. The movement in faith initially resides in the will because the will chooses to assent, and by so choosing, it moves the intellect to move to assent to what it *f-sees*.

As mentioned earlier (in section 3.1.2.4), the assent of faith is held by Aquinas to produce certitude because it engenders firmness of adherence to the proposition assented to. Further, the assent of faith is held to be firmer than that of *perfect scientia* or understanding, and faith is held by Aquinas to be infallible. These latter claims made by Aquinas put faith in a rather extraordinary epistemic position—he even seems to hold that faith is more epistemically secure than understanding or *perfect scientia*. We shall devote the rest of this section to examining these epistemic properties of faith.

That faith should be more firmly adhered to than under-standing of self-evident propositions seems counterintuitive. When we understand a proposition or when we have one demon-strated to us so that we have *perfect scientia*, we *p-see* its truth: we "see" that it is true, why it is true, and further we cannot even entertain the idea that the truth of the proposition could be otherwise. This would seem to generate certitude of the highest degree. Faith, on the other hand, being a product of the will choosing to assent, would seem to have less certitude, particularly since the intellect is not determined by the object—one who has faith can still continue to entertain intellectually the idea that the proposition is false. And yet faith, according to Aquinas, has more certitude than understanding. Here he explains:

> [O]ther things being equal, vision is more certain than hearing. But if the thing that is heard far exceeds the vision of the seer, in this way what is heard is more certain than what is

seen. Just so someone with little knowledge (*scientiae*) might be more certain of what he hears from another, who is most learned (*scientissimo*), than of what might seem to him according to his own reason. And much more is a man more certain of what he hears from God, who cannot fail, than of what he sees with his own reason, which can fail.[91]

What Aquinas here refers to as vision and hearing we have been discussing as *p-vision* and apprehending by testimony. Aquinas seems to make the following argument:

(ia) If testimony is not more reliable than vision, then assent from vision has *more* certitude than assent from testimony.

(ib) If testimony is more reliable than vision, then assent from vision has *less* certitude than assent from testimony.

(ii) The source of assent from *scientia* is *p-vision*.

(iii) The source of assent from faith is the testimony of God.

(iv) God is infallible.

(v) *P-vision* is fallible.

∴ (vi) The testimony of God is a more reliable source than *p-vision*.

∴ (vii) Assent from faith has more certitude than assent from *scientia*.

---

[91] "ad secundum dicendum quod, ceteris paribus, visio est certior auditu. sed si ille a quo auditur multum excedit visum videntis, sic certior est auditus quam visus. sicut aliquis parvae scientiae magis certificatur de eo quod audit ab aliquo scientissimo quam de eo quod sibi secundum suam rationem videtur. et multo magis homo certior est de eo quod audit a deo, qui falli non potest, quam de eo quod videt propria ratione, quae falli potest." (ST II-II.4.8 ad 2)

In the passage above, Aquinas provides justification for pre-mises (ia) & (ib): generally *p-vision* is more reliable than testimony (which explains why assent from *p-vision* generally has more certitude than assent from testimony), but there can be cases in which one has very weak or limited *p-vision* while simultaneously having testimony from a reliable source—and in this case assent from the testimony has more certitude than from the *p-vision*. But this reasoning seems unsound. If one has *p-vision*, that is, one sees why a proposition is true, then it seems one would have under-standing of it. And should one perform a proper demonstration from this, then one would have *perfect scientia*. Even if my perceptiveness were limited, so that many things that are evident by *p-vision* to others are not so to me, it would seem that when I do have *p-vision*, I will also have certitude, and that this certitude would far exceed that which I would have from relying on the testimony of any expert. What seems to be true about the case that Aquinas describes is that the authority of an expert can provide more certitude about P when we lack *p-vision* about P, even though P is something for which *p-vision* may be possible. The lesson of this case would seem to be that assent based on expert testimony has more certitude than assent based on a *mistaken* apprehension that one had *perfect scientia*—that when the intellect cannot obtain for itself *perfect scientia*, then expert testimony is the best source of certitude available.

Perhaps, however, we can understand Aquinas to be making exactly this point. When he says, in the passage above, that reason can be mistaken, perhaps he is not asserting what I have presented as: (v) *p-vision* is fallible; instead, he may be advocating: (v') human reason is fallible in self-attributions of *perfect scientia*. In the previous chapter, we saw that Aquinas does hold (v'),[92] and in

---

[92] See section 2.4.2.

the context of matters of faith, the fallibility of reason appears to be even more common:

> Human reason is much deficient in divine things. A sign of this is that the philosophers, investigating human things naturally, erred in many things and held opinions (*senserunt*) contrary to themselves. Divine things had to be handed down to them in the manner of faith, as being said by God, who cannot lie, so that there might be indubitable and certain apprehension of God among men.[93]

Aquinas's example comparing the expert and one's own reason would work as follows. Though we are fallible in self-attributions of *perfect scientia*, the fallibility is not absolute—we have certain talents and training that make demonstrations about certain topics infallible (e.g., simple arithmetical demonstrations), but with topics that are well beyond our skills or expertise we are very susceptible to attributing *perfect scientia* falsely to ourselves—we are quite fallible. In these latter cases, *believing* on the authority of an established expert should yield more certitude than by our own reasoning. If this is Aquinas's point, then he is not making the argument presented in (i) through (vii), but rather this modified argument:

(ia)   If testimony is not more reliable than vision, then assent from vision has *more* certitude than assent from testimony.

---

[93] "ratio enim humana in rebus divinis est multum deficiens, cuius signum est quia philosophi, de rebus humanis naturali investigatione perscrutantes, in multis erraverunt et sibi ipsis contraria senserunt. ut ergo esset indubitata et certa cognitio apud homines de deo, oportuit quod divina eis per modum fidei traderentur, quasi a deo dicta, qui mentiri non potest." (ST II-II.2.4)

(ib)   If testimony is more reliable than vision, then assent
       from vision has *less* certitude than assent from
       testimony.

(ii') The source of assent from *perfect scientia* is human
       reason.

(iii) The source of assent from faith is the testimony of God.

(iv)   In all matters, God is infallible.

   (v')   Concerning matters of faith, human reason is
             fallible in self-attributions of *perfect scientia*.

∴ (vi')   Concerning matters of faith, the testimony of God
             is a more reliable source than human reason.

∴ (vii')   The assent to matters of faith by means of faith
             has more certitude than such assent by means of
             human reason.

Thus, the assent of faith has more certitude than the assent
stemming from human reason because it is more reliable. The
assent of faith is based on God's informing you of what to *believe*
(via the light of faith which identifies the matters of faith to be
believed), and God never lies and is never wrong, so one can have
absolute certitude that these propositions are true. Assent from
human reason, on the other hand, can be misplaced—when it
comes to matters of the divine, our intellectual capacities are
rather limited, and when we assent to some proposition on the
basis of what we think is a demonstration, we may in fact be
mistaken.

Notice that in the revised argument above, premise (iii)
asserts that the testimony comes directly from God. If the
testimony were given through intermediaries, then assent would
have certitude only if the intermediaries were infallible, at least in
transmitting God's message. Aquinas raises this same worry: "to
assent to the testimony of a man or an angel would lead infallibly
to the truth only in so far as we considered the testimony of God

speaking in them."[94] But how would a person know that the testimony of a man or an angel is a result of God speaking in them? With the evidence of signs, for example, that the man or angel performs miracles, one could know that the figure serves as God's messenger; however, this leads us back to the veracity argument, and assent on this basis does not constitute faith. This seems to lead us back to the dilemma we faced with demonic faith: if we have proof that the testimony comes from God, then we do not have human faith, but if we have human faith, then we do not know that the testimony comes from God, and thus faith would seem to lack certitude.

The key to the certitude of faith is God's grace. Though we may initially apprehend a proposition on the basis of the testimony of other humans (or angels, or Scripture), our assent is not caused by this testimony, but by some inward cause. If one has faith formed by charity, then one has a friendship with God, and this serves as a direct connection to Him, thereby ensuring that what is *believed* is true. For those who do not have faith formed by charity, but have lifeless faith, God infuses them with the light of faith. This illumination of what should be *believed* comes directly from God and, again, will guarantee the truth of what is *believed*.

3.4. Conclusions

According to the account given by Aquinas, faith is a rather extraordinary act. In order to have faith about some proposition, one does not need evidence that proves the proposition is true, and yet faith has certitude and is infallible. It acquires these characteristics as a result of God's gratuitous grace acting within

---

[94] "unde neque hominis neque angeli testimonio assentire infallibiliter in veritatem duceret, nisi in quantum in eis loquentis dei testimonium consideratur." (QDV 14.8)

humans: the grace of charity brings humans into a special loving relationship with God, and the grace of the light of faith allows humans to infallibly identify what should be *believed*. Not only is faith infallible and has certitude, but even more so than understanding and *perfect scientia*—the ideal epistemic states obtainable by the natural operations of the intellect. Similar to *perfect scientia*, faith has rather ideal epistemic qualities, and thus it is not clear that many people even have the sort of faith Aquinas describes.

In order to have faith formed by charity, and thus the virtue of faith, not only must one have a special loving relationship with God, but the goods one desires must be properly ordered. According to Aquinas, the wayfarer who has charity "makes an earnest endeavor to give his time to God and Divine things, while scorning other things except in so far as the needs of the present life demand." A weaker form of charity allows one to give one's "whole heart to God habitually, that is, by neither thinking nor desiring anything contrary to the love of God."[95] Thus, charity, even among self-ascribed Christians, is a difficult state to achieve, particularly since charity is lost should one sin.[96]

Lifeless faith requires that one have the light of faith infused by God. Aquinas holds that this is "common to all members of the Church."[97] However, once someone *disbelieves* an article of faith,

---

[95] "uno modo, sic quod totum cor hominis actualiter semper feratur in deum. et haec est perfectio caritatis patriae, quae non est possibilis in hac vita, in qua impossibile est, propter humanae vitae infirmitatem, semper actu cogitare de deo et moveri dilectione ad ipsum. alio modo, ut homo studium suum deputet ad vacandum deo et rebus divinis, praetermissis aliis nisi quantum necessitas praesentis vitae requirit. et ista est perfectio caritatis quae est possibilis in via, non tamen est communis omnibus caritatem habentibus. tertio modo, ita quod habitualiter aliquis totum cor suum ponat in deo, ita scilicet quod nihil cogitet vel velit quod sit divinae dilectioni contrarium. et haec perfectio est communis omnibus caritatem habentibus." (ST II-II.24.8)

[96] See ST II-II.24.11.

[97] ST II-II.4.5 ad 4.

he or she becomes a heretic, and the gratuitous grace of the light of faith is withdrawn. The faithful is one "who inheres in the doctrine of the Church, as in an infallible rule, [and thereby] assents to all that the Church teaches. If he holds and does not hold whatever he wants from among what the Church teaches, he does not inhere in the teaching of the Church as in an infallible rule, but rather by his own will."[98] Once someone no longer *believes* even one proposition taught by the Church (which is held to align with what the light of faith illuminates), then one loses faith and only has opinion in what one holds. At first, this condition on faith appears to be excessively stringent: one who disagrees with the Church that contraception or premarital sex are in fact sinful would under this account not have faith *at all*—he merely has opinions. Aquinas is perhaps not quite as draconian as this in his Quodlibetial Question, "Whether those listening to different teachers of Theology who have contrary opinions are excused from sin if they follow the false opinions of their teachers." In his response to the question, Aquinas holds that following such opinions are acceptable only if they do not pertain to "faith or good morals."[99] So some Scriptural interpretations or rules of conduct that disagree with official Catholic doctrine might not prevent one from having faith;[100] however, Protestant rejections of the sacrament of the Eucharist presumably would result in one *disbelieving* a matter of faith held by the Church, and

---

[98] "manifestum est autem quod ille qui inhaeret doctrinae ecclesiae tanquam infallibili regulae, omnibus assentit quae ecclesia docet. alioquin, si de his quae ecclesia docet quae vult tenet et quae vult non tenet, non iam inhaeret ecclesiae doctrinae sicut infallibili regulae, sed propriae voluntati." (ST II-II.5.3)

[99] See Quodlibetal Questions III, q. 4, a. 2.

[100] Would, for instance, advocacy for the use of contraceptives or for the poverty of clergy fall into this category? Aquinas is not clear on what counts as relating to "good morals."

thus prevent one from having faith at all, according to Aquinas's account.[101]

The virtue of faith would appear to be a rare and difficult state to obtain. But even the habit of faith would appear not to be had by a significant number of self-ascribed Christians when they *disbelieve* some proposition pertaining to "faith or good morals." By Aquinas's account of faith, then, most contemporary self-ascribed Christians would not seem to have it, nor perhaps ever have had it. This consequence could be construed as a virtue of the account: Aquinas does speak of both *believing* and of opining about matters of faith, so perhaps having faith is a lofty goal to which Christians must aspire, but for most it is something they have not yet achieved. The apparent rarity of faith can also be construed as a weakness of the account: many would be inclined to hold that most Christian believers do, in fact, have faith, and any account which produces a different result must be incorrect.[102]

In pointing out the inadequacies of an Intellectualist interpretation of Aquinas, we earlier cited a number of questions raised by Stump that the Intellectualist interpretations were incapable of answering:

> First, if there is an omniscient and omnipotent God, why would he want human relationships with him to be based on faith? Why wouldn't he make his existence and nature as obvious and uncontroversial to all human beings as the

---

[101] Although Aquinas holds that the Sovereign Pontiff has the authority to draw up new creeds (ST II-II.1.10) he does not hold that the matters of faith are subject to the whim of the Church. The truths of faith, being of and from God, are substantially unchanging (ST II-II.1.7) though the explicit presentation of them is subject to change and addition by the Church.

[102] On the other hand, Aquinas frequently discusses (see, for instance, ST I.1.1) that without faith truths about God would be available only to a few (namely, those capable of performing and understanding the proofs). This would seem to imply that truths about God are instead available to many, which would seem to imply that Aquinas thinks that many do have faith.

existence of their physical surroundings is? Second, why should having faith be meritorious, as Christian doctrine maintains it is? And why should faith be supposed to make acceptable to God a person whom God would otherwise reject? Finally, why is it that epistemological considerations seem to play so little role in adult conversions?[103]

Aquinas's account of faith, as presented here, allows us to answer these questions. Stump holds that God would want relationships with Him to be based on faith, and that faith is meritorius because "faith [is] the beginning of a moral reform of the will, of a kind that simple knowledge of the propositions of faith by itself could not bring about."[104] The account of faith we have given here (which is largely consistent with Stump's) easily explains this. We can pursue the virtue of faith, and its component charity, and by doing so we not only bring ourselves closer to God but develop habits of increasingly well-ordered desires while diminishing the desire to sin. A faith based on charity promotes unity with God, whereas simple propositional acceptance of matters of faith does not. Stump's answer to the final question is: "On Aquinas's account of faith, what is happening in such cases (or, at any rate, in the case of true conversions) is not that the intellect is weighing and judging epistemological considerations but that the will is drawn to a love of God's goodness and in consequence moves the intellect to assent to the propositions of faith."[105] This, too, is the answer one would expect given our interpretation of Aquinas's account of faith.

---

[103] Stump, "Aquinas on Faith and Goodness," (1991) 179-80.
[104] Ibid., 207.
[105] Ibid.

4

INTERACTION OF FAITH AND REASON

In chapters 2 and 3 we examined Aquinas's accounts of reason and faith, respectively. According to Aquinas, *scientia* (the product of demonstrative reasoning), faith (the product of *believing*), and opinion (the product of dialectical or probable reasoning) can all be placed along one epistemic continuum. *Perfect scientia*, as we discussed in chapter 2, is an epistemic state that involves an apprehension of a proposition, certitude in the necessity of the proposition, and perfect apprehension of the truth of the proposition (i.e., an apprehension of why the proposition is true). Faith involves apprehension of the proposition as well as certitude but lacks perfect apprehension of its truth, and opinion lacks both certitude and perfect apprehension of its truth.

We also saw in chapter 3 that these three epistemic states are mutually exclusive—one can have faith, *scientia*, or opinion about a proposition but cannot simultaneously be in more than one of these epistemic states with respect to any particular proposition. Since Aquinas holds that faith is necessary for salvation but reasoning to divine matters is not,[1] we need to understand what role Aquinas thinks reason does or ought to play for Christian philosophers or theologians. In this chapter, we will examine Aquinas's account of the roles for reason and faith with regard to divine matters. In section 4.1, we will consider Aquinas's view that, for certain matters of faith, reason is simply incapable of

---

[1] See, for example, ST I.1.1 and SCG I.4.

providing us with *scientia*. We will look closely at Aquinas's discussion of the possible eternity of the world as an instance of how he understands reason to be limited in matters of faith. In sections 4.4 and 4.5, we will consider some roles that Aquinas does believe reason can play with respect to matters of faith. We will look closely at Aquinas's Five Ways (his proofs for the existence of God) in order to understand better how Aquinas thinks that reason can play a role in faith.

4.1. Limitations of reason in divine matters

Aquinas accepts an Aristotelian account of cognition. Thus, according to Aquinas, our intellects are seriously limited in what we can know about God.

In brief, Aquinas's Aristotelian account of cognition is roughly as follows. Objects make impressions on the external senses; these impressions are copied and transmitted to the intellect as likenesses, or phantasms (*phantasmata*). By abstracting from these phantasms we can apprehend in the intellect the form and accidents of the object sensed. What the senses respond to are individual particulars, but what the intellect apprehends are intelligible species, that is, universals apprehended by means of abstraction.[2] Thus, apprehending that humans are rational animals is a result of first sensing one or more particular humans, forming phantasms of them in the intellect, and then abstracting from these phantasms to apprehend the intelligible species, or form, of a human—and, for instance, that the form of human includes rationality.

Mathematical objects are a special case, yet our apprehension of their forms also depends on our first sensing particular objects.

---

[2] For Aquinas's account of cognition, see ST I.84. See also Kretzmann, "Philosophy of Mind," in *Cambridge Companion to Aquinas*, ed. Kretzmann and Stump (1993).

Mathematical objects, such as triangles, are only accidentally constituted by their particular matter (e.g., some triangular stone), whereas ordinary objects (e.g., Socrates, a house) depend essentially on the matter that constitutes them, since it is this matter that makes them the particular objects they are. In the case of mathematical objects, once we abstract away all the accidents relating to the particular matter, we are left with those accidents, such as quantity, that depend only on intelligible matter.[3] Though mathematical objects do not depend essentially on particular matter, our knowledge of them does, in that we first perceive sensible objects and abstract from them an intelligible species (e.g., triangles).

These apprehended universals serve as the principles of demonstration, so, for instance, from the universal that humans are rational animals we might be able to demonstrate that horses are not human.[4] If we were unable to abstract from phantasms to the intelligible species of a thing, we would be unable to develop any demonstrations about that thing; in other words, our ability to have *perfect scientia* about things depends on our abilities to apprehend something about these universal essences. According to this account of cognition, we are unable to have *perfect scientia* about God, since He is not composed of sensible matter.[5] Aquinas observes:

> For the human intellect is not able to reach a comprehension (*capiendam*) of the divine substance through its natural power. For, according to its manner of cognizing (*cognitio*) in the present life, the intellect depends on the sense for the origin of knowledge; and so those things that do not fall under the

---

[3] For Aquinas's explanation of how we come to apprehend mathematical forms, see DT 5.3.

[4] For Aquinas's account of demonstration, see section 2.4.1.

[5] See ST I.3.1-2.

senses cannot be grasped by the human intellect except in so far as the cognition (*cognitio*) of them is gathered from sensible things. Now, sensible things cannot lead the human intellect to the point of seeing in them the nature of the divine substance; for sensible things are effects that fall short of the power of their cause.[6]

We cannot apprehend the essence of God, not only because He is not sensible, but also, as Aquinas observes in the last sentence from the passage above, because His sensible effects inadequately represent their cause, God. Effects of God are created, finite, and limited, and what we can discern from them by way of abstraction are forms that are also limited. But God and His power are unlimited, so the forms abstracted from God's effects do not accurately reflect God as He is—that is, they do not reveal His essence. Thus, in virtue of our current cognitive apparatus,[7] we cannot apprehend the essence of God, and thus we cannot have *perfect scientia* of God's essence.

Given our cognitive limitations, *perfect scientia* of divine matters that depend on understanding God's essence is unavailable to us. These limitations also restrict in principle our ability to have *perfect scientia* of other matters of faith that depend on understanding God's essence. For instance, that the world was created with a beginning, and thus has existed with a finite duration in time, is also something that Aquinas believes we cannot have *scientia* about. In the next section, we will examine

---

[6] "nam ad substantiam ipsius capiendam intellectus humanus naturali virtute pertingere non potest: cum intellectus nostri, secundum modum praesentis vitae, cognitio a sensu incipiat; et ideo ea quae in sensu non cadunt, non possunt humano intellectu capi, nisi quatenus ex sensibilibus earum cognitio colligitur. sensibilia autem ad hoc ducere intellectum nostrum non possunt ut in eis divina substantia videatur quid sit: cum sint effectus causae virtutem non aequantes." (SCG I.3 n.3)

[7] In the afterlife, we acquire a new cognitive apparatus. See, for instance, CT 164 ff.

Aquinas's treatment of the creation of the world as a case study in how demonstrative reasoning is incapable of producing *scientia* about truths of certain matters of faith. Later, in section 4.4, we will examine what reason can yield in matters of faith.

4.2. Limitations of reason in the matter of the creation of the world

For early theologians, a key topic involving the intersection of philosophy and Christian doctrine was the creation of the world. In *Hexaemera* (treatises on the first six days of creation found in Genesis 1), theologians attempted to reconcile the account of creation given in Genesis with accounts given by philosophers and, frequently, with the account in Plato's *Timaeus*. Until the twelfth century, Plato's cosmogonic account was the primary philosophical account that was considered by theologians.[8] Unlike Plato's, Aristotle's views on the origins of the world conflicted with Christian doctrine, particularly in that he seems to have embraced the view that the world was sempiternal.[9] In response to this apparent incompatibility between Aristotelian cosmogony and the Christian doctrine on the creation of the world in time

---

[8] Though Aristotle's logic was well known, his works of philosophy were lost to the Latin West. Between the middle of the twelfth and the middle of the thirteenth centuries, most of Aristotle's philosophical works were translated into Latin and disseminated among Christian theologians. For a listing of Aristotle's works available in translation (in Latin) to later Medieval scholars, see Dod, "*Aristoteles Latinus*," in *The Cambridge History of Later Medieval Philosophy*, ed. Kretzmann et al. (1982) 74-79.

[9] Sempiternity is different from eternity, which applies to God, in that something that is sempiternal exists for all time and has a "moving now" that changes with the passage of time. God's eternity, by contrast, involves an "ever-present now" that is independent of the passage of time. For a good explanation of the Medieval distinction between sempiternity and eternity, see Stump and Kretzmann, "Eternity," *Journal of Philosophy* 78/8 (1981): 429-58. For simplicity, I shall use "eternity" with respect to the world to mean "sempiternity," and I shall use "eternity" with respect to God to mean "eternity" proper.

philosophers and theologians of the twelfth and thirteenth centuries divided into two camps: eternalists presented arguments that purported to show that the world had existed forever (for instance, Siger of Brabant and Boethius of Dacia, who were inspired by Averroes), whereas temporalists advocated either by appeal to doctrine or arguments that the world was created in time with a beginning (a view that was part of the orthodox Catholic doctrine and was held by the late thirteenth century theologians Giles of Rome, Stephen Tempier, Robert Grosseteste, John Pecham, Bonaventure, and Aquinas, to name a few).[10]

The question of the eternity of the world was of great concern to many thirteenth-century Christian philosophers and theologians. In *Collationes in Hexaemeron*, Bonaventure details three major errors made by philosophers: (1) the eternalist error, which held that the duration of the world was everlasting, and led to (2) the error of the unicity of the intellect, and both led to (3) the error in which it was denied that there was neither happiness nor punishment in the afterlife. Of those who hold these views, Bonaventure says, "These men, therefore, have fallen into errors, nor have they been 'separated from the darkness'; and such errors as these are the very worst. Nor has the abysmal pit been as yet locked up."[11]

An orthodox response to the eternalist position was to condemn it. In 1270 and 1277, several eternalist positions were condemned in Paris. On pain of excommunication, these eternalist

---

[10] For a very detailed and interesting categorization of the eternalists and temporalists, as well as other stances with respect to the eternity of the world, see Kovach, "The Question of the Eternity of the World in St. Bonaventure and St. Thomas—A Critical Analysis," in *Bonaventure & Aquinas: Enduring Philosophers*, ed. Shahan and Kovach (1976).

[11] Bonaventure, *Collationes in Hexaemeron* VI.5.

positions were not to be held or advocated.[12] By contrast, some Christian temporalist theologians pursued less drastic and more philosophical approaches to eternalist positions. Among these approaches were three courses of action that did not conflict with Christian doctrine: (1) deny that Aristotle actually held that the world was eternal, (2) refute Aristotelian (or neo-Aristotelian) arguments that purported to demonstrate the eternity of the world, and (3) offer counter-arguments that purported to demonstrate the temporality of the world. Bonaventure, for instance, was agnostic with respect to the first option, allowing that Aristotle may or may not have argued for an eternal world, and actively pursued the second and third. By pursuing the latter two, Bonaventure represented the period's most common Christian theological position. Aquinas, on the other hand, embraced the first and second options.

Despite the common stance that the eternalist position was a very grave error, Aquinas's response to eternalist arguments was temperamentally rather mild. Although Aquinas rejected the eternalist position, he did so largely on philosophical grounds, and he did not often make a point of chastising eternalists for their theological errors. In the *Summa theologiae*, for instance, when Aquinas considers the various arguments advanced to show that the world has existed forever, he responds with philosophical rebuttals, pointing out the philosophical errors. He also frequently appeals to the authority of Aristotle in giving his answers.[13]

In contrast, when Aquinas responds to temporalist arguments, his criticisms are sometimes quite virulent. He often expresses the view that bad arguments advanced in support of the

---

[12] For an account of the condemnations in Paris, see Wippel, "The Condemnations of 1270 and 1277 at Paris," *Journal of Medieval and Renaissance Studies* 7 (1977): 169-201.

[13] See ST I.46.1. Similarly, see SCG II.31-37.

faith are worse than none at all, and that this is presicely what the temporalists are doing: "And it is useful to consider this, lest anyone, presuming to demonstrate what is of faith, should bring forward reasons that are not cogent, so as to give occasion to unbelievers to laugh, thinking that on such reasons we believe things that are of faith."[14] In the *Summa contra gentiles*, for instance, when Aquinas considers temporalist arguments, he shows that the arguments fail. The terms he uses are particularly negative: he describes these arguments as "lacking cogency" and "weak."[15] Further, Aquinas's only polemical work on the topic, *De aeternitate mundi*, is not directed at eternalists but at those advancing temporalist arguments. Of these he comments sarcastically, "Therefore they who do descry such inconsistency [between eternity and creation] with their hawk-like vision are the only rational beings, and wisdom was born with them!"[16] Given the concern that many of Aquinas's contemporaries had with the eternalist error, his mild treatment of eternalists conjoined with his near-hostility to those advancing temporalist demonstrations is, to say the least, quite surprising.[17]

---

[14] "et hoc utile est ut consideretur, ne forte aliquis, quod fidei est demonstrare praesumens, rationes non necessarias inducat, quae praebeant materiam irridendi infidelibus, existimantibus nos propter huiusmodi rationes credere quae fidei sunt." (ST I.46.2)

[15] SCG II.38; see also DAM 12.

[16] "ergo illi qui tam subtiliter eam percipiunt, soli sunt homines, et cum illis oritur sapientia." (DAM 9)

[17] I am persuaded (as are many others) by Brady's ("John Pecham and the Background of Aquinas's *De Aeternitate Mundi*" [1974]) argument that the target of Aquinas's *De aeternitate mundi* was his contemporary in Paris, John Pecham. In his disputed question on the eternity of the world (see Pecham, *Questions Concerning the Eternity of the World* [1993]) Pecham argues the Franciscan/Bonaventurean line that a world with a finite duration can be demonstrated (and he proceeds to do so). Aquinas's treatise appears to be targeted at Pecham's arguments.

Setting aside the more personal nature of Aquinas's attacks on the temporalists, an important question remains for our understanding of Aquinas's epistemological account of faith and reason: why does Aquinas strive so ardently to discount demonstrations that prove the finite duration of the world, especially since he agrees with the conclusion, namely that the world is finite in duration?[18] One pragmatic answer to this question was given above: advancing bad arguments in support of the faith makes Christian theologians look bad. But Aquinas has a more principled response: the finite duration of the world is an article of faith,[19] and as such, it is something that *cannot* be demonstrated; if we are to have certitude about it, it must be by faith, not by proof. In the next section we examine why Aquinas believes that the duration of the world cannot be demonstrated.

4.3. *Why the duration of the world cannot be demonstrated*

Though Aquinas considers several arguments purporting to prove either the finite or infinite duration of the world and refutes each in turn, Aquinas offers systematic arguments as to why the duration of the created world cannot be demonstrated. He finds that neither the temporality nor the eternality of the created world can be demonstrated but his arguments employ premises about God that will be accepted only by religious believers, so these

---

[18] There is, of course, the related question: why does Aquinas strive to discount demonstrations that prove the eternity of the world? This has a straightforward answer, and one that is not particularly interesting as far as my project is concerned—Aquinas rebuts demonstrations that prove the eternity of the world because their conclusions contradict faith and thus he has certitude that the conclusions of these demonstrations must be false. Aquinas could have left his response at that, but he seems keen on helping to eliminate the philosophical errors that led to these demonstrations, which helps explain his careful, temperamentally mild, philosophical rebuttals to the eternalist arguments.

[19] For Aquinas's views on the articles of faith, see ST II-II.1.6-10.

arguments must be directed toward them. Aquinas considers three arguments against any possibility of demonstration regarding the eternity or temporality of the world. These are the argument from faith, the argument from a consideration of creatures, and the argument from a consideration of God.

4.3.1. The argument from faith

In the *Summa theologiae*, Aquinas considers the position that the eternity of the world cannot be demonstrated because the non-eternity of the world is an article of faith. This argument, however, is advanced as part of the *sed contra* response to the question, and Aquinas seems to advance it not so much as his own but as an argument given on theological authority. In this argument he observes, "The articles of faith cannot be proved demonstratively, because faith is of 'things that appear not' according to Hebrews 11:1."[20] Presumably, what he means by this is that articles of faith involve things not seen, that is, things for which we cannot have *scientia*, and that are thus not demonstrable. The argument continues by observing that God's creation of the world in time *is* a matter of faith, one revealed to us by Moses, who "prophesied about the past when he said, 'In the beginning God created heaven and earth.'" Aquinas concludes: "Therefore the inception of the world is known exclusively by revelation. Accordingly it cannot be proved demonstratively."

Despite the fact that this argument appeals to scriptural authority (which, presumably, Aquinas's temporalist peers would respect), most temporalists would remain unconvinced that demonstrations about the beginning of the world cannot be given. That the temporality of the world is an article of faith does not seem to warrant concluding that matters of faith concerning

---

[20] "fidei articuli demonstrative probari non possunt, quia fides de non apparentibus est, ut dicitur ad hebr. xi." (ST I.46.2 sed contra)

creation are known *exclusively* by revelation. To be sure, Aquinas's account of faith, as we saw in the last chapter, holds that faith and *scientia* are mutually exclusive. However, it does not follow from this that what is held by faith by one person *could not* be held by *scientia* by another. John Pecham, a contemporary of Aquinas and Bonaventure and a temporalist, holds this view. He says, "The creation of the world in time, although it is an article of faith, can, it seems, still be investigated by reason. And this is not in prejudice of the faith, provided that assent is given to it not because of faith but rather we come to an understanding of it with the help of faith."[21] This argument by authority does not seem sufficient to refute temporalist arguments, and thus it must be bolstered by additional arguments that show that demonstrations about the duration of the world cannot be given.[22] The next two arguments, which are Aquinas's own, do this.

---

[21] "creatio mundi ex tempore quamvis sit articulus fidei, tamen ratione, ut videtur, potest investigari. Nec hoc est in praeiudicium fidei, dum no propter rationem fidei assentitur, sed merito fidei ad eius intelligeniam pervenitur." (*Quaestiones de aeternitate mundi*, q. 2, responsio) Though Pecham here merely states that the question of the eternity of the world can be "investigated" (*investigari*) by reason (something Aquinas also accepts) he has a stronger claim in mind—he actually goes on to demonstrate that the world cannot be eternal (something Aquinas does not think can be done).

[22] Aquinas also has an argument from authority to help convince the eternalists that no demonstration of the age of the world can be given. He points out that the arguments given by Aristotle that appear to prove that the world is eternal, are not, in fact, intended to be demonstrations. He gives three reasons for thinking this:

"First, because, both in *Physics VIII* and in *De Caelo I* he advances some opinions as those of Anaxagoras, Empedocles and Plato, and brings forward reasons to refute them. Secondly, because wherever he speaks of this subject, he quotes the testimony of the ancients, which is not the way of a demonstrator, but of one persuading what is probable. Thirdly, because he expressly says in Book I of the *Topics* that there are dialectical problems, of which we do not have proofs, such as, 'whether the world is eternal.'" (ST I.46.1)

4.3.2. The argument from a consideration of creatures

One way in which the duration of the world might be demonstrated would be to consider the essence or nature of the world (or some creatures in it) and to demonstrate from this nature that it has either a finite or infinite duration. Such a demonstration, because it would explain why the duration is as it is (by appeal to the nature of the entity) would provide us with *perfect scientia* about the age of the world. Aquinas argues that no such demonstration could be provided by considering the world (or any creatures for that matter) because the nature of demonstration does not permit such a consideration. He says, "For the principle of demonstration is the essence (*quod quid est*) of a thing. Now everything according to the notion of its species abstracts from here and now; hence it is said that 'universals are everywhere and always.' Hence it cannot be demonstrated that man, or heaven, or a stone did not always exist."[23] This passage appeals to Aquinas's theory of cognition and its consequence for demonstration, as discussed earlier—if we cannot form universals that contain information about the duration of something, we cannot form demonstrations concerning its duration.

Some help in understanding this argument is given in *De potentia dei*. Aquinas considers whether a creature's nature necessitates the form it takes once the creature has been created.

As Aquinas points out, one does not appeal to the testimony of the ancients (in the case of the argument from faith, these include Gregory and Moses, and in this case, Aristotle) to give a demonstration. So by Aquinas's own standards, the argument from faith has not yet proven that we cannot demonstrate the age of the world, but has merely given us reasons to believe that such demonstrations *may* not be available to us.

[23] "demonstrationis enim principium est quod quid est. unumquodque autem, secundum rationem suae speciei, abstrahit ab hic et nunc, propter quod dicitur quod universalia sunt ubique et semper. unde demonstrari non potest quod homo, aut caelum, aut lapis non semper fuit." (ST I.46.2)

He answers in the affirmative but observes that God can choose which nature to create:

> [A]ll existing things have a definite quantity by nature. For, just as the divine power is not restricted to one quantity rather than to another, so it is not restricted to a nature (*naturam*) requiring a particular quantity rather than to a nature requiring a different quantity. And so the same question [why the world is of some particular size] recurs with respect to nature as to quantity, even though we should grant that the nature of heaven is not wholly indifferent to quantity, or that it has no capacity for any other than its present quantity.[24]

Consider a world that God could create (for example, our world). Its nature (call it A) includes a determinate size (i.e., quantity) for the world (let us dub this size α). We can also consider a different world that God could create, one with a different nature (B) and different size (size β). If God were to create A, it would be true that A must be of size α, and it is also true that if our world has that nature (A), then our world is necessarily of size α. But it does not follow that the world God creates is *necessarily* size α, unless it were impossible for God to create B (or any other alternatives to A with a size different than α).

On the other hand, Aquinas holds that duration, unlike quantity, is extraneous to a thing's nature:

---

[24] "Nec obstat, si dicatur quod talis quantitas consequitur naturam caeli vel caelestium corporum, sicut et omnium natura constantium est aliqua determinata quantitas, quia sicut divina potentia non limitatur ad hanc quantitatem magis quam ad illam, ita non limitatur ad naturam cui debeatur talis quantitas, magis quam ad naturam cui alia quantitas debeatur. Et sic eadem redibit quaestio de natura, quae est de quantitate; quamvis concedamus, quod natura caeli non sit indifferens ad quamlibet quantitatem, nec sit in eo possibilitas ad aliam quantitatem nisi ad istam." (DPD 3.17)

For time, like place, is extraneous to a thing. Consequently even heaven, which has no capacity for a different quantity or a different accident intrinsically inhering, has such capacity with regard to place and position, since it has local motion; and also with regard to time, since time ever succeeds time, just as there is succession in movement and locality. Hence neither time nor locality can be said to result from the nature of heaven, as was stipulated in the case of quantity. Thus it is clear that the prefixing of a definite quantity of duration for the universe, as also of a definite quantity of dimension, depends on the mere will of God. Accordingly we cannot arrive at any necessary conclusion about the duration of the universe, so as to be able to prove demonstratively that the world has existed forever.[25]

Here Aquinas argues that time and spatial location, because these change, are not part of the intrinsic nature of a thing. Thus, even were we to understand the nature of the world, we still would not be able to demonstrate what duration in time it has (or would have, for a possible nature, were it to exist) since, as Aquinas asserted in the passage from the *Summa theologiae* above, "the principle of demonstration is the essence of a thing." We cannot perform a demonstration *propter quid* from the nature of the world to *perfect scientia* about its duration because the nature of the world does not contain information about its duration.

---

[25] "Nam tempus est extrinsecum a re, sicut et locus; unde etiam in caelo, in quo non est possibilitas respectu alterius quantitatis vel accidentis interius inhaerentis, est tamen in eo possibilitas respectu loci et situs, cum localiter moveatur; et etiam respectu temporis, cum semper tempus succedat tempori, sicut est successio in motu et in ubi; unde non potest dici, quod neque tempus neque ubi consequatur naturam eius, sicut de quantitate dicebatur. Unde patet quod ex simplici Dei voluntate dependet quod praefigatur universo determinata quantitas durationis, sicut et determinata quantitas dimensionis. Unde non potest necessario concludi aliquid de universi duratione, ut per hoc ostendi possit demonstrative mundum semper fuisse." (DPD 3.17)

4.3.3. The argument from a consideration of God

Though we cannot have *perfect scientia* about the duration of the world by considering the nature of the world, perhaps we could obtain it by considering the manner in which God creates. As Aquinas observed in the passage from *De potentia dei* above, God chooses what natures to create just as he chooses what durations these objects will have. If for some reason it were necessary that God, as creator, should choose a world with a particular (finite) duration, then it might be possible to demonstrate from this necessity of creation to a conclusion about the duration of the world. Aquinas argues that if there were some reason for God to be limited to choosing to create a particular nature, it must lie in God's power, His goodness, or His will. In *De potentia dei* he rules out the first two: "...a reason for the definite disposition of the universe cannot be discerned either on the part of the divine power, which is infinite, or on the part of the divine goodness, which has no need of created things, the reason for it must be found in the sheer will of the Creator."[26] God's power cannot be what limits Him to create this world (with its finite duration), since His power is unlimited—His power is sufficient to create a different world with an infinite duration. Similarly, God cannot be constrained to create this world by His goodness, since His goodness does not require the creation of this or any other world—that is, it is not necessary that God create a world of finite duration because of His goodness, since God's goodness is unaffected by creation.

---

[26] "unde, cum nec etiam ex parte divinae potentiae quae est infinita, nec divinae bonitatis, quae rebus non indiget, ratio determinatae dispositionis universi sumi possit, oportet quod eius ratio sumatur ex simplici voluntate producentis ut si quaeratur, quare quantitas caeli sit tanta et non maior, non potest huius ratio reddi nisi ex voluntate producentis." (DPD 3.17)

In the *Summa theologiae*, by making an appeal to God's freedom, Aquinas argues that the duration of the world cannot be demonstrated:

> For the will of God cannot be investigated by reason, except as regards those things which God must will of necessity, and what He wills about creatures is not among these, as was said above. But the divine will can be manifested to man by revelation, on which faith rests. Hence that the world began to exist is an object of faith, but not of demonstration or *scientia*.[27]

Because God is free to will as He wishes, unless He is absolutely necessitated to do otherwise, God was free to make the world eternal if He so wished. But how can we be sure that God is not necessitated to make the world temporal? Earlier in the *Summa*, Aquinas gives an argument proving that God's will is not necessitated with respect to created things. God's will has His goodness as its proper object, and thus He necessarily wills the being of His own goodness. Aquinas adds, "But God wills things apart from Himself in so far as they are ordered to His own goodness as their end."[28] That is, to the extent that God wills concerning anything outside of Himself, the final cause of the act of will is God's goodness. Aquinas observes that if anyone wills towards an end and that end is attainable in some other way than by willing it, then that act of will is not necessary in order for the end to be obtained: "But we do not will necessarily those things without which the end is attainable...." Finally, Aquinas observes, "Hence, since the goodness of God is perfect and can exist without

---

[27] "voluntas enim dei ratione investigari non potest, nisi circa ea quae absolute necesse est deum velle, talia autem non sunt quae circa creaturas vult, ut dictum est. potest autem voluntas divina homini manifestari per revelationem, cui fides innititur. unde mundum incoepisse est credibile, non autem demonstrabile vel scibile." (ST I.46.2)

[28] "alia autem a se deus vult, inquantum ordinantur ad suam bonitatem ut in finem." (ST I.19.3)

other things, inasmuch as no perfection can accrue to Him from them, it follows that for Him to will things other than Himself is not absolutely necessary." Thus, the final cause of God's acts of will is His goodness, and His goodness can be obtained without acts of creation; therefore no act of creation is necessary for God to perform.

God's creating a world of a finite duration was not necessitated by God's act of creation, for God's power allowed Him to create worlds with other natures (and other durations), God's goodness allowed Him not to create at all, and God, in willing to create, did so freely, since the end of His willing would have been achieved whether or not He created. There was nothing necessary about God's act of creation, and thus there can be no necessary first principles about God's creating by which a demonstration *propter quid* could be formed to demonstrate the duration of the world.

4.3.4. Another type of demonstration of the duration of the world

In the last two sections we considered two ways in which the duration of the world might have been demonstrated: from a consideration of the nature of the world itself, and from a consideration of God's creative act. Concerning God's creative act, no demonstration *propter quid* is possible since we cannot have any understanding of the immediate premises concerning God that would be necessary for demonstration *propter quid*. Because God's essence is unknowable to us, we cannot demonstrate conclusions that follow from His essence. Further, we cannot demonstrate them from what must necessarily be true of God's act of creation (and hence, subject to *perfect scientia*), since it is not necessary that God create at all, much less that He create a world of any particular duration. We also cannot construct a demonstration *propter quid* about the duration of the world because if we examine the essence of the world itself, the universals that we abstract from our experience of the world do not contain information about its duration in time, and thus we have no immediate principles about the world's duration from which to construct such a demonstration. Though Aquinas has ruled out demonstrations *propter quid*, he has not yet ruled out demonstrations *quia*, some proof that shows *that* the world must be eternal or temporal but not *why*. Van Steenberghen raises precisely this difficulty for Aquinas:

> He well knows that besides the kind of demonstrations which Aristotle proposes as [demonstration *propter quid*], there are other types of valid demonstration: for instance, demonstrating a cause from an effect [demonstration *quia*], the only kind of demonstration which makes it possible to prove God's existence. He should have shown that no type of demonstration can enable one to prove that the world began.[29]

Demonstrations of causes from effects are a species of demonstration *quia*, the sort of demonstrations that produce *scientia quia*, that is, knowledge *that* the conclusion is true but not knowledge *why* it is true.[30] We cannot have *perfect scientia* about the duration of the world, since we cannot see why the world should have the duration it does. We might be able to have *scientia quia* about the duration of the world if we were able to infer from our observations of the world, of creation, or of duration in time that this world *must* have been created in a certain way (for instance, with a finite duration).

Though throughout his works Aquinas does consider and rebut demonstrations *quia* in favor of a finite world, he does not systematically rule them out until *De aeternitate mundi*. This

---

[29] Van Steenberghen, "The Eternity of the World," ed. Wissink (1980) 23.

[30] For Aquinas's account of demonstration and *scientia quia*, see section 2.4.

polemical text, which is clearly aimed at Christian theologians,[31] is primarily concerned with demonstrations *quia* for a finite duration of the world—if a demonstration can be provided that shows that it is impossible for the world to be infinite in duration, then such a demonstration would also show *that* the world must be finite in duration. Such a *deductio ad impossible*[32] would, if successful, prove that the world has a finite duration and thus establish the correctness of the temporalist position. Aquinas, following distinctions previously made in *De potentia dei*,[33] observes that there are two ways in which an eternal, created world can be impossible: "Now if it is said that this is impossible, this will be said either [1] because God could not make something which always existed, or [2] because, even if God could make it, it could not be made."[34] That God lacks the power to create an eternal world is rejected, since, as we observed before, God can create any nature, and natures do not entail their durations—thus God has the power to create a world with an infinite duration. However, if such a world could not be made (not as a limitation of God's power but as some problem with such a world), then it would follow that this world (which has been made) must be finite in duration. There are, Aquinas says, only two reasons why a world of infinite duration might not be able to be made: "…either [2a]

---

[31] See note 17, above.

[32] William de la Mare, criticizing Aquinas in 1278/1279, uses this term to describe these sorts of arguments. See Hoenen, "The Literary Reception of Thomas Aquinas' View on the Provability of the Eternity of the World in De La Mare's *Correctorium* (1278–9) and the *Correctoria Corruptorii* (1279–Ca 1286)," in *The Eternity of the World*, ed. Wissink (1990) 48.

[33] See DPD 3.14.

[34] "si autem dicatur hoc esse impossibile, vel hoc dicetur quia deus non potuit facere aliquid quod semper fuerit, aut quia non potuit fieri, etsi deus posset facere." (DAM 1)

because of a lack of passive potency, or [2b] because of incompatibility in the concepts involved."[35]

One reason to think that a world of infinite duration could not be made would be that there could be no appropriate passive potentiality, that is, no matter from which a world of infinite duration could be made. Under Aristotelian metaphysics, substances are created when form (the active principle) informs matter (the passive potency). One problem with a world of infinite duration would seem to be that, since the world has existed forever, there would seem to be no time prior to the world's existence for there to be passive potency from which the world is made.

In response to this argument, Aquinas appeals to angelic creation—he explains that angels are not made out of matter (they have no passive potency), yet they are capable of being made by God. This would be one way in which an infinite world could exist—if it were created in some manner like the angels, then no prior passive potency would be required.[36] Aquinas also considers the heretical position that there could have been eternally existing passive potency from which the world was made. Though this view is heretical,[37] Aquinas observes that such an account (which an Aristotelian eternalist might advance) is nevertheless metaphysically possible, and thus such a world would be capable of being made.

The last way [2b] in which a world of infinite duration might be shown to be impossible would be to show that there was a contradiction involved in a created, eternal world. The contra-

---

[35] "si autem dicatur quod hoc non potest fieri, hoc non potest intelligi nisi duobus modis, vel duas causas veritatis habere: vel propter remotionem potentiae passivae, vel propter repugnantiam intellectuum." (DAM 2)

[36] And this would seem to conform to the orthodox position of the doctrine of creation *ex nihilo*.

[37] It is heretical because such a passive potency is prior to creation, and thus uncreated. And thus there would be something that God did not create.

diction can be expressed in the form of a demonstration:

(1)   For any x, if the concepts involved in x are
       incompatible, then x is impossible.
(2)   The concepts "the world has existed forever" and
       "the world was created by God" are incompatible.
∴ (3) A world created by God that has existed forever
       is impossible.

This argument (if successful) counts as a demonstration *quia* because the conclusion would be necessarily true, and hence we would have certitude that a created eternal world could not exist. However, the argument cannot count as a demonstration *propter quid*, because, as Aquinas argued in the previous sections, our knowledge of the truth of (2) (if we indeed have such knowledge) is not ultimately a result of understanding the essence of the world or of God's act of creation. By proving that creation and infinite duration are incompatible, we can conclude that the world is finite in duration. Aquinas's goal is to show that premise (2) is false, and thus that the syllogism above is not a demonstration at all. He says, "The whole question comes to this, whether the ideas, to be created by God according to a thing's entire substance, and yet to lack a beginning in duration, are mutually repugnant or not."[38]

Aquinas asserts that there are only two ways in which the concepts in (2) could be mutually incompatible.[39] He says, "...a

---

[38] "in hoc ergo tota consistit quaestio, utrum esse creatum a deo secundum totam substantiam, et non habere durationis principium, repugnent ad invicem, vel non." (DAM 3)

[39] Aquinas does not seem to consider in DAM that (2) could be true because one of the concepts to be conjoined is itself self-contradictory, thus either "the world has existed forever" or "the world was created by God" would be self-contradictory. Perhaps he does not consider this because he feels he has already resolved this possibility in earlier texts. Clearly, all

contradiction could arise only...because an efficient cause must precede its effect in duration, or because non-existence must precede existence in duration...."[40] In order to show that (2) cannot be true, Aquinas proceeds to argue that the concepts are not incompatible in either of these ways.

These two possible proofs of premise (2) can be summarized as follows:

(a)   All efficient causes are prior in duration to their effects.

(b)   If God is the creator of the world, then God is the efficient cause of the world.

∴ (c) If God is the creator of the world, then God's efficient cause is prior in duration to the existence of the world.

(d)   If something is prior in duration to x, then x has not existed forever.

∴ (e) If God is the creator of the world, then the world has not existed forever.

Christians would reject out of hand as heretical the view that "the world was created by God" is self-contradictory (and Aquinas shows that this is not self-contradictory by arguing that God created the world in ST I.44.1). Our discussion of the argument from a consideration of creatures above does seem to show that an eternal world is not self-contradictory; the nature of the world, as Aquinas has argued, does not contain its duration of existence, and thus having an infinite duration would seem to be compatible with the essence of the world. Another approach to asserting the self-contradictory nature of a world with infinite duration centers on arguments that show an absurdity in there being an actual number of infinite days. These sorts of arguments are not dealt with systematically but one by one (see, for example, SCG II.38) and thus I shall not discuss them in detail here. Some scholars, however, find Aquinas's responses seemingly inconsistent (see Van Steenberghen, "Eternity of the World," 16-18) or unsatisfying (see Kovach, "Question of the Eternity of the World in St. Bonaventure and St. Thomas—A Critical Analysis," 175-76).

[40] "si enim repugnant, hoc non est nisi propter alterum duorum, vel propter utrumque: aut quia oportet ut causa agens praecedat duratione; aut quia oportet quod non esse praecedat duratione." (DAM 3)

(f)　　All things that are made from nothing have non-existence prior in duration to existence.

(g)　　If God is the creator of the world, then the world is made from nothing (*ex nihilo*).

∴ (h) If God is the creator of the world, then the non-existence of the world is prior in duration to its existence.

(i)　　If something is prior in duration to x, then x has not existed forever.

∴ (j) If God is the creator of the world, then the world has not existed forever.

Aquinas's rejects the principle (a) that all efficient causes must precede their effects in time. Though he agrees that all efficient causation that produces its effect by *motion* (*motum*) precedes the effect in time, he claims that efficient causes that produce effects *instantaneously* need not precede their creation in time. Thus, if God acted instantaneously, God's act of creation need not precede the created being in time. To understand why God could have acted instantaneously in creating the world, we turn to Aquinas's account of creation in the *Summa theologiae*.[41] In the ordinary causation resulting in motion (that is, change), there is change from a former state to a latter state. Woodworkers change wood into furniture, nature changes seed into animals, etc. But according to Aquinas, creation is not a real change; it is merely a change in how we think of something. When something is created there is not a preexisting thing that was changed; instead, with creation the entire substance, both form and matter, is produced. Change transforms something that exists, but creation produces a new existent where previously there was nothing. When things are produced by creation rather than change, becoming and being are simultaneous—there is no time between a

---

[41] See ST I.45.2 ad 2-3.

match becoming lit and its being lit, or between a mind forming a concept and having one. This is because the causal act of creation involves no intermediary—no stuff that needs to be transformed. "In things of this kind, what is being made, is; but when we speak of their being made, we mean that they are from another, and that previously they did not exist. Hence, since creation is without motion, a thing is being created and has been created at the same time."[42] God creates the world, He does not change something into the world; thus, His efficient causation of the world would not be prior in time to it, but rather could be simultaneous with it.

In the second argument, the claim is that the world is made from nothing. If the world is made from nothing, or non-existence, then non-existence precedes existence in duration, and thus the world has had a beginning in duration. The argument holds that the world is made *from* some N (namely, "non-existence"), so N must have preceded the world. Since the world is preceded by N, the world cannot have existed forever. Aquinas has two responses to this line of argument. Aquinas's first response is that the first premise is not necessarily true because "made from nothing" could mean something other than the world is made from non-being. Aquinas quotes Anselm in order to explain the error: "…[for something to be said] to have been made from nothing, is reasonable if we understand that the thing was, indeed, made, but that there was nothing from which it was made. In a like sense we may say that, when a man is saddened without cause, his sadness arises from nothing. In this sense, therefore, no absurdity will follow if the conclusion drawn above is kept in mind, namely, that, with the exception of the supreme essence, all things that exist were made by it out of nothing, that is, not out of

---

[42] "et in his, quod fit, est, sed cum dicitur fieri, significatur ab alio esse, et prius non fuisse. unde, cum creatio sit sine motu, simul aliquid creatur et creatum est." (ST I.45.2 ad 3)

something."[43] The temporalist is confused in holding that the proposition "the world was created from nothing" requires the following interpretation: $\exists x$ (w was created from x) and x is non-existence. But, as Aquinas points out, it is possible for the proposition "the world was created from nothing" to be interpreted as: $\sim \exists x$ (w was created from x), that is, "the world was not created from something." And since this is a possible interpretation of creation *ex nihilo*, nothing at all is logically entailed to have preceded in duration the existence of the world, and hence one cannot demonstrate that the world had a beginning in duration.

In Aquinas's second response to the argument, he concedes we *might* wish to assert that creation *ex nihilo* be understood to mean that the world was made from non-being.[44] Even if we were required to interpret creation *ex nihilo* in this way, it does not follow, Aquinas argues, that non-being precedes the world in *duration*. That is, even if the world is created from non-being, it need not come after non-being *in time*. Being created from non-being could be understood temporally, but it also could be understood as expressing a *conceptual* priority. Created beings are nothing before they are made to exist—their existence depends wholly on their being made—so if uncreated natures are not made

---

[43] "tertia, inquit, interpretatio, qua dicitur aliquid esse factum de nihilo, est cum intelligimus esse quidem factum, sed non esse aliquid unde sit factum. per similem significationem dici videtur, cum homo contristatus sine causa, dicitur contristatus de nihilo. secundum igitur hunc sensum, si intelligatur quod supra conclusum est, quia praeter summam essentiam cuncta quae sunt ab eadem, ex nihilo facta sunt, idest non ex aliquo; nihil inconveniens sequetur." (DAM 6). In this passage Aquinas is quoting Anselm from *Monologium*, 8. The same position expressed in Aquinas's own words can be found in SCG II.38 ad 2.

[44] Perhaps such an assertion would be driven by theological concerns, for instance, if there were reason to think that other interpretations of creation *ex nihilo* would be heretical.

to exist, they will not exist. Aquinas says, "But a creature does not have existence except from another; regarded as left simply to itself, it is nothing; prior to its existence, therefore, nothingness is its natural lot.... We maintain that its nature is such that it would be nothing if it were left to itself...."[45] By an analogy with the illumination of the moon,[46] Aquinas explains why this fact about created natures shows that they *could be* eternal in duration. Suppose that the moon were always illuminated by the sun—that is, suppose the light of the sun (and the existence of the moon) were eternal and that the sun were always shining on the moon. The moon in this case would have always been illuminated. However, the moon, of its own nature, is not illuminated—it is dark, and only receives illumination from a light source. If the light source were removed, the moon would become dark. In this sense, we could talk of the moon being made light *from* darkness, that is, it is by nature dark, while at the same time we could hold that no darkness of the moon preceded in time its illumination. Similarly, Aquinas argues, we can conceive of created beings in the same way—they are by nature nothing, and it is from this nature, this non-being, that an existent creature is made. The non-existent nature of a thing does not precede the created, existent thing in time, just as the darkness of the moon (in the case presented) would not precede its illumination in time; rather,

---

[45] "esse autem non habet creatura nisi ab alio; sibi autem relicta in se considerata nihil est: unde prius naturaliter est sibi nihilum quam esse. nec oportet quod propter hoc sit simul nihil et ens, quia duratione non praecedit: non enim ponitur, si creatura semper fuit, ut in aliquo tempore nihil sit: sed ponitur quod natura eius talis esset quod esset nihil, si sibi relinqueretur." (DAM 7)

[46] Actually, Aquinas uses for his example the illumination of air, but he also observes that his argument works even more clearly with the illumination of the planets. I will discuss the illumination of the moon, rather than of the air, since to modern ears it sounds odd to talk about illuminated and dark air.

since the creature is by nature nothing, its non-being is conceptually prior to its being made, similar to the case in which a by-nature-dark moon is conceptually prior to the moon's being illuminated. Thus, even if we interpret creation *ex nihilo* as creation from a non-existent nature, it does not logically follow that such a nature *must* precede existence in time, and thus we cannot demonstrate that the propositions "the world is made from nothing" and "the world has existed forever" are incompatible.

By showing that the first premise of each of these two purported demonstrations *quia* is in fact not necessarily true, Aquinas shows that these temporalist arguments can provide no *scientia* concerning the age of the world. However, Aquinas seems only to have shown that *these two* sorts of arguments fail to work—his response to them does not obviously rule out the possibility of constructing another kind of argument that an eternal world is self-contradictory.[47] And yet Aquinas seems to claim confidently (in the passage quoted earlier) that a contradiction could arise *only* if the cause precedes its effect or if nothingness precedes existence in time. The source of Aquinas's confidence that only these two cases could yield a contradiction is not clear. If Aquinas thinks that these two arguments are the only reasonably good ones advanced, then he has not in principle ruled out that other arguments for a contradiction are possible, and thus he has not ruled out the possibility that a world of finite duration could be shown by a demonstration *quia*. There is some reason to interpret Aquinas in this way: after presenting and rejecting the arguments against infinite duration due to precedence in time, Aquinas appeals to the authority of Augustine and other Church fathers as well as philosophers in that these people also saw no contradiction in an eternal created world. This seems to imply that

---

[47] For instance (as was noted in note 39 above) that an eternally created world is impossible because any actual infinite is impossible.

Aquinas holds that since these arguments do not work, and since authorities have found no contradiction, there is none to be found. Thus, by this reasoning, Aquinas would hold that no contradiction could be (would be?) found in a created, eternal world.

Under this interpretation, Aquinas's argument that an eternal world is not self-contradictory is rather weak, since it merely seems to show that no one has, at least thus far, proven that it is self-contradictory. As an interpretation of Aquinas this is unsatisfying, because it is uncharacteristic for Aquinas to rely on authority in order to draw a conclusion to a philosophical argument. Instead, Aquinas typically will first prove his point and then appeal to authority in order to bolster his position, rather than appeal to authority in order to justify his conclusion. If Aquinas thinks there is no contradiction in an eternal world, either he thinks so because no one has been able to demonstrate one, or else he has a more principled reason why no contradiction could be found. The latter option is philosophically stronger and more consistent with Aquinas's philosophical practices. It seems that if we can easily interpret Aquinas this way, we ought to.

In his arguments from a consideration of creatures and of God, Aquinas shows that the duration of the world is neither demonstrable by a consideration of its *final* cause (i.e., God's intention in creating the world) nor of its *formal* cause (i.e., the nature of the world itself). In *De aeternitate mundi*, Aquinas considers only two possible arguments for the incompatibility of a created world and an eternal world—that some cause must be prior in time to the world's existing or that non-being must be. In rebutting the first argument, Aquinas gives a treatment of the *efficient* cause of the world, namely how God creates the world, and shows how a finite duration of the world cannot be demonstrated from it. In rebutting the second, Aquinas considers the *material* cause of the world, namely that from which the world is made, and also shows how a finite duration of the world cannot be demonstrated from it. In his arguments from creatures and from God in the *Summa theologiae* and his responses to these two arguments in *De aeternitate mundi*, Aquinas shows that no demonstration about the duration of the world can be given by considering final, formal, efficient, and material causes. This list is exhaustive; thus, in responding to the two arguments in *De aeternitate mundi*, Aquinas rules out the possibility of any explanation involving necessary causes of the world's duration and hence any demonstration concerning the duration of the world.

Without some ability to demonstrate causally the duration of the world, we can have no *scientia* about its duration. Whether the world is finite or infinite in duration then must be held either by opinion or faith. The arguments that Aquinas presents to show that temporalist arguments cannot be demonstrations are largely philosophical (they extensively employ an Aristotelian meta-physics), but they do include premises that would be accepted only by Christians.[48] As such, these arguments can persuade only Christians and must therefore be directed toward them. Arguments made by eternalists (who clearly advocate a heretical and thus presumably non-Christian view) are not treated quite so systematically by Aquinas. Because Aquinas has faith (and thus certitude) that the world is *not* eternal, he can be sure that all eternalist demonstrations are wrong. Aquinas's approach to these arguments is more piecemeal but also wholly philosophical—he points out the philosophical errors made in eternalist demonstrations and rebuts them one by one.

---

[48] Consider, for example, Aquinas's view that God has the power to create any nature, including a world with an infinite duration; and his discussion of angelic creation as a model for the possibility of an eternal world (discussed earlier in this section).

4.4. *The role of* scientia *in divine matters*

As we saw in the last section, Aquinas takes great pains to show that the world, which as a matter of faith is held to have had a beginning and a finite duration in time, cannot be demonstrated as such. Aquinas's position is fairly controversial, and theologians of the period strongly criticized his position.[49] Why Aquinas so strenuously defended such a theologically controversial position is not immediately clear. A further, and perhaps more perplexing, mystery is why Aquinas strongly attacked temporalists who tried to demonstrate the truth of their position (with whom he agreed that the world was finite in duration) while maintaining a rather mild response to eternalists who tried to prove a heretical position.

A ready response to these questions would be to hold that Aquinas's epistemology required this position. According to Aquinas's Aristotelian account of cognition and his Aristotelian epistemological account of *scientia*, the human mind is simply incapable of proving truths about the duration of the world (and, presumably, truths about the other articles of faith). This philosophical result corresponds nicely with Aquinas's account of faith as an epistemic state concerning "things that appear not" and that is incompatible with *scientia*—if we simply cannot have *scientia* about divine matters, then the faith we do have about them (particularly since it is epistemically stronger than the other

---

[49] For instance, in 1278–1279, not long after Aquinas's death, the Franciscan William de la Mare wrote a scathing critique of Aquinas views, *Correctorium Fratris Thomae*. In this work de la Mare holds that Aquinas's view that the articles of faith (including the notion that the world was created with a finite duration) cannot be proven is false; is contrary to Scripture, the Saints, and the doctors; nourishes doubt; and is harmful rather than conducive to faith, and that the arguments Aquinas gives are neither philosophically nor theologically viable. (For an examination of de la Mare's *Correctorium*, see Hoenen, "Literary Reception," 1990.)

option, opinion), would seem to be epistemically reasonable.[50] Under this interpretation, Aquinas is forced to take on the temporalist mainstream because he is theologically as well as epistemologically obligated to do so.

This interpretation runs into difficulties, however, when we consider that there are, according to Aquinas, some matters of faith that *can* be demonstrated. The existence of God, for example, seems to be a matter of faith that Aquinas himself demonstrates in his famous Five Ways. If faith concerns what cannot be proven, then it seems odd that Aquinas would prove that God exists, and further that He is simple, etc. These proofs would seem to undermine the epistemological motivation for taking on the temporalists that was suggested by the interpretation above. Further, if epistemological considerations led Aquinas to conclude that the duration of the world (or the Trinity, or the Incarnation, etc.) could not be demonstrated, then why is it that similar considerations did not lead Aquinas to conclude that the existence of God (or His simplicity, etc.) also could not be demonstrated? To say the least, it seems odd that Aquinas would so *tenaciously* argue against the demonstrability of a created, finite world while at the same time demonstrate other matters of faith. The Five Ways represent a special, interesting case concerning the role reason plays in faith for Aquinas. In the next section, we turn to a detailed examination of the Five Ways, in particular focusing on how Aquinas uses them with respect to faith and how his approach to the existence of God differs from that he took with the duration of the world.

---

[50] For a more thorough discussion of the epistemic reasonableness of faith, see chapter 5.

4.4.1. Reason and scientia of the divine: The Five Ways

Near the beginning of the *Summa contra gentiles*, Aquinas makes it clear that some matters concerning the divine are subject to reason while others are not:

> There is a twofold mode of truth in what we profess about God. Some truths about God exceed all the ability of the human reason. Such is the truth that God is triune. But there are some truths which the natural reason also is able to reach. Such are that God exists, that He is one, and the like. In fact, such truths about God have been proved demonstratively by the philosophers, guided by the light of the natural reason.[51]

Aquinas goes on to explain that we cannot have *scientia* about certain truths about God due to the limitations of our cognitive apparatus, as we discussed above (in section 4.1). Though Aquinas holds that we cannot have *perfect scientia* about God (because we cannot form any demonstrations from God's essence), he does claim that we can have *scientia quia* concerning God—that is, we can have *scientia that* God exists by forming demonstrations from effects to their divine cause.

> Now, in arguments proving the existence of God, it is not necessary to assume the divine essence or quiddity as the middle term of the demonstration.... In place of the quiddity, an effect is taken as the middle term, as in demonstrations *quia*. It is from such effects that the meaning of the name *God* is taken. For all divine names are imposed either by removing the

---

[51] "est autem in his quae de deo confitemur duplex veritatis modus. quaedam namque vera sunt de deo quae omnem facultatem humanae rationis excedunt, ut deum esse trinum et unum. quaedam vero sunt ad quae etiam ratio naturalis pertingere potest, sicut est deum esse, deum esse unum, et alia huiusmodi; quae etiam philosophi demonstrative de deo probaverunt, ducti naturalis lumine rationis." (SCG I.3 n2)

effects of God from Him or by relating God in some way to His effects.

It is thereby likewise evident that, although God transcends all sensible things and the sense itself, His effects, on which the demonstration proving His existence is based, are nevertheless sensible things. And thus, the origin of our knowledge in the sense applies also to those things that transcend the sense.[52]

From this (and similar considerations discussed in ST I.2.2), Aquinas proceeds to present five ways in which the existence of God is proven via a demonstration *quia*—in the first, for instance, he proceeds from an effect, namely that something is in motion (and that this motion is evident to the senses), and from this effect demonstrates the existence of its ultimate cause, the unmoved mover, i.e. God.

This account presented in the *Summa contra gentiles* does not provide an answer to the puzzles raised at the beginning of this section, however. Aquinas strenuously argues that we can have neither *perfect scientia* nor *scientia quia* about the duration of the world in time, and this would seem to be motivated by the argument from faith—theological commitments would seem to require that faith is of things unseen. Yet, here Aquinas clearly holds that, concerning God, we can have *scientia quia* that He

---

[52] "in rationibus autem quibus demonstratur deum esse, non oportet assumi pro medio divinam essentiam sive quidditatem, ut secunda ratio proponebat: sed loco quidditatis accipitur pro medio effectus, sicut accidit in demonstrationibus quia; et ex huiusmodi effectu sumitur ratio huius nominis deus. nam omnia divina nomina imponuntur vel ex remotione effectuum divinorum ab ipso, vel ex aliqua habitudine dei ad suos effectus.

patet etiam ex hoc quod, etsi deus sensibilia omnia et sensum excedat, eius tamen effectus, ex quibus demonstratio sumitur ad probandum deum esse, sensibiles sunt. et sic nostrae cognitionis origo in sensu est etiam de his quae sensum excedunt." (SCG I.12 n8-9)

exists (though not *perfect scientia*).[53] We seem to have an unresolved puzzle in Aquinas—either matters of faith cannot be demonstrated at all (the theological commitment of the argument from faith), in which case Aquinas should hold that we cannot demonstrate God's existence; or some matters of faith can be demonstrated and others cannot, and we need to understand which are demonstrable and which are not (and also why Aquinas bucked the commonly held position by holding that the duration of the world is one of those matters that cannot be demonstrated).

Some Aquinas scholars resolve this puzzle by arguing that the Five Ways were never presented as demonstrations for the existence of *God*; rather, they either prove the existence of some entity (an unmoved mover, uncaused causer, etc.) that may or may not be God,[54] or they are intended to reveal truths not about God but about the nature of existence, causation, etc.[55] Aquinas does clearly seem to claim that he is demonstrating the existence of God, so before we entertain such interpretations, we should

---

[53] In SCG I.14 ff, Aquinas provides additional and different ways in which we can have *scientia quia* about God. In these chapters, rather than arguing from effects to causes, as with the Five Ways, he argues by way of "remotion"; that is, he proves truths about God by showing what God is *not*.

[54] Kretzmann (*The Metaphysics of Theism: Aquinas's Natural Theology in Summa contra gentiles I*, 1997, 88) for instance, observes that the arguments for the existence of God really only prove the existence of a metaphysical entity Kretzmann calls "alpha." Later arguments by Aquinas fill out the Christian character of this entity. Similarly, see Davies, *The Thought of Thomas Aquinas* (1992) 26.

[55] Though many interpret the Five Ways as proving the existence of the Christian God, or at least of some entity (an unmoved mover, uncaused causer, etc.) some have argued that the Five Ways are not intended to prove the existence of an entity; rather, they establish something not about God but about other things, such as truths about natural causation (see, for instance, Fogelin, "A Reading of Aquinas's Five Ways," *American Philosophical Quarterly* [1990]: 305-313) or the nature of finite being (see the discussion of Mascall's views in Kennick, "A New Way with the Five Ways," *Australasian Journal of Philosophy* 38 [1960]: 225-33).

investigate whether the puzzles raised can be resolved while taking Aquinas's claims about the Five Ways at face value.

In the *Summa theologiae*, Aquinas considers the objection that the existence of God cannot be demonstrated, for faith is of things unseen and demonstration produces *scientia*. Aquinas's response creates a distinction between two kinds of divine matters:

> The existence of God and other like truths about God, which can be known (*nota*) by natural reason, are not articles of faith, but are preambles (*praeambula*) to the articles; for faith presupposes (*praesupponit*) natural cognition (*cognitionem*), even as grace presupposes nature, and perfection the perfectible. Nevertheless, there is nothing to prevent a man, who cannot grasp a proof, accepting, as a matter of faith, something which in itself is capable of being scientifically known and demonstrated.[56]

As we see here, Aquinas distinguishes between two kinds of matters of faith—articles and preambles. Preambles are those matters of faith that can be known by natural reason, articles those known only by faith. The preambles also seem to be prior to the articles—they somehow come before the articles, just as "faith presupposes natural cognition, even as grace presupposes nature, and perfection the perfectible."

One way of interpreting the preamble/article distinction that should be avoided is a *logical* one. Since the preambles are prerequisites for the articles, and since believers who cannot demonstrate the preambles must presuppose them, it would seem natural to conclude that Aquinas is characterizing a logical rather

---

[56] "ad primum ergo dicendum quod deum esse, et alia huiusmodi quae per rationem naturalem nota possunt esse de deo, ut dicitur rom. i non sunt articuli fidei, sed praeambula ad articulos, sic enim fides praesupponit cognitionem naturalem, sicut gratia naturam, et ut perfectio perfectibile. nihil tamen prohibet illud quod secundum se demonstrabile est et scibile, ab aliquo accipi ut credibile, qui demonstrationem non capit." (ST I.2.2 ad 1)

than epistemic distinction between preambles and articles. For example, I cannot believe the article of faith that God is triune without believing the preamble that God exists. When I say that my belief that God is triune presupposes my belief that God exists, it seems natural to infer that I am calling attention to a logical relation between these two statements. Under this interpretation, the preambles are distinguished from the articles because in order for the articles to be true, the preambles must be true (though not vice-versa).

However, the passages in *Summa contra gentiles* clearly point to an epistemic rather than a logical distinction. In chapter 9, Aquinas notes that the truth of things is not "twofold on the part of God, who is one simple Truth, but on the part of our knowledge, as our cognitive faculty has different aptitudes for the knowledge of divine things." Further, in chapter 3, after Aquinas first introduces the concept of the twofold truth of divine things, he goes on to discuss how angelic natural knowledge is greater than that of humans, implying that the dividing line between knowable and not-knowable for angels would be different than it is for human beings. If the twofold truth of divine things in the *Summa contra gentiles* corresponds to the distinction between preamble and article, then the distinction is clearly made on epistemic, not logical, grounds, for the distinction is drawn in different places for angels and humans.

That the difference between preamble and article is meant to be epistemic seems borne out in the *Summa theologiae* as well. After defining articles of faith as being enumerated on epistemic grounds, Aquinas discusses two ways in which the articles of faith can be considered:

> [T]he formal account of the object of faith can be understood in two ways. One way, on the part of the very thing believed. And in this way the formal account of all

believable things is one, namely, the first truth. And in this way articles are not distinguished. The formal account of believable things can be taken in another way, on our part. And in this way the formal account is that the believable is something not seen. And in this way the articles of faith are distinguished, as has been said.[57]

On the part of the formal object of faith, that is, God, not only is there no logical distinction between articles, but there would be no logical distinction between articles and preambles—each truth about God entails and is entailed by the others (and strictly speaking cannot be distinguished from the others). The second way of considering articles is from our point of view, and in this way the preambles would be distinguished from the articles, for they would be seen (by those who have proven them) whereas the articles would be unseen—but this is an epistemic distinction.

A distinction between preambles and articles would give Aquinas room to wriggle out of the puzzle raised earlier. The solution would proceed as follows: even though faith is of things unseen, faith concerns *articles*,[58] and the existence of God can be demonstrated because it is a *preamble*. At this point, Aquinas's solution to our puzzle is not very satisfying because it remains exposed to the obvious objection that, if anything, the preamble "God exists" is central to faith. In order for the article/preamble distinction to be a valuable solution to our puzzle, we need to understand better why Aquinas counts some propositions as

---

[57] "ad secundum dicendum quod ratio formalis obiecti fidei potest accipi dupliciter. uno modo, ex parte ipsius rei creditae. et sic ratio formalis omnium credibilium est una, scilicet veritas prima. et ex hac parte articuli non distinguuntur. alio modo potest accipi formalis ratio credibilium ex parte nostra. et sic ratio formalis credibilis est ut sit non visum. et ex hac parte articuli fidei distinguuntur, ut visum est." (ST II-II.1.6 ad 2)

[58] That faith is primarily concerned with *articles* is advanced by Aquinas in ST II-II.1.6-7.

articles and others as preambles. We take this up in the next section.

4.4.2. The existence of God as a part of faith

The Five Ways, Aquinas's proofs for the existence of God, are taken by many philosophers to be intended to provide some sort of epistemic *justification* for faith. This could provide a ground for counting God's existence as epistemically distinct from articles of faith. If faith needs epistemic justification, it is perhaps to be found in demonstrable preambles—whereas faith itself is concerned with indemonstrable articles. The interpretation might go something like this: faith without some sort of rational justification is unreasonable and epistemically inappropriate, and Aquinas presented the Five Ways as a means of providing just such a rational justification for faith. Anthony Kenny expresses exactly this position in *The Five Ways*:

> To me it seems that if belief in the existence of God cannot be rationally justified, there can be no good reason for adopting any of the traditional monotheistic religions. A philosophical proof of God's existence from the nature of the world would not be the only form such a rational justification might take: a man might, for instance, come to accept the existence of God through believing something in the world to be a revelation from God...Those philosophers and theologians who still consider belief in God to need rational justification frequently offer the arguments of Aquinas as such a justification.[59]

If the Five Ways are Aquinas's attempt to rationally justify faith, and if these proofs are unsound, then faith would fail to be made reasonable by them. A great deal of work in philosophy has

---

[59] Kenny, *The Five Ways: St. Thomas Aquinas' Proofs of God's Existence* (1969) 4.

been devoted to understanding and attacking or defending the soundness of the Five Ways, presumably precisely because they are seen (if sound) to provide epistemic justification for faith.[60]

Given my interpretation of Aquinas's account of faith, we run into an immediate problem in interpreting Aquinas in Kenny's way, for faith is not had by means of proof and yet Aquinas, as is well known, offers five proofs for the existence of God. Further, he clearly identifies his proofs as demonstrations *quia* (which produce *scientia quia*),[61] and the last chapter argued that faith could not be *scientia quia*. This difficulty is compounded when we consider numerous claims Aquinas makes, such as "it is impossible to have faith and *scientia* about the same thing."[62] It would seem that one cannot have faith about matters for which one has a proof, such as the existence of God. This seems, to say the least, a peculiar result of Aquinas's account of faith as I have interpreted it. In contrast, many interpreters of Aquinas take his proofs to be the basis for beliefs in the existence of God.[63] But if my interpretation is correct and the Five Ways are not intended by Aquinas to be the basis of *faith*, then what are they for?

There is some disagreement among Aquinas scholars about what the Five Ways actually prove, but the following claims are

---

[60] Typical of this view is that held by Clark (*Religion, Reason and Revelation*, 1961). He says, "Now, if the cosmological argument (leaving the ontological argument out of consideration) is invalid, either Christianity has no rational foundation, or a meaning for reason must be found that is independent of Thomistic philosophy" (35).

[61] See ST I.2.2

[62] See QDV 14.9.

[63] Jenkins (*Knowledge and Faith in Thomas Aquinas*, 1997) conveniently cites several texts that offer the Evidentialist Interpretation. (See his note 14 on p. 252). They are: Hick, *Faith and Knowledge* (1966) 20-21; Penelhum, "The Analysis of Faith" (1977) 145; Plantinga, "Reason and Belief in God" (1983) 40-47; and Pojman, *Religious Belief and the Will* (1986) 32-40. I add to this list Kenny, *The Five Ways* (1969) 4, who also very clearly advocates an Evidentialist line.

clearly found in his works: Aquinas provides demonstrations *quia*[64] (demonstrations from effects to causes) that establish or at least are related to the existence of what Christians call God;[65] the result of these demonstrations is not an article of faith (because it is known by natural reason), but instead is a "preamble to the articles" (*praeambulum*);[66] however, if these preambles were not known by natural reason, they could be held by faith.[67]

Aquinas makes it quite clear that the preambles can be assented to by either of two epistemic means, demonstration *quia* or faith, but for a given person one cannot have both faith and demonstration of a preamble.[68] When it comes to preambles there would seem to be four epistemic scenarios: (1) a person first demonstrates the preambles and later comes to have faith in them, (2) a person first has faith in the preambles and later comes to demonstrate them, (3) a person has faith in the preambles and never demonstrates them, or (4) a person demonstrates the preambles and never has faith in them. For Aquinas, (1) is

---

[64] ST I.2.2: "Demonstration...through the effect...is called a demonstration *quia*;... Hence the existence of God, in so far as it is not self-evident to us, can be demonstrated from those of His effects which are known to us."

[65] ST I.2.3: "The existence of God can be proved in five ways.... Therefore it is necessary to arrive at a first mover, moved by no other; and this everyone understands to be God.... Therefore it is necessary to admit a first efficient cause, to which everyone gives the name of God.... Therefore we cannot but admit the existence of some being having of itself its own necessity, and not receiving it from another, but rather causing in others their necessity. This all men speak of as God.... Therefore there must also be something which is to all beings the cause of their being, goodness, and every other perfection; and this we call God.... Therefore some intelligent being exists by whom all natural things are directed to their end; and this being we call God."

[66] ST I.2.2 ad 1: "The existence of God and other like truths about God, which can be known by natural reason, are not articles of faith...."

[67] ST I.2.2 ad 1: "...there is nothing to prevent a man, who cannot grasp a proof, from accepting, as a matter of faith, something which in itself is capable of being *scientia* and demonstrated."

[68] See ST II-II.1.5.

impossible (assuming the demonstrations have not been undermined[69]), for one cannot go from *scientia* that something is true to a lack of *scientia* (as would be required to have faith) that it is true. Of the remaining three possibilities, only one seems a likely scenario for how the Five Ways are to be used: (3) is of no interest here, for it would not seem to bear any relevance to our trying to determine the purpose of the Five Ways, and (4) seems highly unlikely as an explanation for the Five Ways; Aquinas would not propose proofs for the sake of people who might believe in God through proofs rather than faith, since he thinks that faith is necessary for salvation[70] and that belief motivated by proof is without merit.[71] Thus, it would seem that Aquinas introduces the Five Ways for the sake of those who already have faith in the preambles. This is borne out by Aquinas's claims regarding the purpose of the *Summa theologiae*. In the prologue, he claims that the text is a work of sacred doctrine (*sacra doctrina*) intended for the instruction of beginning theology students, all of whom would presumably have faith in the preambles (e.g., in the existence of God, etc.).

Why should the faithful need or want proofs for what they already *believe*? The Five Ways appear to comprise demonstrations of philosophical (or natural) theology in which Aquinas argues to theological conclusions (e.g., that God exists) without employing any revealed truths in his arguments. This interpretation, that the Five Ways are intended to be a project in philosophical theology, leaves something to be desired. For, in question 1, immediately preceding the Five Ways, Aquinas clearly holds that sacred

---

[69] For example, we might undermine a demonstration previously held by forgetting it, or by some other mental defect by which we fail to see the truth of that which previously was evident to us.

[70] See ST II-II.2.4.

[71] See ST II-II.2.10.

doctrine (which is the enterprise of the *Summa theologiae*) is a science in which demonstrations proceed *from* divinely revealed truths,[72] rather than a science in which demonstrations proceed *to* divine truths. If the Five Ways are to be understood as part of an enterprise of philosophical theology, then we are confronted with the trouble of needing to understand why Aquinas sets up the *Summa* as a project of sacred doctrine and then immediately proceeds to do philosophical theology.

This tension in Aquinas is not easily resolved. In question 1, Aquinas does seem to hold that philosophical theology is different from sacred doctrine:

> Sciences are differentiated according to the different natures of knowable things. For the astronomer and the physicist both may prove the same conclusion—that the earth, for instance, is round; the astronomer by means of mathematics (that is, by abstracting from matter), but the physicist by means of matter itself. Hence there is no reason why those things which are dealt with in the philosophical sciences, so far as they can be known by natural reason, may not also be taught us by another science so far as they fall within revelation. Hence theology which pertains to sacred doctrine differs in genus from that theology which is part of philosophy.[73]

---

[72] See ST I.1.8.

[73] "ad secundum dicendum quod diversa ratio cognoscibilis diversitatem scientiarum inducit. eandem enim conclusionem demonstrat astrologus et naturalis, puta quod terra est rotunda, sed astrologus per medium mathematicum, idest a materia abstractum; naturalis autem per medium circa materiam consideratum. unde nihil prohibet de eisdem rebus, de quibus philosophicae disciplinae tractant secundum quod sunt cognoscibilia lumine naturalis rationis, et aliam scientiam tractare secundum quod cognoscuntur lumine divinae revelationis. unde theologia quae ad sacram doctrinam pertinet, differt secundum genus ab illa theologia quae pars philosophiae ponitur." (ST I.1.1 ad 2)

From this passage, it would seem to follow that the Five Ways, as a product of natural reason, would be part of philosophical theology, not sacred doctrine. But in the prologue to question 2, in which Aquinas introduces the Five Ways, he clearly seems to beleive that the Five Ways are part of sacred doctrine: "Because the chief aim of sacred doctrine is to teach the knowledge of God, not only as He is in Himself, but also as He is the beginning of things and their last end...we must consider whether God exists...."[74] The Five Ways, because they are known by natural reason, do not seem to be a part of sacred doctrine, and yet Aquinas clearly seems to hold that the existence of God (shown by the Five Ways) is the first thing sacred doctrine must consider. How are we to resolve this apparent conflict?

Interpreters have not been unified in deciding how to understand Aquinas on this issue.[75] At the risk of entering a centuries-old debate, I offer the following interpretation.[76] Immediately prior to presenting the Five Ways, Aquinas describes his approach:

> When the existence of a cause is demonstrated from an effect, this effect takes the place of the definition of the cause in

[74] "quia igitur principalis intentio huius sacrae doctrinae est dei cognitionem tradere, et non solum secundum quod in se est, sed etiam secundum quod est principium rerum et finis earum, et specialiter rationalis creaturae, ut ex dictis est manifestum; ad huius doctrinae expositionem intendentes...primo considerandum est an deus sit...." (ST I.2 prol.)

[75] For instance, Wallace, *The Role of Demonstration in Moral Theology: A Study of Methodology in St. Thomas Aquinas* (1962) 63, examines how Gabriel Vasquez holds that the Five Ways are primarily philosophical, whereas Cajetan argues that philosophical proofs like the Five Ways are properly theological. Gilson seems to have changed his mind from something like the former view to the latter, as is discussed in Houser (1996) 103.

[76] Which is roughly similar to views held by Francisco Muniz (presented and expanded by Wallace, *Role of Demonstration* [1962] 63-68) and Houser (Trans-Forming Philosophical Water into Theological Wine: Gilson and Aquinas," 1996) though my approach is somewhat different.

proof of the cause's existence. This is especially the case in regard to God....[77]

Aquinas here holds that in demonstrations of the Five Ways, *a posteriori* effects serve in the place of definitions. In question 1, Aquinas discusses the usefulness of such an approach:

> Although we cannot know of God what He is, nevertheless in [sacred] doctrine we make use of His effects, either of nature or of grace, in place of a definition, in regard to whatever is treated of in this doctrine concerning God, even as in some philosophical sciences we demonstrate something about a cause from its effect, by taking the effect in place of a definition of the cause.[78]

Because God's essence is ineffable, Aquinas holds that we cannot know what God is; however, by means of demonstrations from effects, we are able to consider things about God—for instance, that He is an unmoved mover. Consideration of these things, as we saw in the prologue to question 2 (above), is instrumental in achieving the goals of sacred doctrine. If we understand the premises of the Five Ways to be primarily part of one of the philosophical sciences, then we can understand why Aquinas uses the Five Ways, a product of natural reason, in a work concerned with revealed theology. He says:

> This science [i.e., sacred doctrine] can in a sense take from the philosophical sciences, not as though it stood in need of them, but only in order to make its teaching clearer. For it takes

---

[77] "ad secundum dicendum quod cum demonstratur causa per effectum, necesse est uti effectu loco definitionis causae, ad probandum causam esse, et hoc maxime contingit in deo." (ST I.2.2 ad 2)

[78] "ad primum ergo dicendum quod, licet de deo non possimus scire quid est, utimur tamen eius effectu, in hac doctrina, vel naturae vel gratiae, loco definitionis, ad ea quae de deo in hac doctrina considerantur, sicut et in aliquibus scientiis philosophicis demonstratur aliquid de causa per effectum, accipiendo effectum loco definitionis causae." (ST I.1.7 ad 1)

its principles not from other sciences, but immediately from God, by revelation. Therefore it does not take from other sciences as from the higher, but makes use of them as of the lesser, and as handmaidens; just as the master sciences make use of the sciences that supply their materials, as political of military science. That it thus uses them is not due to its own defect or insufficiency, but to the defect of our intellect, which is more easily led by what is known through natural reason (from which proceed the other sciences), to that which is above reason, such as are the teachings of this science.[79]

The Five Ways, though they seem to prove *that* God exists, more importantly for a student of sacred doctrine, help the student consider God in new ways. For instance, the First Way proves from the existence of moving things the existence of an unmoved mover. Aquinas recognizes that these proofs are employed by philosophers as well as Christian theologians[80]—these arguments do not seem to prove clearly that a uniquely *Christian* God exists, which seems to be why the conclusion of each argument is not about the existence of God but about the existence merely of *some* entity. The First Way, for instance, concludes with "Therefore it is necessary to arrive at a first mover

---

[79] "ad secundum dicendum quod haec scientia accipere potest aliquid a philosophicis disciplinis, non quod ex necessitate eis indigeat, sed ad maiorem manifestationem eorum quae in hac scientia traduntur. non enim accipit sua principia ab aliis scientiis, sed immediate a deo per revelationem. et ideo non accipit ab aliis scientiis tanquam a superioribus, sed utitur eis tanquam inferioribus et ancillis; sicut architectonicae utuntur subministrantibus, ut civilis militari. et hoc ipsum quod sic utitur eis, non est propter defectum vel insufficientiam eius, sed propter defectum intellectus nostri; qui ex his quae per naturalem rationem (ex qua procedunt aliae scientiae) cognoscuntur, facilius manuducitur in ea quae sunt supra rationem, quae in hac scientia traduntur." (ST I.1.5 ad 2)

[80] Though he does not credit the First Way to Aristotle in ST, he does so explicitly in SCG I.13.

which is moved by no other."[81] That the First Way seems to prove only the existence of an unmoved mover is unproblematic for Aquinas, for the Five Ways, as I have argued, are intended for those who already have faith. For the faithful student of sacred doctrine who already *believes* that the Christian God exists, this unmoved mover, the creator of all motion, is, of course, God Himself. And this is why Aquinas concludes the First Way with the observation, "And this [the unmoved mover] everyone understands to be God." Each of the Five Ways has this form—an entity is proven to exist, and this entity is then identified (without proof) as God. Without an implicit appeal to faith, these proofs do not demonstrate the existence of the Christian God, and thus they do not and can not justify faith. Their importance is in what they allow the faithful to learn about God. The First Way, for instance, reveals to the student of sacred doctrine that God is unmoved, that He started motion without moving, and that motion requires God. From the unmoved mover argument, we learn some additional truths about God and creation. The Five Ways (and other demonstrations) provide an opportunity for students of sacred doctrine to understand better the matters of faith they already accept.[82] In these proofs, reason investigates what faith already accepts to be true.

For Aquinas, a further reason for studying proofs of what one already believes is that they provide for personal improvement. Studying these proofs helps promote the contemplative life because it helps train the intellect and helps remove obstacles to contemplation of the divine—namely those erroneous arguments

---

[81] The other Ways conclude similarly; see ST I.2.3.

[82] For others who have also argued that the five ways primarily serve to aid understanding of God, see Velecky, *Aquinas's Five Arguments in the Summa Theologiae Ia 2, 3* (1994) 63ff; W. J. Hankey, *God in Himself: Aquinas' Doctrine of God as Expounded in the Summa Theologiae* (1987) 42ff; and Davies, *The Thought of Thomas Aquinas* (1992) 26.

offered against the faith.[83] Further, the study of them "turns the mind away from lustful thoughts, and tames the flesh on account of the toil that study entails...It also helps to remove the desire of riches...It also helps to teach obedience...."[84] For those whose lives are devoted to the service of God, Aquinas cautions that these proofs should be pursued only insofar as doing so aims at sacred doctrine. Otherwise, those who pursue reason run the risk of becoming impious.[85]

If, as I have argued, the proofs of the existence of God are not presented by Aquinas in order to provide an epistemic justification of faith, nor is the existence of God presented in order to identify the logical presuppositions of the articles of faith, then what exactly does Aquinas mean when he labels the existence of God (and other demonstrable conclusions) *preambles*—that is, in what sense do they *presuppose* the articles of faith? As the previous chapter argued, faith, according to Aquinas, is an epistemic state independent from *scientia*—faith neither depends on *scientia*, nor vice versa. However unique faith is, it occupies a place on an epistemic spectrum ranging from opinion to *scientia*—as a part of this epistemic scale, faith is as much a component of reason as is *scientia*. Recall that reason, for Aquinas, "denotes a transition from one thing to another by which the human soul reaches or arrives at cognition of something else."[86] Faith, in this way, is as much an act of reason as *scientia*. Understood in this way, then, faith is presupposed by natural cognition in that our natural reasoning

---

[83] The proofs might also play some role in converting unbelievers by removing obstacles that prevent them from having faith—for instance, the belief that God *cannot* exist. See ST II-II.2.10 ad 2, SCG I.9.

[84] In ST II-II.188.5.

[85] See ST II-II.188.5.ad 3.

[86] "ratio vero discursum quemdam designat, quo ex uno in aliud cognoscendum anima humana pertingit vel pervenit." (QDV 15.1) See section 2.1 for a discussion of Aquinas's account of reason.

powers serve as a necessary precondition for having faith at all (as well as for *scientia* and opinion), just as human nature is a necessary precondition for grace and the existence of a substance is a necessary precondition for its being perfected. The difference between article and preamble, then, is that articles of faith require our having faith in order to count them as being *known* (that is, cognized with certitude), whereas preambles do not require faith but merely the exercising of our natural reasoning powers (that is, our ability to perform demonstrations). They are preambles not in the sense of being prior in the chain of epistemic justification but of being prior in the sense of depending on a more "primitive" (i.e., natural) cognitive operation.

The existence of God, as well as other demonstrable proofs, are distinguishable from articles of faith in that they do not require faith in order for them to be known (that is, to have *scientia* about them). It does not follow from this, however, that matters of faith, such as the existence of God, concern things that are seen; for faith, as it is defined by Aquinas, requires that we neither see why nor that a proposition is true but merely *f*-see that it is to be *believed*. When we have faith about God's existence, the truth of this proposition is unseen; when we see the truth of God's existence (through, for example, the Five Ways), we no longer have faith about it.

4.4.3. The puzzle of the duration of the world resolved

This interpretation of the Five Ways and of the preambles shows that the Five Ways do not undermine the argument from faith posited earlier. Faith, for Aquinas, is a cognitive state that essentially requires that its object be unseen, and the duration of the world, unlike the existence of God, is an article of faith, that is, it is knowable only by means of faith. But why, returning to the puzzle posed earlier, is Aquinas so adamant that the duration of the world is an article of faith, especially considering the controversy surrounding this view? Although Aquinas identifies in the *Summa contra gentiles* a twofold mode of truth about what we can know about God and in the *Summa theologiae* refines this distinction to one of preambles and articles, he does not provide a systematic account of which propositions count as preambles and which as articles. Theologically, there does not seem to be great significance to some proposition being counted as a preamble versus as an article. That God exists is demonstrable and thus a preamble, but that the world was created with a beginning in time is not, at least according to Aquinas. But nothing of great theological importance seems to rest on Aquinas's position on whether the duration of the world is an article or preamble—no heresy or theological error seems to follow from allowing that the duration of the world *could* be demonstrated (even if, at least so far, it has not been). The problem Aquinas has with this view, then, must be philosophical.

As we saw earlier (in section 4.3.4), Aquinas's most exasperated response to temporalist proofs occurs in his *De aeternitate mundi*. In this polemical treatise, Aquinas is primarily concerned with the arguments that the world could not be eternal because either God's efficient causation of the world was temporally prior to it or the non-existence of the world was temporally prior to it. Aquinas's response to these arguments, and his exasperation with their proponents, is due to the philosophically limited views these arguments advance. The Aristotelian causation implied by the first account is too limiting for Aquinas's purposes. If he allows that efficient causes must always be temporally prior to their effects, then his Christian-Aristotelian synthesis is deprived of the ability to posit creation as a miraculous and special form of causation. Further, according to Aquinas this view of causation is philosophically just plain wrong, as his counterexamples of instant illumination are intended to show. If, on the other hand, he allows that non-existence must temporally precede existence, as the Neo-Platonic temporalists argue, then Aquinas becomes constrained in his ability to use an Aristotelian metaphysics in support of his theological endeavors. In each case, the temporalists, by asserting that they can demonstrate that the world is finite in duration, have, at the same time, limited the metaphysical options available to Aquinas. This, I believe, is why he finds these arguments so tiresome and why he attacks them so vigorously—they, at root, challenge the validity of Aquinas's approach of freely employing a modified Aristotelianism to help understand and explain theological problems.

4.5. Probable reasoning about divine matters

In addition to providing demonstrations about divine matters, Aquinas clearly employs reasoning (and sometimes proofs) to refute arguments against faith, as he does when he argues against each of the purported demonstrations advanced in favor of the eternity of the world. Aquinas also observes a mode of argumentation that can be employed even for matters for which we can know only by faith:

> [T]here are certain probable (verisimilis) arguments that should be brought forth in order to make divine truth apparent (manifestandam). This should be done for the training and consolation of the faithful, and not with any idea of refuting those who are adversaries. For the very inadequacy of the arguments would rather strengthen them in their error, since they would imagine that our acceptance of the truth of faith was based on such weak arguments.[87]

---

[87] "sunt tamen ad huiusmodi veritatem manifestandam rationes aliquae verisimiles inducendae, ad fidelium quidem exercitium et solatium, non autem ad adversarios convincendos: quia ipsa rationum insufficientia eos

As we saw with the Five Ways, in the case of preambles, demonstrations can be provided for the faithful to help them investigate truths they already believe. So too can probable arguments be given for the same purpose. These arguments, if they were not being provided to those who already had faith, would merely result in opinion, since their premises are merely probable—that is, they are not necessarily true. Thus, Aquinas warns, we should not offer them to nonbelievers, since they may recognize that these arguments are not compelling (they do not yield certitude) and may seem weak if used for apologetics. In the case of the duration of the world, though Aquinas strenuously argues that no demonstration is possible, he does find some probable arguments persuasive, as for instance the following:

> [I]n the production of things the end of God's will is His own goodness as it is manifested in His effects. Now, His power and goodness are made manifest above all by the fact that things other than Himself were not always in existence. For this fact shows clearly that these things owe their existence to Him, and also is proof that God does not act by a necessity of His nature, and that His power of acting is infinite. Respecting the divine goodness, therefore, it was entirely fitting that God should have given created things a temporal beginning.[88]

---

magis in suo errore confirmaret, dum aestimarent nos propter tam debiles rationes veritati fidei consentire." (SCG I.9 n.2)

[88] "finis enim divinae voluntatis in rerum productione est eius bonitas inquantum per causata manifestatur. potissime autem manifestatur divina virtus et bonitas per hoc quod res aliae praeter ipsum non semper fuerunt. ex hoc enim ostenditur manifeste quod res aliae praeter ipsum ab ipso esse habent, quia non semper fuerunt. ostenditur etiam quod non agit per necessitatem naturae; et quod virtus sua est infinita in agendo. hoc igitur convenientissimum fuit divinae bonitati, ut rebus creatis principium durationis daret." (SCG II.38 n.15)

Since God's end in creating is the manifestation of his goodness, anything that reveals this goodness is fitting (but not necessary) to that end. Finite temporal created beings imply, to Aquinas, an infinite, eternal creator. By reasoning from the temporal existence of the world, we come to comprehend God better. This comprehension is not *scientia*, for many of the premises in the above argument are merely probable and not necessary (e.g., that divine power is made manifest by the creation of finite temporal beings), and it is not clear that anyone would have any reason for believing the premises to be true, except as they are matters of faith that have already been accepted.

5

PUTTING IT ALL TOGETHER: AQUINAS'S SOLUTION TO THE PROBLEM OF FAITH AND REASON

5.1. An Aristotelian epistemology

As we discussed in chapter 2, Aquinas adopts an Aristotelian framework for his epistemology. This is particularly significant when we try to understand and evaluate Aquinas' solution to the problem of faith and reason. A Christian philosopher who is concerned about charges that faith is epistemically irresponsible may attempt to develop accounts of faith and reason in order to defend epistemic compatibilism.[1] Compatibilist solutions to the problem of faith and reason run the risk of appearing to be *ad hoc*, particularly if the accounts of faith and reason that are provided seem motivated more by apologetics than by developing an adequate account of religious epistemology. Epistemic compatibilism can be easily had, but at the risk of being philosophically uninteresting. Consider, as an example, the following solution to the problem of faith and reason.

Suppose we stipulate that faith is a special case of ordinary belief: faith is belief justified by the evidence of miracles and by the evidence adduced by creation scientists. Suppose further that I

---

[1] Recall from chapter 1 that epistemic compatibilism is the position that one can be epistemically responsible in believing propositions pertaining to the divine on the basis both of faith and reason.

claim that the results of modern scientific inquiry that seems to contradict the claims of faith (e.g., the theory of evolution) have no better evidence in support of them than does faith, and in fact the evidence for evolution is less "strong" than the evidence for creation science. When two accounts (evolution, creation science) conflict, as many scientific theories do, it is (we might claim) epistemically responsible to believe the one that has the strongest evidence, which in this scenario would seem to be creation science. Faith under this story would be epistemically responsible, and we might also hold that scientific approaches to matters pertaining to the divine would also be epistemically responsible, if the science weren't so bad (if, for example, scientists didn't keep neglecting the evidence in favor of creation science and against evolution). In order to defend such a solution to faith and reason adequately, we would need to establish the truth of a number of claims—that there is evidence of miracles and for creation science, that such evidence exceeds that of evolution, etc. But there is an underlying and more fundamental problem with this solution and others like it—it seems to assume an epistemology that guarantees epistemic compatibilism. Under this hypothetical solution, faith and reason turn out to be compatible—in fact, they appear to be funda-mentally the same: faith is belief justified by sufficient evidence, and so is reason (or science). But surely this solution is inadequate for precisely the same reason it succeeds in establishing epistemic compatibilism—we don't really think that faith and reason (or science) are basically the same.

When Aquinas adopts Aristotle's epistemology and his conditions for *scientia* and demonstration, opinion and probable arguments, Aquinas avoids the worry that his account of reason is an *ad hoc* construction motivated by apologetics. Aristotle's philosophy represented a major source of tension between faith and reason (in this case, philosophy) in the thirteenth century.

Aristotelian incompatibilists were inclined to favor Aristotle's philosophy over Christian faith, theist incompatibilists the reverse. As a compatibilist solution, starting with Aristotle immediately deprives secular critics of the ability to charge Aquinas of employing an *ad hoc* epistemology for the sake of Christian apologetics.[2] Using an Aristotelian epistemology is not merely a means to avoid criticism for Aquinas, however. We can infer from his extensive employment of Aristotelian notions in his responses to theological questions that Aquinas found Aristotle to be largely correct in a significant number of philosophically and theologically relevant areas. Earlier we discussed how using Aristotelian epistemology helps Aquinas avoid some ready criticism that might be leveled against other solutions to the problem of faith and reason. The main question remains: how exactly did Aquinas use Aristotle's epistemology, and what role did it play in his solution?

As discussed in chapter 2, Aquinas adopts Aristotle's account of *scientia* from the *Posterior Analytics*. Aquinas, following Aristotle, recognizes that *perfect scientia* is the ideal form of knowledge, and that it has three components—cognition, certitude, and perfect apprehension of the truth. Aquinas also accepts Aristotle's account of opinion (and its variants—doubt, suspicion, etc.) and notes that opinion lacks certitude and perfect apprehension of the truth. Thus far, Aquinas's epistemology is Aristotle's. Aquinas notices however, that there is room for a possible third epistemic state between *scientia* and opinion—one that has certitude but lacks perfect apprehension of the truth, namely, the epistemic state Aquinas calls *credere*; this is the state I have been referring to

---

[2] Though, as we shall see in section 5.5.1, Aquinas's use of an Aristotelian account of cognition earns him some severe criticism from fellow theologians.

as *belief* (distinct from ordinary non-italicized 'belief').[3] The job for Aquinas is to explain how Christian faith exemplifies that epistemic state Aristotle apparently overlooked (or could not foresee). If Aquinas can adequately explain not only that *belief* is possible, but also that the Christian view of faith conforms to it, then he will have succeeded in "Aristotelianizing" faith. This represents a move in the direction of establishing the epistemic compatibilism of faith and reason, since it establishes that faith as well as reason (as exemplified by *scientia* and opinion) occupy positions on an epistemic spectrum—a spectrum established by philosophers who were not motivated by Christian apologetics.

5.2. An Aristotelianized faith

As discussed in chapter 3, Aristotle's epistemology distinguishes between *scientia* and opinion, and there are two forms of *scientia*: *scientia propter quid* and *scientia quia*. *Scientia propter quid* is the ideal form of knowledge and includes three components: (1) cognition of the proposition, (2) certitude of the proposition, and (3) perfect apprehension of the truth of the proposition. *Scientia quia* satisfies the first two criteria but not the third—it is a form of knowledge in that one with *scientia quia* has knowledge *that* something is true but not knowledge *why* it is true. Opinion fails to meet both of the latter two criteria and thus fails to be a form of knowledge at all. Aquinas picks out *belief* as an epistemic state between *scientia* and opinion. *Belief* has certitude, as do both varieties of *scientia*, though it lacks perfect apprehension of the truth. Perfect apprehension of the truth, that is, understanding

---

[3] I presume that Aquinas never entertained a fourth possible epistemic state: one has perfect apprehension of the truth but lacks certitude. Certitude establishes that a proposition is true and could not be otherwise (i.e., is necessary); perfect apprehension of the truth reveals *why*. I assume Aquinas thought it obvious that if you knew *why* something was necessarily true, then you would automatically know that it was necessarily true.

what causes something to be true and why these causes make something true, is a result of intellectual vision—characterized in section 3.1.2.4 as *perfect-* or *p-vision*. This intellectual vision, which is a cognition illuminated by the natural light of reason, is the ability to "see" that and why something is true. For instance, we see that self-evident truths (e.g., the principle of non-contradiction) are true, and in seeing that they are true, we are compelled to assent to them. Further, the assent is accompanied with certitude—we are unable to conceive that the truth of the proposition could be otherwise—that is, we conceive the proposition as being necessarily true. Aquinas observes that *belief* as well as opinion lack such intellectual vision—the sorts of things about which we have *belief* or opinion are not those that we see to be true.

With opinion, we accept the truth of a proposition without having any certitude of it—not only do we not see why the proposition is true, but we also do not comprehend that the proposition could not be false. With *belief*, on the other hand, though we do not see why the proposition is true, we do hold that it could not be otherwise. In cases of *belief*, because we lack p-vision, our assent to the proposition is not compelled by our seeing that the proposition is true. Aquinas reasons that if the intellect is not compelled to assent by the object (the proposition), then it must be compelled by something else. When it is compelled by the will (in a special way), we have *belief*. The will compels the intellect to assent, according to Aquinas, through the following process: we apprehend some proposition and we apprehend that assenting to the proposition would be good for us; from these apprehensions we begin to desire to assent to the proposition, then choose to assent, and finally do assent.[4] Faith, as

---

[4] Though it is clear Aquinas thinks that *belief* (*credere*) has certitude ("But the act of believing has firm adherence to one alternative, in which the

a special form of *belief*, thus occupies the same place in Aristotle's epistemic spectrum as *scientia quia*.

What gives faith its certitude and what differentiates it from *scientia*, according to Aquinas, is that the *belief* is a result of grace, not of evidence. The faithful do not come to *believe* matters of faith because conclusive evidence has been presented to them—if that were the case, then these people would have *scientia*, not faith. In order for someone to have faith that some proposition is true, that person cannot have compelling evidence of its truth. Instead, the will moves the intellect to assent, and the will is helped to move by the grace of God. Though faith lacks the compelling evidence of *scientia*, it has an alternate route to certitude. Along with God's grace comes an interior light of faith analogous to the light of reason. Just as the light of reason illuminates propositions so that we can "see" that they are true (*p-seeing*), the light of faith illuminates propositions so that we can "see" that they are something we ought to *believe* (*f-seeing*). Once the faithful see what is to be *believed*, and have a will that is prepared by grace to choose to *believe* such propositions, they do so *believe*. And their faith has certitude because the source of the light of faith and the grace that helps guide the will both come from God, the most reliable source of truth there is.

Thus, the certitude of faith differs in an important way from the certitude of *scientia*. Aquinas says:

> Certitude can mean two things. The first is firmness of adherence, and with reference to this, faith is more certain than any understanding [of principles] and scientific knowledge. For the first truth, which causes the assent of faith, is a more

---

believer agrees with the knower [*sciente*] and the one who understands" [ST II-II.2.1]) I am not clear as to what other instances may count as *belief* other than faith. Given that faith is my particular interest here, I shall limit my discussion to faith in particular rather than *belief* in general.

powerful cause than the light of reason, which causes the assent of understanding or *scientia*. The second is the evidence of that to which assent is given. Here, faith does not have certainty, but *scientia* and understanding do. It is because of this, too, that understanding has no discursive thought.[5]

There are two different types of certitude: the certitude of faith is a firmness of adherence to a proposition resulting from the process of grace-aided *belief*, and the certitude of *scientia* is an evidence that compels assent. What these two have in common is that the intellect is determined to one side of a contradiction, that is, those who have faith as well as those who have *scientia* equally hold that what they believe cannot be false. If each type of certitude is reliable, then the certitude of faith and the certitude of *scientia* are epistemically on a par. And thus Aquinas can hold faith to be on the same Aristotelian epistemological spectrum as *scientia* and opinion.

5.3. Limitations of reason

Thus far we have seen how Aquinas construes faith to fit into the epistemology established by Aristotle. This does not, in itself, provide a solution to the problem of faith and reason. Just as Aristotelian mathematicians would hold other mathematicians to be epistemically irresponsible should they construct an opinion-based (rather than a *scientia*-based) mathematics, so philosophers could hold the faithful to be epistemically irresponsible for believing on faith what they should instead believe by means of

---

[5] "ad septimum dicendum, quod certitudo duo potest importare: scilicet firmitatem adhaesionis; et quantum *ad hoc* fides est certior etiam omni intellectu et scientia, quia prima veritas, quae causat fidei assensum, est fortior causa quam lumen rationis, quae causat assensum intellectus vel scientiae. importat etiam evidentiam eius cui assentitur; et sic fides non habet certitudinem, sed scientia et intellectus: et exinde est quod intellectus cogitationem non habet." (QDV 14.1 ad 7)

demonstration. Aquinas blunts such criticisms by arguing that natural reason is inherently limited in its abilities to understand many matters of the divine, and, at least when *scientia* is impossible, having faith about these matters is epistemically the best we can do. Aquinas shows that faith is epistemically responsible at least for propositions that natural reason cannot demonstrate, which I shall call the Scope Strategy.

The strategy is to argue that the scope of natural reason is limited when it comes to divine matters. As was discussed throughout chapter 4, Aquinas adopts an Aristotelian account of cognition, a move that blocks criticism of Aquinas as having developed an *ad hoc* account of cognition for the sake of apologetics. Using this Aristotelian account, Aquinas argues that we cannot have any understanding about the divine essence; *perfect scientia* about any divine matters is unavailable to us, because we cannot know *why* God did something without first knowing God, and this we cannot do. The truth of some divine matters, however, we can infer, but only so as to acquire *scientia quia*. From effects we can deduce their causes (thus performing a demonstration *quia*) and thus know *that* the causes exist but not *why* the causes brought about the effects. If we are careful Aristotelian scientists, we will then see that natural reason can lead us to *scientia* that God exists, and also that He is an unmoved mover, etc. We will also see that natural reason *cannot* lead us to *scientia* about certain other divine matters, including not only the Christian mysteries but also the duration of the universe. Aquinas's Scope Strategy in a nutshell is this: he employs Aristotelian accounts of epistemology and cognition to show that according to such accounts, natural reason is limited in the scope of what it can generate *scientia* about. For any proposition P that falls outside the scope of natural reason, if P can be had by faith, then one can have certitude that P, and thus it would appear that the best epistemic state a human could have vis-à-vis P would be faith.[6] This achieves a degree of epistemic compatibilism between faith and reason, for even if faith were generally found to be epistemically inadequate when had instead of reason (such a position will be considered in the next section), at least in cases where reason cannot go, having faith would seem to be epistemically responsible. Even for divine matters that *are* accessible to natural reason, Aquinas thinks that it would be epistemically responsible still to have faith about these matters. This approach I call the Pragmatic Strategy.

In many places throughout his writings, Aquinas expresses the view that it is often the case that one ought to have faith about provable divine matters. His reasons for holding this view are: (1) because proofs about divine matters require a great deal of other knowledge, *scientia* about such matters would come only late in life; (2) many people do not have the time, inclination, or mental ability to perform such proofs; and (3) philosophers have often made mistakes when reasoning about the divine.[7] Aquinas's

---

[6] As Aquinas points out, those who have experienced the beatific vision, angels, and God are capable of having *p-vision* of certain divine matters that we, as ordinary mortal humans, are not. See, for instance, ST I.57.3.

[7] "...it is necessary for man to accept in the way of faith not only the things that are above reason, but also the things that can be known by reason. And this for three reasons. First, so that man might come more quickly to the apprehension of divine truth. The body of knowledge that has the task of proving that God exists and other such things about God, is proposed to men for learning last, many other sciences being presupposed. And so man could not come to the apprehension of God during his life except after a long time. Second, so that the apprehension of God be more common. Many cannot make progress in the study of knowledge, either because of dullness of wit; or because of other occupations and the necessities of temporal life; or even because of laziness in learning. All of them would be entirely cheated of the apprehension of God unless divine things were proposed to them in the manner of faith. Third, on account of certainty. Human reason is much deficient in divine things. A sign of this is that the philosophers, investigating human things naturally, erred in many things and held opinions contrary to

concern here is that without faith, a significant number of people would lack the appropriate sorts of beliefs needed for salvation—pragmatically, faith is preferable to natural reason. This strategy also would seem to satisfy Alston's account of practical rationality discussed in chapter 1. Recall that for Alston, a person is counted as a practically rational believer (and in this way counted as epistemically responsible) when he/she has belief-forming practices that satisfy the following conditions: (i) they do not lead to massive inconsistencies, (ii) there is no reason to think them unreliable, (iii) there are no alternative practices (that we know of) that are more reliable, and (iv) changing to some other practice would be massively disruptive and difficult. If faith indeed yields certitude, then faith immediately satisfies (i) and (ii). Aquinas in (3) above (and discussed in detail in section 3.3) holds that faith *is* more reliable than natural reason when it comes to divine matters, and thus his account satisfies (iii). Finally, I take it that in order to save the most number of people we can, and given Aquinas's observations (1) and (2), to shift from requiring people to believe on the basis of faith to believing on the basis of proofs of natural reason would be massively disruptive and difficult; thus his account satisfies (iv). So it would appear that even though some matters of faith are accessible by natural reason, the faithful are practically rational when they believe those matters on faith alone, and, at least to this extent, are epistemically responsible in their beliefs.

5.4. Faith and reason are compatible

A common mistake in interpreting Aquinas is to conclude that the Five Ways set out to prove the existence of God in order

---

themselves. Divine things had to be handed down to them in the manner of faith, as being said by God, who cannot lie, so that there might be indubitable and certain apprehension of God among men." (ST II-II.2.4)

to provide rational justification for faith. If we construe rational justification as we did in section 1.2.1, then faith (understood as that Aristotelianized unique epistemic state) is not rationally justified. Recall that in that chapter, a belief P was counted as epistemically responsible and rationally justified just in case there was sufficient evidence for P. And a belief that P was held to have sufficient evidence if P was either: foundational (i.e., properly basic) or believed on the basis of foundational beliefs that inductively, deductively, or abductively supported P. Faith fails to satisfy either of these conditions. First, faith does not seem to be properly basic, for faith is a result of a complex process of grace and the will moving the intellect to assent. Properly basic beliefs do not require any support for them—like self-evident beliefs, when we apprehend them, we see that they are true and accept them as such. This is not the case with the beliefs of faith.[8] Second, believing by faith is not believing on the basis of some evidence from which one deduces the truths of faith. The Five Ways at first appear to provide such evidence—for instance, from the evidence that something is moving, we deduce that God exists. One might think that our belief that God exists is therefore rationally justified by the proofs based on such evidence. However, as I argued in chapters 3 and 4, the Five Ways cannot have been given in order to provide this sort of rational justification for *faith*—for faith is of things unseen, that is, only when we lack a proof for P can we have faith that P.

---

[8] This is an oversimplification. As I argue in the response to the first objection in section 5.5.2 below, there is a sense, I think, in which faith *is* properly basic.

On the other hand, the Five Ways *can* be used to provide rational justification for certain sorts of belief.[9] There can be those who believe that God exists without having faith (understood as Aquinas does). These persons, if they believe on the basis of some sort of proof (whether it be the Five Ways, evidence of miracles, etc.), can presumably count themselves as rationally justified in believing that God exists. Proofs of the existence of God (and other sorts of proofs or evidence) can thus be advanced to justify beliefs about divine matters, and many contemporary philosophers of religion concern themselves with whether or not such proofs or evidence do, indeed, provide sufficient justification for some religious beliefs. Aquinas's epistemic compatibilism, however, is not this. Aquinas did not seek to show that beliefs concerning divine matters were epistemically responsible; rather, his concern was to show that *faith* was. And faith, strictly speaking, is not justified, because faith lacks sufficient evidence for assent. (Recall the passage from QDV 14 quoted above [in section 5.2] in which Aquinas recognizes that faith lacks the certitude of evidence that *scientia* and understanding have.)

Another role for the Five Ways and other proofs could be to establish *truth* compatibilism. If the Five Ways were taken to be successful, then the truth of at least the existence of God can considered to have been established—secular truth incompatibilism would be significantly diminished as a response to the tension between faith and reason (though one could still be an incompatibilist about the articles of faith). Aquinas does seem to speak as if the Five Ways are indeed proofs that establish the existence of God,[10] and further that these proofs are advanced to

---

[9] However, I do not believe that this is the intended purpose of these proofs. See chapter 4.

[10] See ST I.2.2.

remove obstacles to the faith.[11] Aquinas seems to advance them, at least in part, so that proofs against the faith (e.g., the problem of evil) have a counterpart. Once the truths of faith are established as at least possible, then one will be more easily motivated to rebut disproofs against faith. And, of course, Aquinas will hold that all such disproofs of articles of faith are erroneous or not actually demonstrations. In section 2.4.2, we surveyed a number of ways in which arguments could fail to be demonstrations; in section 3.3, we saw how Aquinas argued that natural reason is often deficient in divine matters; and in chapter 4, we examined some ways in which reason was incapable of demonstrating conclusions about the divine. Considerations such as these give Aquinas the confidence to believe that disproofs of matters of faith must fail. Armed with (what he considers to be) successful proofs of matters of faith, Aquinas can confidently hold a truth compatibilism—that is, that the truths of faith are fully compatible with the truths that result from reason, since any incompatibility will be a result of error.

Aquinas seems to hold to a different standard for rational justification than the one advanced in section 1.2.1 and discussed in earlier paragraphs. The chapter 1 account assumes that a belief P is rationally justified if and only if there is sufficient evidence for P. By this standard of rational justification, faith is not justified because, as Aquinas holds, faith lacks this degree of evidence. It seems, however, that according to Aquinas it is not evidence that yields rational justification but certitude—the apprehension that some proposition is necessarily true. What distinguishes opinion from *scientia* and understanding is certitude—the latter two states have it, the former does not. Understanding has certitude because it is properly basic; we simply "see" (that is, we *p-see*) that what we understand cannot be otherwise. *Scientia* derives its certitude

---

[11] See ST II-II.2.10 ad 2.

from demonstrations (deductive inferences) from propositions that, ultimately, are grounded in propositions we understand. This model of understanding and *scientia* does seem to conform to the version of Classic Foundationalism laid out in chapter 1.2.A:

(CF)   S's belief that P is epistemically *responsible* if and only if there is sufficient evidence for P. There is sufficient evidence for P if and only if either:
  (1) P is properly basic (i.e., P is self-evident, incorrigible, or evident to the senses for S), or
  (2) P is believed on the evidential basis of other beliefs that are epistemically responsible and that support P deductively, inductively, or abductively.

Understanding satisfies condition (1), *scientia* (2). For Aquinas, however, faith also has certitude, and it has this certitude despite a lack of evidence. Faith is neither properly basic nor evidentially supported by properly basic propositions, yet faith has certitude. And certitude of faith is clearly held by Aquinas to be sufficient for epistemic responsibility, since Aquinas holds that faith, with its certitude, is at least if not more reliable than *scientia* (see, for instance, section 3.3).

Classic foundationalism is thus too limiting an account of epistemic responsibility, because faith, due to its certitude, should count as epistemically responsible. Rather than CF, Aquinas seems rather to hold a position closer to the following; let us call it Faith-Inclusive Foundationalism (FIF):[12,13]

---

[12] I should note that Aquinas does not explicitly argue for epistemic responsibility or rational justification. Although I think this account is consistent with the views held by Aquinas, he did not seem particularly concerned with explicitly developing an account of epistemic justification.

(FIF)   S's belief that P is epistemically responsible if and only if S has certitude that P. S has certitude that P if and only if either:

(1) S *p-sees* that P is true (that is, S understands P: S sees by natural reason that P is true, why P is true, and needs no further evidence in support of P [and P is properly basic]), or

(2) S *f-sees* that P is true (that is, S sees by the light of faith that P is to be *believed*, and S assents to P on this basis—S has faith that P), or

(3) P is believed on the evidential basis of other beliefs that are epistemically responsible and that support P by demonstration.[14]

Why should we be inclined to favor FIF over CF? As was discussed in section 3.1.2.4, the role of evidence in the operation of the intellect is to move the intellect to be settled to one side of a contradiction. According to Aquinas, this settling, or determination, is certitude. And it is in virtue of having this certitude that *scientia* can be seen to be necessary, itself a necessary

---

[13] See Stump (1992) for an interesting survey of views on Aquinas as a Foundationalist. Stump does not believe that Aquinas accepts CF, but it seems that she would also reject Aquinas as holding FIF. Her positions depends on a substantially different approach and interpretation to Aquinas's epistemology than my own, and for this reason, I do not have the room to rebut her views here.

[14] There seem to be three sorts of certitude had by derivative means. *Perfect scientia* is acquired when one demonstrates from propositions understood to conclusions. *Scientia quia*, on the other hand, is had when one demonstrates from propositions intellectually assented to, but not understood (for example, propositions known to be true because proved by some other scientist or proved in the past, or propositions evident to the senses, e.g., something is moving). The science of sacred doctrine involves demonstrations from propositions that are *f-seen* to conclusions that are proven, but not themselves seen.

condition for distinguishing *scientia* from mere opinion. Evidence, then, can be instrumental for certitude, but it is certitude, the determination of the intellect to one thing, that is the epistemically relevant factor in *scientia*. The movement of the will in faith also determines the intellect to one thing, and this is why faith also has certitude. Seeing by the light of faith and by the light of natural reason are two means by which the intellect is steered to certitude, but it is only with certitude that an epistemic state becomes "respectable"—that is, becomes more than mere opinion. FIF, then, is preferable to CF for two reasons: first, it acknowledges that it is certitude, not evidence, that is the epistemically interesting aspect of *scientia* and understanding; second, it notes that there are two means of achieving such certitude—via the intellect by *p-seeing* and via the will and grace and by *f-seeing*.

If we count FIF rather than CF as the correct version of foundationalism, then we can count faith as rationally justified. Those who are inclined to cringe when justification is separated from evidence will recoil from describing Aquinas's faith as rationally justified. So be it. Even if faith is not to be counted as rationally justified, it seems clear that Aquinas's faith, at least under an Aristotelian epistemology, should not be counted as epistemically irresponsible. If Aquinas's account is correct, then what gives *scientia* its epistemic credentials is certitude—because faith has certitude, it, too, should be counted as equally epistemically responsible. Because faith does not violate the epistemic norms of reason under Aristotle, Aquinas seems to have achieved an epistemic compatibilism between faith and reason.

By employing an Aristotelian epistemology and account of cognition, and by introducing an Aristotelianized faith, Aquinas also achieves an epistemic compatibility between faith and reason along the lines of Plantinga's version of epistemic responsibility as having warrant. Recall from section 1.2.3 that according to

Plantinga, "a belief has warrant for a person S only if that belief is produced in S by cognitive faculties functioning properly (subject to no dysfunction) in a cognitive environment that is appropriate to S's kind of cognitive faculties, according to a design plan that is successfully aimed at truth."[15] Aristotle's account of cognition nearly guarantees that our faculties will, under ordinary circumstances, function properly and will be successfully aimed at the truth. For, according to Aristotle, our faculties are determined teleologically, and nothing exists naturally that cannot perform its proper function. As Aquinas observes in his commentary on Aristotle's *Metaphysics*:

> ...the desire to know belongs by nature to all men.
> ...each thing naturally desires its own perfection...since the intellect, by which man is what he is, considered in itself is all things potentially, and becomes them actually only through *scientia*...so each man naturally desires *scientia* just as matter desires form.
> ...each thing has a natural inclination to perform its proper operation...Now the proper operation of man as man is to understand, for by reason of this he differs from all other things. Hence the desire of man is naturally inclined to understand, and therefore to possess *scientia*.
> ...a natural desire cannot exist in vain.[16]

---

[15] Plantinga, *God and Other Minds* (2000) 156.

[16] "proponit igitur primo, quod omnibus hominibus naturaliter desiderium inest ad sciendum.

cuius ratio potest esse triplex: primo quidem, quia unaquaeque res naturaliter appetit perfectionem sui. unde et materia dicitur appetere formam, sicut imperfectum appetit suam perfectionem. cum igitur intellectus, a quo homo est id quod est, in se consideratus sit in potentia omnia, nec in actum eorum reducatur nisi per scientiam, quia nihil est eorum quae sunt, ante intelligere, ut dicitur in tertio de anima: sic naturaliter unusquisque desiderat scientiam sicut materia formam.

secundo, quia quaelibet res naturalem inclinationem habet ad suam propriam operationem: sicut calidum ad calefaciendum, et grave ut deorsum

Aquinas (following Aristotle) holds that natural faculties and functions are, by definition, incoherent if their function is, in principle, unobtainable. A faculty with a certain specific function F exists in order to achieve F (achieving F is its final cause). If F is in principle unobtainable, that is, if the natural desire of the faculty (to achieve F) could never be achieved, then the natural desire of F would be in vain—the faculty would have a final cause that could not be a final cause—and this is incoherent.[17] The proper function of man is to understand and reason, and the final cause of the understanding and reasoning is the truth, so in order for our intellectual faculties *not* to be in vain, we must be capable of using them to achieve the truth; in fact, they must be designed so that with them, we can achieve the truth. As Aquinas says,

---

moveatur. propria autem operatio hominis inquantum homo, est intelligere. per hoc enim ab omnibus aliis differt. unde naturaliter desiderium hominis inclinatur ad intelligendum, et per consequens ad sciendum.

tertio, quia unicuique rei desiderabile est, ut suo principio coniungatur; in hoc enim uniuscuiusque perfectio consistit. unde et motus circularis est perfectissimus, ut probatur octavo physicorum, quia finem coniungit principio. substantiis autem separatis, quae sunt principia intellectus humani, et ad quae intellectus humanus se habet ut imperfectum ad perfectum, non coniungitur homo nisi per intellectum: unde et in hoc ultima hominis felicitas consistit. et ideo naturaliter homo desiderat scientiam. nec obstat si aliqui homines scientiae huic studium non impendant; cum frequenter qui finem aliquem desiderant, a prosecutione finis ex aliqua causa retrahantur, vel propter difficultatem perveniendi, vel propter alias occupationes. sic etiam licet omnes homines scientiam desiderent, non tamen omnes scientiae studium impendunt, quia ab aliis detinentur, vel a voluptatibus, vel a necessitatibus vitae praesentis, vel etiam propter pigritiam vitant laborem addiscendi. hoc autem proponit aristoteles ut ostendat, quod quaerere scientiam non propter aliud utilem, qualis est haec scientia, non est vanum, cum naturale desiderium vanum esse non possit." (M I.1.1-4)

[17] See ST I.77.3—powers are ordered to their acts, and acts of active powers are distinguished by their ends; thus powers are essentially distinguished and determined by their ends.

Now it is clear that as truth is the good of the intellect, so falsehood is its evil, as the Philosopher says....as regards its proper object the intellect is always true; and hence it is never deceived of itself, but whatever deception occurs must be ascribed to some lower power, such as the imagination or the like. Hence we see that when the natural power of judgment is free we are not deceived by such images, but only when it is not free, as is the case in sleep.[18]

Thus when the intellect is operating under its own power, that is, when it is functioning properly, it designed to aim at the truth; the operations of the Aristotelian intellect thus, under Plantinga's account, have warrant.

By fitting faith into Aristotelian epistemology and cognition, Aquinas is able to argue that faith has the same sort of warrant that understanding and *scientia* have. As discussed in the detailed account of faith in chapter 3, both the will and the intellect are involved in the act of faith. In the case of faith, unlike cases of understanding or *scientia*, the will moves the intellect to be determined to one thing, that is, to certitude. At root, however, the act of faith is an act of intellect, and just as the final cause of *scientia* and understanding is the truth, so too with faith.[19] Just as *scientia* and understanding have warrant, so too and for the same reasons will faith have warrant. The difference between faith and *scientia* is that the latter will be functioning properly when its power is not impaired by a lower power, such as the imagination. Faith, on the other hand, functions properly when the will is

---

[18] "manifestum est autem quod, sicut verum est bonum intellectus, ita falsum est malum eius, ut dicitur in vi ethic....manifestum est autem ex praemissis quod intellectus circa proprium obiectum semper verus est. unde ex seipso nunquam decipitur, sed omnis deceptio accidit in intellectu ex aliquo inferiori, puta phantasia vel aliquo huiusmodi. unde videmus quod, quando naturale iudicatorium non est ligatum, non decipimur per huiusmodi apparitiones, sed solum quando ligatur, ut patet in dormientibus." (ST I.94.4)

[19] See ST II-II.4.2.

moved by grace and directed by the light of faith (rather than directed by other motives or for other reasons).[20] God's role in faith presumably ensures that faith is functioning properly; thus we may presume that, for Aquinas, faith will *always* have warrant. If we understand faith and *scientia* to be success terms (as I believe Aquinas does), then they each, by definition, have warrant, for when the intellect is not properly aimed at the truth or when we fail to function properly (either in the manner of reasoning or in our relation to God), we are always left with, at most, mere opinion. To say that someone has *scientia* or faith is to imply proper function and a state that grasps the truth, that is to say, that these states always have warrant.

We see, therefore, that Aquinas reconciles faith and reason according to each of the three ways outlined in chapter 1 for epistemic compatibilism.[21] He finds faith to be epistemically responsible because it is practically rational to believe—faith seems a far more efficient and effective means of forming beliefs about propositions concerning God and His actions. If, following Aquinas, we accept a Faith-Inclusive Foundationalism, then faith would also seem to be rationally justified. Even if we do not accept FIF, faith from *f-seeing* seems at least epistemically responsible because it has certitude. Finally, because faith is an act of the intellect of a similar sort to *scientia* and understanding, each will be epistemically responsible because each has warrant. As I have also suggested, the Five Ways would appear to ground claims of truth compatibilism. Finally, though we shall not discuss it here, it is quite clear that Aquinas holds that there is moral compatibilism

---

[20] See ST II-II.6.1.

[21] However, it may be that Aquinas's approach seems to us to be an adequate reconciliation of faith and reason only if we accept an Aristotelian account of epistemology and cognition. This issue will be taken up later in the third objection in section 5.5.2 below.

between faith and reason. Aquinas finds there to be value in our natural reason, even in reasoning about divine matters, and Aquinas certainly holds that faith will not be immoral. It appears then that Aquinas holds faith and reason to be fully compatible.

5.5. Objections and replies

As we discussed at the beginning of this chapter, solutions to the problem of faith and reason run the risk of being *ad hoc* if the account of reason and/or faith that is provided seems motivated primarily by apologetics. By employing the account of episte-mology and cognition of the leading reason-based threat to Christianity at the time, Aquinas avoids the charge of advancing this sort of *ad hoc* solution. However, precisely for employing Aristotle's (pagan) epistemology, Aquinas runs into criticism from his fellow theologians, both Medieval and more recent. In the next section we will look at Christian responses to Aquinas's Aristotelian account of reason. In section 5.5.2, we will raise more general philosophical problems with Aquinas's solution to the problem of reason and faith.

5.5.1. Christian responses to Aquinas's account of reason

Two key elements in Aquinas's epistemic compatibilism between faith and reason are his use of the Scope Strategy, in which he limits the scope of what reason can grasp, and his modification of Classic Foundationalism into what I have termed Faith-Inclusive Foundationalism, in which beliefs count as rationally justified not because they have sufficient evidence but because they have certitude. Each of these elements relies significantly on Aristotelian philosophy. In order to limit the scope of reason, Aquinas employs an Aristotelian account of cognition (in chapter 4, we discussed how he uses this account to argue that reason cannot prove the duration of the world). In support of his certitude-based foundationalism, Aquinas employs an Aristotelian epistemology in which certitude plays a crucial role in picking out epistemically responsible states. Aquinas's account of reason based on an Aristotelian cognition/epistemology was by no means universally accepted among Medieval Christian theologians, and aspects of Aquinas's account of reason would certainly seem inappropriate to later philosophers who no longer accepted Aristotelian accounts of cognition or epistemology.

Aristotle's *Posterior Analytics*, long unavailable to the Latin West, was translated into Latin in 1159, and Robert Grosseteste appears to have written the first full commentary around 1225.[22] I have provided, in chapter 2, my interpretation of *scientia* as Aquinas understood it from his commentary on the *Posterior Analytics*. I have argued that what was key to this concept, particularly for his solution to the problem of faith and reason, was that *scientia* was composed of three cognitions: apprehension, certitude, and perfect apprehension of the truth. Each Medieval philosopher who wrote at any length on Aristotelian *scientia* appears to have differed with Aquinas, at least slightly, in how *scientia* and demonstration are to be understood. It would take far too long to survey the differences between Aquinas's account of *scientia* and that of his contemporaries and later Scholastics, particularly since much has been written on the subject.[23] Instead,

---

[22] Dates from Serene, "Demonstrative Science," in *The Cambridge History of Later Medieval Philosophy*, ed. Kretzmann et al. (1982) 498.

[23] For a good survey of Medieval views on *scientia*, see Serene, "Demonstrative Science." Marrone ("Concepts of Science among Parisian Theologians in the Thirteenth Century," in *Knowledge and the Sciences in Medieval Philosophy*, ed. Tyorinoja et al. [1990]) also has a useful survey of views held by theologians in Paris shortly following Aquinas's death. Adams (*William Ockham* [1987], ch. 14) provides a particularly detailed look at the views of Henry of Ghent, Duns Scotus, Ockham, et al.

I shall claim that the basic outline of Aquinas's epistemology became a commonly held view, at least until the waning years of Aristotelianism and the rise of new approaches to natural philosophy and logic after around 1600. My support for this claim will be thinly documented here, though I think evidence for later views that are fundamentally congruent with those of Aquinas are easily found. I offer only one bit of evidence here for my claim.

In 1589, during his first teaching position at the University of Pisa, Galileo himself wrote a commentary on the *Posterior Analytics*. As William Wallace argues,[24] Galileo's commentary was largely cribbed from lectures by his professor Paulus Vallius. As excerpts from the Vallius lectures (plagiarized and published by Ludovico Carbone) show, the account of Aristotelian epistemology that Galileo learned and in turn presumably taught was, though perhaps more nuanced, fundamentally unchanged from Aquinas's account. What follows are a number of passages concerning the Vallius-Carbone text that exemplify the similarities between the late-sixteenth-century interpretation of *scientia* and demonstration and Aquinas's account provided in chapter 2:

> Vallius-Carbone define evidence as a certain clarity and perspicuity whereby an argument or sign is able to elicit conviction in the intellect, much the way in which a visible object seen at a proper distance and under appropriate light elicits conviction in the power of sight. It is not the same as certitude, since one can have certitude without evidence, as in divine faith, but one cannot have evidence without an accompanying certitude.[25]

> Vallius-Carbone define certitude as a firmness of the intellect in knowing that eliminates doubt or wavering about

---

[24] See Wallace, *Galileo's Logic of Discovery and Proof* (1992) xiii. All claims interpreting Galileo that follow are from this source.

[25] Wallace, *Galileo's Logic*, 95.

the know-ledge obtained; it differs from truth in that truth can be accompanied by doubt whereas certitude cannot. There are, moreover, two kinds of certitude: one is said to be extrinsic because, although the intellect gives its assent, it does so prompted by a command of the will; the other is intrinsic because the intellect gives assent on its own, forced as it were by the evidence presented or by its own reasoning, so that only a person deprived of the natural light would hold the contrary. The two certitudes differ in various ways: the extrinsic type can be false, as in the case of unfounded human faith, whereas the intrinsic cannot; the extrinsic necessarily depends on the will, whereas the intrinsic can actually be opposed to the will; the extrinsic does not invoke the natural light of the intellect, whereas the intrinsic does; and the extrinsic lacks evidence, whereas the intrinsic depends on it.[26]

[Quoting Vallius-Carbone:] Demonstration is a syllogism composed of necessary propositions wherefrom something is concluded necessarily and evidently through causes or effects. Note here that there are three kinds of demonstration: one is said to be most perfect and most powerful (*potissima*); a second is demonstration of the reasoned fact (*propter quid*); a third, demonstration of the fact (*quia*). Three functions are attributed to demonstration. The first is to show the existence of an effect and its reason why, as is done in most powerful demonstration. The second is to manifest the cause of a thing, and demonstration of the reasoned fact does that. The third is to show the existence of a cause through an effect, and that is what is done by demonstration of the fact.[27]

The careful reader will note that these views of Vallius-Carbone/Galileo do not match those of Aquinas's precisely. However, they are sufficiently similar to justify, I believe, the

---

[26] Ibid., 96.
[27] Ibid., 65.

claim that Aquinas's accounts of *scientia*, demonstration, and certitude were widely acceptable to Medieval and later theologians and philosophers. If views quite similar to Aquinas's were part of the sixteenth-century logic curricula, then Aquinas's views were not (at least until after 1600) considered particularly controversial.

Even if I am correct in holding that it was the case that Aquinas's interpretation of Aristotelian *scientia* and demonstration was not particularly radical, his embracing of Aristotelian cognition engendered a significant amount of controversy. Recall the brief account of cognition advanced in discussing the eternity of the world in chapter 4, which I repeat again here.

In brief, Aquinas's Aristotelian account of cognition is roughly as follows. Objects make impressions on the external senses and these impressions are copied and transmitted to the intellect as likenesses, or phantasms (*phantasmata*). By abstracting from these phantasms we can apprehend in the intellect the form and accidents of the object sensed. What the senses respond to are individual particulars, but what the intellect apprehends are intelligible species, that is, universals apprehended by means of abstraction.[28] Thus, when we apprehend that humans are rational animals, this is a result of first sensing one or more particular humans, forming phantasms of them in the intellect, and then abstracting from these phantasms to apprehend the intelligible species, or form, of a human—and, for instance, that it includes rationality.

This power we have of apprehending intelligible species is that of the *agent intellect* (*intellectus agens*). Our intellect has both a passive and an active component. The intellect is passive, in part,

---

[28] For Aquinas's account of cognition, see ST I.84. See also Kretzmann, "Philosophy of Mind," in *Cambridge Companion to Aquinas*, ed. Kretzmann and Stump (1993).

for its ability to receive. Just as the senses passively receive impressions of objects, the passive intellect receives likenesses from these impressions. But these impressions are corporeal, and thus the intellect must actively make these impressions intelligible (that is, turn them into phantasms) so that they can become, as a result of abstraction, species that are intelligible. Our agent intellect is the power that converts the raw matter of thought into the intelligible species that we apprehend; it is not only a power, but active in that it draws us from passively receiving information to actively apprehending it. As Aquinas argues:

> But since Aristotle did not allow that forms of natural things subsist apart from matter, and as forms existing in matter are not actually intelligible, it follows that the natures or forms of the sensible things which we understand are not actually intelligible. Now nothing is reduced from potency to act except by something in act; just as the senses are made actual by what is actually sensible. We must therefore assign on the part of the intellect some power to make things actually intelligible, by the abstraction of the species from material conditions. And such is the necessity for positing an agent intellect.[29]

This view of cognition was sometimes vehemently rejected by Medieval theologians who preferred a more Augustinian/

---

[29] "sed quia aristoteles non posuit formas rerum naturalium subsistere sine materia; formae autem in materia existentes non sunt intelligibiles actu, sequebatur quod naturae seu formae rerum sensibilium, quas intelligimus, non essent intelligibiles actu. nihil autem reducitur de potentia in actum, nisi per aliquod ens actu, sicut sensus fit in actu per sensibile in actu. oportebat igitur ponere aliquam virtutem ex parte intellectus, quae faceret intelligibilia in actu, per abstractionem specierum a conditionibus materialibus. et haec est necessitas ponendi intellectum agentem." (ST I.79.3)

Avicennan account of cognition. Timothy Noone neatly summarizes one main contrasting position:[30]

> *Augustinisme avicenissant* involves the following claims: 1) God is identified as the agent intellect spoken of by Aristotle and is further thought of as functioning as the *Intelligentia agens* of Avicenna; 2) the human mind is essentially passive and is identified with the *intellectus possibilis* of Avicenna and Aristotle; and 3) human intellectual knowledge involves seeing things in the intelligible world under the light of divine illumination, although the mature Bacon allows some role for innate ideas in this process.[31]

The main difference between Aquinas's account of cognition and the Augustinian/Avicennan account is that the agent intellect is a power of man in the former and a power of God in the latter. This difference has serious repercussions for philosophy and theology. Under Aquinas's account of cognition, intelligible species can be known by the unaided human intellect—we can have understanding and *scientia* about these matters. (However, our intellectual powers in discerning the natures of things is often weak: "But, our cognition [*cognitio*] is weak to such a point that no philosopher would be able to investigate perfectly the nature of a single fly. Thus one reads that one philosopher spent thirty years in solitude that he might know [*cognosceret*] the nature of a bee."[32])

---

[30] For variations on and criticisms of Aristotelian cognition, see Kuksewicz, "Criticisms of Aristotelian Psychology and the Augustinian-Aristotelian Synthesis," in *The Cambridge History of Later Medieval Philosophy*, ed. Kretzmann et al. (1982) and Pasnau, *Theories of Cognition in the Later Middle Ages* (1997).

[31] Noone, "The Franciscans and Epistemology: Philosophy and Theology on the Issue of Universal Causality," in *Medieval Masters: Essays in Memory of Msgr. E. A. Synan*, ed. Houser (1999) 68.

[32] "Sed cognitio nostra adeo debilis est quod nullus philosophus potuit perfecte inuestigare naturam unius musce; unde legitur quod unus

Part and parcel of this account of cognition is a rejection of separate Platonic forms as unnecessary.[33]

On the other hand, the Augustinian/Avicennan account of cognition embraces a Platonic account of forms, or similar variations thereof (Bonaventure, for example, holds them to be ideas in God, identical with God's essence[34]). God illuminates these forms or ideas for us so that we can "see" them. Because the agency involved in understanding is God's, it follows that the human mind is incapable, without divine illumination, of understanding even the truths of natural philosophy. According to this view, our intellects are naturally inadequate for understanding. Once we think with the aid of divine illumination, we can finally understand. But without illumination, and further without faith, we cannot understand.

> The mind has, as it were, eyes of its own, analogous to the soul's senses. The certain truths of the sciences are analogous to the objects which the sun's rays make visible, such as the earth and earthly things. And it is God himself who illumines all.... Having eyes is not the same thing as looking, and looking is not the same as seeing. The soul therefore needs three things: eyes which is can use aright, looking and seeing. The eye of the mind is healthy when it is pure from every taint of the body, that is, when it is remote and purged from desire of mortal things. And this, faith alone can give in the first place.[35]

Augustine characterizes the natural (unilluminated) state of the intellect as needing "healing." According to Augustine, only

---

philosophus fuit triginta annis in solitudine ut cognosceret naturam apis." (*The Sermon-Conferences of St. Thomas Aquinas on the Apostles' Creed*, I.4.)

[33] See ST I.79.3, I.84.1.

[34] See Quinn, *The Historical Constitution of St. Bonaventure's Philosophy* (1973) ch. 7.

[35] Augustine, *Soliloquies* VI, 12.

once the eye of the mind has been healed are we capable of understanding. This healing is accomplished by joining with God—that is, by faith:

> Reason is the power of the soul to look, but it does not follow that every one who looks, sees. Right and perfect looking which leads to vision is called virtue. For virtue is right and perfect reason. But even looking cannot turn eyes already healed to the light unless these three things are present: faith that believes that the object to which our looking ought to be directed can, when seen, make us blessed; hope which is assured that vision will follow right looking; love which longs to see and to enjoy.[36]

Once one has healed the eye of the mind and is capable of looking and seeing, there is, in principle, no reason why God could not reveal any truth about any created thing. Thus, for example, the finite duration of the world *could* be proven, were one properly illuminated by God when constructing the demonstration. A second consequence is that, though the Five Ways could perhaps serve as demonstrative grounds for beliefs in divine matters, according to Aquinas (but not, however, as grounds for faith), they cannot serve as grounds according to the Augustinian account—for the intellect without faith would presumably be too damaged and unilluminated so that *scientia* about God's existence would be impossible under these circumstances. Finally, faith is an operation of the intellect according to Aquinas and is, in principle, independent of other operations of the intellect,[37] but for the Augustinian account, faith is presumably a precursor to *any* operation of the agent intellect—

---

[36] Ibid., VI, 13.

[37] However, Aquinas acknowledges that from faith and the gratuitous grace of God we can acquire the gifts of understanding and *scientia*—basically improvements in our ability to understand and to demonstrate.

that is, any ability to have understanding or *scientia* of intelligible species.

The Augustinian/Avicennan account of cognition, then, should be seen as a serious competitor to Aquinas's Aristotelian account—one that, if held, would block Aquinas's solution to the problem of faith and reason. Aquinas's insertion of faith into the Aristotelian epistemology of understanding and *scientia* appears, as I have argued, to have been fairly well received and seems to have had a long-lasting influence. Aquinas's account of cognition, particularly the roles of the active and passive intellect, seem to not have had such influence. As I have discussed above and Noone (1999) and Kuksewicz (1982) observe, the thirteenth century saw strong challenges to Aquinas's account, both from the Augustinian/Avicennan camp and from Aristotelian modifications of Aquinas's account. Philosophers and theologians of the fourteenth and fifteenth centuries, though concerned with human cognition, were less concerned with the human soul and its faculties, particularly that of the agent intellect. Accounts of Ockham, Peter Auriol, Durand, et al., essentially changed the nature of the subject, developing non-Thomistic accounts of cognition.[38] Recall that Aquinas's Scope Strategy relied on his account of cognition, but his certitude-based foundationalism does not. Were we to reject Aquinas's Aristotelian account of cognition, we might have to abandon one part of the solution to the problem of faith and reason (essentially that part discussed in chapter 4) but could still maintain, on Aquinas's behalf, an epistemic compatibilism between faith and reason.[39]

---

[38] See Kuksewicz, "Criticisms of Aristotelian Psychology," 628.

[39] An interesting research project, but one far too lengthy for this book, would be to examine how Aquinas's specific and detailed account of faith was actually received. After the Medieval era, and continuing to this day, there are numerous theological interpretations of faith that conflict in some way with the account given by Aquinas. My training in theology is inadequate,

No theist solution to the problem of faith and reason will be fully adequate that has an account of faith in which nobody has it. Although Aquinas avoids the charge of an *ad hoc* solution from the side of secular philosophy by largely employing the account of reason in vogue among philosophers at the time, he would still be vulnerable to criticism from theists were he guilty of developing an empty account of faith merely to show that it was epistemically compatible with Aristotelian reason. Criticism of Aquinas's account of faith, at least among Aquinas's peers and later Medieval theologians, is hard to pinpoint—in part, perhaps, because few Medieval theologians seem to have provided nearly as thorough an account of faith as did Aquinas (and thus, there are few points of contrast), and further because Aquinas took pains to show that his account of faith matched the characterization given in Scripture in Hebrews 11:1: "Faith is the substance of things to be hoped for, the evidence of things that appear not." As far as Aquinas's account of faith holds that faith lacks sufficient evidence (things that appear not), and that faith is the ground for salvation (the substance of things hoped for), presumably no Medieval theologian would disagree with him. Further, Aquinas's account of faith held that it is a result of a free choice of will, which deserves merit for such faith, while at the same time having certitude; these are positions that would be welcomed by the orthodoxy. As to exactly how the statement in Hebrews is to be

---

however, to attempt to provide useful explanations of these various views, to show how they contrast with Aquinas's, or to defend Aquinas's account in light of these latter day competitors. I leave it to the more theologically trained reader to evaluate Aquinas's account herself. (I shall note, however, that given his position as a Doctor of the Catholic Church, his enormous influence on the Dominican order, and serving as the inspiration for latter-day Thomists, his account of faith would seem not to be too objectionable to many Christians. As was discussed in chapter 1.3, Aquinas's approach to faith and reason also held a special place in *Fides et ratio* of John Paul II.)

explained by an account of faith, Aquinas has done so, but it is very difficult to see precisely how this account was received.

5.5.2. Philosophical problems with Aquinas's solution

In this section, we shall consider three philosophical objections to Aquinas's reconciliation of faith and reason. By no means are these objections exhaustive of the possible criticisms of Aquinas's account; they are, perhaps, the most immediate.

First objection. Aquinas's solution to the problem of faith and reason fails because it does not adequately establish that faith is epistemically responsible, because faith is epistemically circular. This objection is presented by Terence Penelhum:

> Thomas seems to be telling us both that one cannot believe in God unless one believes certain propositions about him, and that when one believes these propositions in faith, one accepts them as coming from him. But there is an obvious circularity about holding both together. One cannot accept a given proposition as coming from God unless one believes that God exists and has spoken; but one cannot (can one?) believe that God exists and has spoken because *these* propositions come from God. Surely at some stage one's assent has to be based on something less explicitly part of the faith than this, or how could it all begin?[40]

Reply to the first objection. In response to the objection that faith is epistemically circular, two solutions are commonly advanced. The first, that the existence of God is not held on faith, but by proof (e.g., by the Five Ways) would seem to be a successful response to the objection. This response acknowledges that faith by itself is epistemically unjustified; fortunately, we have demonstration to provide us with epistemic foundations for belief.

---

[40] Penelhum, "Analysis of Faith in St. Thomas Aquinas," *Religious Studies* 3 (1977): 141.

Proofs establish and justify the existence of God, and once we believe that God exists, then we are justified in believing what God reveals, namely, the articles of faith. This response to the objection is not Aquinas's, and as I argued in chapter 4, the Five Ways were not intended to justify faith. Since, as Aquinas points out, most believers are incapable of understanding proofs for the existence of God (at least until late in life), a consequence of this response would be that the faith of most Christians is irrational, a result that Aquinas would certainly not accept.

A second response to the objection, made famous by Alvin Plantinga, is to hold that belief in the existence of God is properly basic. Recall the formulation of Classic Foundationalism presented earlier in this chapter. Plantinga rejects CF because what it counts as properly basic is too limited:

> But many propositions that do not meet these conditions *are* properly basic for me. I believe, for example, that I had lunch this noon. I do not believe this proposition on the basis of other propositions; I take it as basic; it is in the foundations of my noetic structure. Furthermore, I am entirely rational in so taking it, even though this proposition is neither self-evident nor evident to the senses nor incorrigible for me.[41]

Plantinga proceeds by arguing that much in the same way "I had lunch this noon" is properly basic, so too, because one might experience God, for that person "God exists" is properly basic.[42] Plantinga's claim that "God exists" can be properly basic is a controversial one, and a great deal has been written both in favor of and against it; I leave it to the interested reader to explore the

---

[41] Plantinga, "Reason and Belief in God," (1983) 60.

[42] Plantinga, ibid., 81, acknowledges that, strictly speaking, what is properly basic is some proposition like "God is speaking to me" that entails "God exists." Since the latter proposition is derived from the former, it is not basic; however, we can talk of the latter as being properly basic in most circumstances without running into trouble.

contemporary literature on the subject. What is of particular interest here is whether the view that "God exists" is properly basic can serve as a viable (though controversial) response on behalf of Aquinas to the charge of epistemic circularity. We turn now to this issue.

Earlier I argued that Aquinas did not accept CF but rather a foundationalism based on certitude:

> (FIF) S's belief that P is epistemically responsible if and only if S has certitude that P. S has certitude that P if and only if either:
>
> (1)   S *p-sees* that P is true (that is, S understands P: S sees by natural reason that P is true, why P is true, and needs no further evidence in support of P [and P is properly basic]), or
>
> (2)   S *f-sees* that P is true (that is, S sees by the light of faith that P is to be *believed*, and S assents to P on this basis—S has faith that P), or
>
> (3)   P is believed on the evidential basis of other beliefs that are epistemically responsible and that support P by demonstration.

The analogue to the Plantingan move for FIF would be to argue that the Christian faithful believe that "God exists" with certitude, and thus such beliefs are epistemically responsible. This move at first seems unpromising. To say that we *p-see* that "God exists" is true is to say that the proposition is *understood*—a position held by Anselm but rejected by Aquinas.[43] To say that we *f-see* that "God exists" seems to reintroduce the circularity objection—to *f-see* this proposition would seem to be epistemically circular, since we are influenced to assent to what we *f-see* because

---

[43] See ST I.2.1.

226

God is telling us what to believe, including the proposition "God exists." As to the third condition, to believe "God exists" on the basis of prior faith seems incoherent, and to believe it on the basis of what we *p-see* amounts to proving that God exists—which amounts to the first response to the objection, one we have already rejected. However, for reasons similar to those for which Plantinga rejected CF, we should perhaps reject FIF, at least as it is currently formulated.

As discussed in section 2.3.1, Aquinas does seem to leave room for allowing one to have certitude about propositions concerning contingent matters. And in the Five Ways, Aquinas seems to allow that of propositions that are evident to the senses one also can have certitude. This would seem to suggest that FIF is missing a fourth condition, one in which S's belief that P has certitude about contingent or sensible matters. Exactly how to formulate this additional condition is difficult, particularly since Aquinas is never very clear on exactly how or to what extent sensible evidence provides certitude.[44] However, following Plantinga's reasoning, it seems plausible to hold that "I had lunch this noon" is a proposition about which one would have firm adherence and be determined to its truth and thus would be a proposition about which one could have certitude. Similarly, then, it seems plausible that one could have certitude about "God exists."

Whether or not Aquinas actually embraced this view is hard to determine. The best source for Aquinas's position is found in

---

[44] Formulating this condition is also difficult for contemporary religious epistemology. Audi, "Direct Justification, Evidential Dependence, and Theistic Belief," in *Rationality, Religious Belief, and Moral Commitment*, ed. Audi and Wainwright (1986) 148-49, constructively discusses a number of useful characteristics that could plausibly be claimed to hold of basic beliefs, but to my knowledge precise criteria for properly basic beliefs has yet to be successfully defended.

his reply to an objection very similar to this first objection in *De veritate* 14. I include here the objection and Aquinas's reply:

> Obj. 9. That God exists is an object of faith (*credibile*). However, we do not believe (*credimus*) this because it is acceptable to God, for no one can think that something is pleasing to God unless he first thinks that there is a God to whom it is pleasing. Hence, the judgment by which one thinks that God exists precedes the judgment by which he thinks something is pleasing to God. Nor can the former cause the latter. But we are led to believe something which we do not know through that which we believe is pleasing to God. Therefore, that God exists is believed (*creditum*) and known (*scitum*).

> Ad 9. Someone can begin to believe what he did not believe before but which he held with some hesitation. Thus, it is possible that, before believing in God, someone might think that God exists, and that it would be pleasing to God to have him believe that He exists. In this way a man can believe that God exists because such a belief pleases God, although this is not an article of faith, but preliminary to the article, since it can be proved by demonstration.[45]

---

[45] "Obj. 9. praeterea, deum esse, est quoddam credibile. non autem credimus hoc eo quod sit deo acceptum: quia nullus potest exstimare aliquid esse deo acceptum, nisi prius existimet esse deum qui acceptat; et sic existimatio qua quis existimat deum esse, praecedit existimationem qua quis putat aliquid esse deo acceptum, nec potest ex ea causari. sed ad credendum ea quae nescimus, ducimur per hoc quod hoc credimus esse deo acceptum. ergo deum esse, est creditum et scitum.

"ad nonum dicendum, quod aliquis potest incipere credere illud quod prius non credebat, sed debilius existimabat; unde possibile est quod aliquis antequam credat deum esse, exstimaverit deum esse, et hoc esse ei placitum quod credatur eum esse. et sic aliquis potest credere deum esse, eo quod sit placitum deo, quamvis etiam hoc non sit articulus; sed antecedens articulum, quia demonstrative probatur." (QDV 14.9 ob 9 & ad 9)

The objection here seems to pick out the epistemic circularity that we have identified as the first objection, and it offers as a solution the first response we rejected above—that in order to avoid the circularity, "God exists" must be scientifically known. In response, Aquinas seems to allow that prior to faith one can accept that God exists with some hesitation (*existimatio debilis*) and also believe that accepting His existence would please God. Such a person does not yet have faith, because "God exists" is accepted only hesitantly, although presumably this person could come to have faith (or, alternatively, could come to demonstrate that God exists). John Jenkins offers a useful analogy in order to help explain what Aquinas has in mind with this response:

> This is similar to the case in which a person, George, say, who first has a suspicion that he has a long-lost relative, Uncle Harry, subsequently comes to the firm conviction that such an Uncle Harry exists when he receives a letter from him. George does not, of course, believe Uncle Harry that he exists, but he does come to the firm conviction that Uncle Harry exists because he has taken the communication as genuine. My suggestion is that in a similar fashion one comes to a firm conviction that God exists because one believes that he has received a genuine revelation from God.[46]

If we interpret Aquinas in this way (as I am inclined to do), then Aquinas seems to provide a response to the objection of epistemic circularity very similar in spirit to Plantinga's. We first conjecture and hold, as an opinion only, that God exists. Then, God "speaks" to us in providing the grace that aids the will in assenting to the articles of faith and in providing the light of faith—this "communication" is taken by the believer to be genuine, and as a result the believer comes to believe with firm adherence and certitude what was previously only opined. Faith

---

[46] Jenkins, *Knowledge and Faith in Thomas Aquinas* (1997) 199.

produces two sorts of certitude: first, the certitude that what is to be believed is necessarily true; second, the certitude that it is indeed God that reveals (via the light of faith) these truths. "God exists," then, is not something that is illuminated by the light of faith, and thus the charge of epistemic circularity is avoided; rather, by experiencing the light of faith one directly experiences God and comes to believe in God's existence with certitude, where previously there was only opinion.[47]

In concluding the response to this objection, I would like to point out an important difference between my interpretation of Aquinas offered above and that of Plantinga. Plantinga holds, as I do, that Aquinas believes that "God exists" is basic, but for importantly different reasons. I interpret "God exists" as basic for those who have faith because God's role in faith reveals His existence to the faithful. Plantinga, on the other hand, interprets Aquinas as holding that "God exists" as accompanying more mundane experiences:

> The heavens declare the glory of God and the skies proclaim the work of his hands: but not by way of serving as premises for an argument. Awareness of guilt may lead me to God; but it is not that in this awareness I have the material for a quick theistic argument: I am guilty, so there must be a God.... I don't take my guilt as *evidence* for the existence of God, or for the proposition that he is displeased with me. It is rather that in that circumstance—the circumstance of my

---

[47] Although I favor this interpretation of Aquinas (as does Barad, *Consent: The Means to an Active Faith According to St Thomas Aquinas* [1992], 70, and Pojman, *Religious Belief and the Will* [1986], 36) there is not much textual evidence to support it. The quotation from QDV 14.9 seems to support this interpretation, even though Aquinas's response to the objection is by no means clear, and there seems to be little other evidence to either confirm or disconfirm this interpretation.

clearly seeing my guilt—I simply find myself with the belief that God is disapproving or disappointed.[48]

Now, Plantinga may well be right in claiming that these sorts of experiences provide a basic belief in the existence of God; however, I do not think such a view is attributable to Aquinas. The grounds for attributing this view to Aquinas depend on the claim frequently made by Aquinas that: "To know that God exists in a general and confused way is implanted in us by nature..."[49] (Plantinga quotes this very passage at the outset of the chapter for his passage quoted above). Plantinga seems to interpret the innate knowledge of God referred to in the quoted passage as an innate capacity for knowing God's existence, and various experiences (watching the heavens, guilt) activate this capacity. The knowledge, though activated by experience, is due to an implanted capacity, and thus is basic.

I want to resist Plantinga's interpretation for two reasons. First, it places the locus of the certitude of the existence of God in somewhat mundane experiences, rather than in faith. Faith, as argued above, carries with it awareness (and certitude) of God's existence, and this is in part what makes faith so special. Although the presence of God may not seem important for unformed faith, recall that faith formed by charity involves a relationship between the believer and God. In order for such a relationship to exist, God

---

[48] Plantinga, *Warranted Christian Belief* (2000) 175.

[49] "ad primum ergo dicendum quod cognoscere deum esse in aliquo communi, sub quadam confusione, est nobis naturaliter insertum, inquantum scilicet deus est hominis beatitudo, homo enim naturaliter desiderat beatitudinem, et quod naturaliter desideratur ab homine, naturaliter cognoscitur ab eodem. sed hoc non est simpliciter cognoscere deum esse; sicut cognoscere venientem, non est cognoscere petrum, quamvis sit petrus veniens, multi enim perfectum hominis bonum, quod est beatitudo, existimant divitias; quidam vero voluptates; quidam autem aliquid aliud." (ST I.2.1 ad 1). See also SCG III.38.1 and Aquinas's Inaugural Lecture of 1256 (see Aquinas (1988), 356).

must be present to the believer, and so it makes sense to say that faith presents God to the believer. Second, Plantinga's interpretation relies on Aquinas's view that we have innate knowledge of God, but I want to suggest that Aquinas did not actually have this view. When Aquinas speaks of innate "knowledge" he uses the Latin term *cognoscere* (and its cognates), a term that, I have argued, should be translated not as "knowledge" but as "cognition."[50] To have a general and confused innate cognition that God exists is merely to have a sense that God exists and would not seem to justify belief in God's existence. I may have a confused sense on some particular afternoon that it will rain, but my lack of meteorological knowledge coupled with my previous inattentiveness to indicative signs of rain would seem to indicate that to hold strongly a belief that it will rain would be irrational. Similarly, it would seem, if I were to have a general and confused cognition of God's existence when I look at a beautiful sunset while lacking any demonstration for His existence and also lacking faith, to then firmly believe in God would also be irrational. That *cognoscere* should be translated as I am proposing, rather than as "knowledge," is further supported by Aquinas's response following the one quoted above. In his response to ST I.2.1 objection 1, Aquinas says that we have a general and confused *cognoscere* of God's existence. In his response to objection 2, in which he rejects Anselm's ontological argument, Aquinas notes that some believed God to be a body. That Aquinas first points out that we have a confused *cognoscere* of God's existence and then observes that some believed God to be a body would strongly seem to suggest that *cognoscere* should be translated merely as "cognition," not as "knowledge." This interpretation seems further confirmed by what Aquinas says in DV 14.10:

---

[50] See chapter 2, note 1.

Our understanding does not have a natural determination to matters of faith in the sense that it should know (*cognoscat*) them naturally, but it does in some sense have a natural ordination to a knowledge (*cognoscenda*) of them in so far as nature is said to have an ordination to grace by reason of a divine decree.[51]

Second objection. Since one cannot tell whether one believes according to the light of faith or not, faith cannot produce certitude. Here is the argument: as was discussed in section 3.2.1, Aquinas holds that a heretic who refuses to believe even one article of faith loses the habit of faith and believes matters relevant to faith not according to the light of faith but according to some personal, human standard of judging. But presumably at least some of these heretics still think that their beliefs are formed according to the light of faith—at least some heretics still think of themselves as properly believing Christians. Heretics of this sort cannot tell the difference between believing by faith and believing without faith, and thus faith is phenomenologically indistinguishable from mere opinion. But if one cannot be sure whether or not one has faith (that is, whether one is a heretic of this sort), then faith cannot provide certitude. A second, related argument can be given in light of my response to the first objection. As Robert Audi presents it:

And imagine a cult, say of the Great Oz, who is so conceived that he cannot be God under another name. Suppose its votaries made similar claims about the existence of a natural tendency to form basic Ozistic beliefs and they argued that Hebraic-Christian (and other) influences have prevented widespread realization of this tendency. They might also

---

[51] "ad quartum dicendum, quod ad ea quae sunt fidei, non naturaliter determinatur intellectus quasi ea naturaliter cognoscat; sed quodammodo naturaliter ordinatur in ipsa cognoscenda, sicut natura dicitur ordinari ad gratiam ex divina institutione." (QDV 14.10 ad 4)

maintain that they have Ozian experiences in which they are directly aware of Oz.

...How comforting should it be to know that one's basic religious beliefs have a favorable epistemic status if incompatible, even outlandish, religious beliefs, can also have it?[52]

Nothing, in principle, would seem to prevent Ozians (or Muslims, etc.) from claiming for themselves a light of faith by which they believe with certitude and by which the existence of God is properly basic. But supposing that Ozian beliefs are incompatible with Christian beliefs, it seems that neither the Ozians nor the Christians can reasonably claim that their beliefs have certitude.

Reply to the second objection. As was discussed at the end of section 3.4, Aquinas's stringent account of faith would seem to have the consequence that few self-ascribed Christians do, in fact, have faith. For, as Aquinas claims (and as is pointed out in the objection above), someone who disbelieves even one article of faith lacks faith. Let us accept this consequence of Aquinas's account.[53] Thus, most self-ascribed Christians do not have faith. Yet, according to the objection, many still think that they believe according to the light of faith, and that they have faith. I think that Aquinas would reject this last claim, and thus stop the objection in its tracks here. Those who truly have faith accept all articles of faith according to the light of faith, but according to Aquinas anyone who disbelieves an article of faith must be deciding for himself, on the basis of his own will and judgment, what to accept and what not to accept.[54] When these sorts of believers think that

---

[52] Audi, "Direct Justification," 164-65.

[53] Whether or not such a stringent standard for faith is an advantage or failing of the account is an issue of theology, and so I shall not take it up here.

[54] See ST II-II.5.4; see also 5.4 ad 1.

234

they believe according to the light of faith, they are simply wrong. Their error does not suggest that believing according to one's own will and judgment cannot be distinguished from believing according to the light of faith; rather, it shows that some may claim to believe by the light of faith either facetiously or out of ignorance. Consider the following analogy. Some people (undergraduates in introductory philosophy come to mind) make claims such as "That the number of stars in the sky is infinite is knowable *a priori*." That some falsely claim that propositions are *a priori* does not show that one cannot, in principle, tell the difference between *a priori* and *a posteriori* claims. Rather, it merely shows that those who make the erroneous claims do not know what they are talking about. Similarly, those self-ascribed Christians who disbelieve some article of faith yet claim to believe according to the grace of God and the light of faith do not know what they're talking about—they're making empty claims about their belief formation.

Another analogy to help explain how those who disbelieve one article of faith lack faith is considered by Aquinas in the *Summa theologiae* when he considers the following objection:

> Furthermore, just as man obeys God in believing the articles of faith, so also he obeys in following the commandments of the law. But a man can be obedient to some commandments and not to others. Therefore he can have faith concerning some articles and not others.[55]

In his response to this objection, Aquinas observes that someone who does not obey all the commandments does not *really* obey God. To obey God is to be driven by the motive to obey God

---

[55] "praeterea, sicut homo obedit deo ad credendum articulos fidei, ita etiam ad servanda mandata legis. sed homo potest esse obediens circa quaedam mandata et non circa alia. ergo potest habere fidem circa quosdam articulos et non circa alios." (ST II-II.5.3 ob 3)

completely. One who obeys some but not all the commandments is really being driven by various proximate motives that select which commandments to obey. Just as selective obedience to God is not really obedience, selective belief in articles of faith is not really faith. Whatever it is that motivates a person to disbelieve an article of faith, and thus embrace error, also might mask that person's self-realization that this is what is occurring—and this is why such people still think that they believe according to the light of faith.

As for Ozians, or Muslims or other religious groups whose beliefs are incompatible with those of Christians, I think Aquinas would deny that such groups appeal to belief according to a light of faith. Here, it seems that Aquinas's claim is meant to be factual—Christians believe according to the light of faith; Muslims do not. In *Summa contra gentiles*, Aquinas contrasts the way in which Christians and Muslims come to believe. He sees as the greatest miracle of Christianity the fact that vast numbers of people, both simple and learned, have flocked to the Christian faith despite adversity and persecution, and come to believe truths that exceed reason, but are neither coerced nor enticed by the promise of pleasure. In other words, Christians believe by faith and through God. For Muslims, on the other hand, the motives for belief are different:

> On the other hand, those who founded sects committed to erroneous doctrines proceeded in a way that is opposite to this. The point is clear in the case of Mohammed. He seduced the people by promises of carnal pleasure to which the concupiscence of the flesh goads us. His teaching also contained precepts that were in conformity with his promises, and he gave free rein to carnal pleasure. In all this, as is not unexpected, he was obeyed by carnal men.... Mohammed

forced others to become his followers by the violence of his arms.[56]

Whether or not his assertions about Islam are correct, Aquinas clearly seems to believe that Muslims believe on the basis of motives that are not those corresponding to his account of faith. Muslims (and presumably members of all other religious groups) do not have faith and do not believe by the light of faith—should they claim to do so, they, like the heretics discussed above, claim falsely.[57]

---

[56] "hi vero qui sectas errorum introduxerunt processerunt via contraria: ut patet in mahumeto qui carnalium voluptatum promissis, ad quorum desiderium carnalis concupiscentia instigat, populus illexit. praecepta etiam tradidit promissis conformia, voluptati carnali habenas relaxans, in quibus in promptu est a carnalibus hominibus obediri. documenta etiam veritatis non attulit nisi quae de facili a quolibet mediocriter sapiente naturali ingenio cognosci possint: quin potius vera quae docuit multis fabulis et falsissimis doctrinis immiscuit. signa etiam non adhibuit supernaturaliter facta, quibus solis divinae inspirationi conveniens testimonium adhibetur, dum operatio visibilis quae non potest esse nisi divina, ostendit doctorem veritatis invisibiliter inspiratum: sed dixit se in armorum potentia missum, quae signa etiam latronibus et tyrannis non desunt. ei etiam non aliqui sapientes, in rebus divinis et humanis exercitati, a principio crediderunt: sed homines bestiales in desertis morantes, omnis doctrinae divinae prorsus ignari, per quorum multitudinem alios armorum violentia in suam legem coegit. nulla etiam divina oracula praecedentium prophetarum ei testimonium perhibent: quin potius quasi omnia veteris et novi testamenti documenta fabulosa narratione depravat, ut patet eius legem inspicienti. unde astuto consilio libros veteris et novi testamenti suis sequacibus non reliquit legendos, ne per eos falsitatis argueretur. et sic patet quod eius dictis fidem adhibentes leviter credunt." (SCG I.6 n.4)

[57] Should some religious group have motivations for their beliefs that more closely resemble those that Aquinas claims on behalf of Christians, then the second objection could be reinstated. It seems clear, however, that Aquinas holds that the Christian religion is the only extant one that has motives for belief that are compatible with having faith. I am not clear whether Aquinas held that believers of Eastern Orthodox Christianity had faith or not, but if so, then presumably the differences between views held by Eastern Orthodox

Third objection. Aquinas's solution to the problem of faith and reason fails because it relies on an inaccurate epistemology, as presented by Kenneth Konyndyk:

> One of the more serious objections to Aquinas's solution to the problem of conflicts between faith and science is its reliance on an unacceptable epistemology and an antiquated view of the sciences. Aquinas links a certain deductive structure of science, proceeding as it were axiomatically from postulates and first principles (axioms?), with an epistemology of science or theory of justification. Thus we know scientifically and fully justifiably because we see the links between the claim under consideration and the first principles.... some claims that one would have thought were *per se nota* and candidates for axioms or postulates have been shown to lead to notorious logical paradoxes.... In short, it appears that it will not work to try to get an axiomatic structuring of science to coincide with the sort of theory of justification that Aquinas wants. Because Thomas's arguments for compatibility are based on this structure, rejection of the structure means that certain key premises in his arguments must be rejected.[58]

Rather than delve in detail to Konyndyk's objection, I think we can simplify it for the purposes of this work to the following: "Aquinas's solution depends on Aristotelian accounts of science

---

believers and those of Catholics were not differences centering on the articles of faith.

[58] Konyndyk, "Aquinas on Faith and Science," *Faith and Philosophy* 12/1 (1995): 17. In addition to his criticism of the axiomatic structure of science, Konyndyk criticizes Aquinas for finding no significant epistemic conflict between faith and opinion, since opinion is based on merely probable reasoning (18). However, as Konyndyk observes, nearly all contemporary science fits under opinion by Aquinas's epistemology, and to say that faith and contemporary science have no real tension because faith has certitude whereas contemporary science is merely probable does not seem to dissipate the tension between the two adequately at all.

and epistemology. But Aristotelian science and epistemology are wrong. Therefore, Aquinas's solution is inadequate."

Reply to the third objection. Anachronistic objections such as this are, in some sense, unfair to Aquinas. Aquinas's project was to provide a solution that reconciled faith with the standards of philosophical reason at the time in which he wrote, standards that were exemplified by Aristotle. I have tried to present Aquinas's solution to the reconciliation of Christian faith with Aristotelian reason and have suggested in section 5.5.1 above that his solution was *prima facie* well-received in that its main elements seem still to have been in place at least as late as when Galileo wrote. In this context, Aquinas's solution is impervious to objections of the sort given above. However, we might also wish to evaluate the adequacy of Aquinas's solution in the current climate of tension between faith and reason. By this standard, Aquinas's solution clearly fails, relying as it does on an outdated epistemology, as Konyndyk rightly observes. On the other hand, the main thrust of Aquinas's solution might yet find some purchase in the current debate. In contemporary discussions of religious epistemology, faith is often taken to be un- or under-evidenced belief, whereas science is taken to involve beliefs with sufficient evidence. By such an account, faith clearly seems to be epistemically irresponsible since it lacks sufficient evidence. However, we can jettison Aristotelian epistemology and still adopt Aquinas's account of faith. Faith, fundamentally for Aquinas, is something that has certitude without evidence. Contemporary science has given up on certitude—beliefs of science are no longer held with *scientia* but inductively and contingently. Aquinas's faith, by comparison, is a far stronger and more reliable epistemic state than contemporary scientific belief, so it would seem that we could still argue for epistemic compatibilism between faith and contemporary science—particularly if we adopt some version of the Scope

Strategy that limits the scope of what science can discern, such as that suggested by Evelyn Fox Keller (see chapter 1 footnote 15).

5.6. Concluding remarks

This book has attempted to provide a detailed account of precisely how Aquinas reconciles faith with Aristotelian reason. Such an exegetical enterprise is important for several reasons. First, Aquinas was the first philosopher/theologian to provide a thorough and systematic reconciliation between faith and reason. His exercise is both historically significant and influential to later philosophers and theologians. Such a thoroughly developed solution may serve as a useful standard by which contemporary reconciliations of faith and reason should be developed.[59] Second, as a significant figure in the history of philosophy, Aquinas deserves to be understood correctly. In providing a detailed account of Aquinas's views, I have made my case for correcting a number of common but erroneous interpretations of Aquinas. Finally, though much has been written on Aquinas's account of faith, reason, the eternity of the world, and the Five Ways, my enterprise is to my knowledge the first that tries to provide a complete account of Aquinas's views, bringing together disparate passages by Aquinas that are relevant to faith and reason and synthesizing them into a unified and comprehensible whole. In writing this book, I hope I have achieved these goals.

---

[59] Plantinga, *Warranted Christian* Belief (2000) is a good example of the sort of thorough, systematic solution I am talking about. Efforts like Plantinga's, unfortunately, are few and far between.

BIBLIOGRAPHY

Adams, Marilyn McCord. *William Ockham*. Notre Dame: University of Notre Dame Press, 1987.

———— "Praying the *Proslogion*: Anselm's Theological Method." In *The Rationality of Belief & the Plurality of Faith*, ed. Thomas D. Senor, 13-39. Ithaca: Cornell University Press, 1995.

Aertsen, Jan A. "The Eternity of the World: The Believing and the Philosophical Thomas. Some Comments." In *The Eternity of the World*, ed. Josef Wissink, 9-19. Leiden: E. J. Brill, 1990.

Alston, William P. *Perceiving God: The Epistemology of Religious Experience*. Ithaca: Cornell University Press, 1991.

Anderson, James F. "The Notion of Certitude." *Thomist* 18 (1955): 522-39.

Anscombe, G. E. M. "What Is It to Believe Someone?" In *Rationality and Religious Belief*, ed. C. F. Delaney, 141-51: University of Notre Dame Press, 1979.

Aquinas, Thomas. "Opera Omnia," *Corpus Thomisticum* (from the Leonine texts), http://www.unav.es/filosofia/alarcon/amicis/ctopera.html (accessed June 2011).

————. *Quaestiones Quodlibetales III, Q. 4*. Trans. Alfred J. Freddoso, http://www.nd.edu/~afreddos/translat/aquinas2.htm (accessed June 2011).

————. *Summa Theologiae*, 2 volumes. Trans. Fathers of the English Dominican Province, revised by Daniel J. Sullivan. Great Books edition. Chicago: Encyclopedia Britannica, 1952

————. *Truth: De Veritate*. Trans. James V. McGlynn. Chicago: Henry Regnery Company, 1953.

————. *Theological Texts*. Trans. Thomas Gilby. Oxford: Oxford University Press, 1955.

————. *God*. Volume 1 of *On the Truth of the Catholic Faith: Summa contra gentiles*. Trans. Anton C. Pegis. Garden City NY: Image Books, 1955.

————. *Creation*. Volume 2 of *On the Truth of the Catholic Faith: Summa contra gentiles*. Trans. James F. Anderson. Garden City NY: Image Books, 1956.

————. *On Charity*. Trans. Lottie H. Kendzierski. Milwaukee: Marquette University Press, 1960.

————. *The Division and Methods of the Sciences: Questions V and VI of His Commentary on the De Trinitate of Boethius*. Trans. Armand Maurer. Toronto: Pontifical Institute of Medieval Studies, 1963.

————. *St Thomas Aquinas, Siger of Brabant, St. Bonaventure: On the Eternity of the World*. Trans. Cyril Vollert, Lottie H. Kendzierski, and Paul M. Byrne. Milwaukee: Marquette University Press, 1964.

Aquinas, Thomas. *Commentary on the Posterior Analytics of Aristotle.* Trans. F. R. Larcher. Albany NY: Magi Books, Inc., 1970.

———. *Commentary on the Gospel of John.* Trans. James Weisheipl. Albany NY: Magi Books, 1980.

———. *Faith, Reason and Theology: Questions I-IV of His Commentary on the De Trinitate of Boethius.* Trans. Armand Maurer. Toronto: Pontifical Institute of Medieval Studies, 1987.

———. *The Sermon-Conferences of St. Thomas Aquinas on the Apostles' Creed.* Trans. Nicholas Ayo. Notre Dame: University of Notre Dame Press, 1988.

———. "Inaugural Lecture (1256)." In *Albert & Thomas: Selected Writings,* ed. John Farina, et. al. 355-60. New York: Paulist Press, 1988.

———. *On Faith: Summa Theologiae, Part 2-2, Questions 1-16.* Trans. Mark D. Jordan. Notre Dame: University of Notre Dame Press, 1990.

———. *Light of Faith: The Compendium of Theology.* Trans. Cyril Vollert. Manchester NH: Sophia Institute Press, 1993.

———. *Commentary on Aristotle's Metaphysics.* Trans. John P. Rowan. Notre Dame: Dumb Ox Books, 1995.

———. *Commentary on the Book of Causes.* Trans. Vincent A. Guagliardo, Charles R. Hess, and Richard C. Taylor. Washington DC: Catholic University of America Press, 1996.

———. "On the Principles of Nature." In *Selected Writings,* ed. Ralph McInerny 18-29. New York: Penguin Books, 1998.

———. *Disputed Questions on Virtue: Quaestio Disputata De Virtutibus in Communi and Quaestio Disputata De Virtutibus Cardinalibus.* Trans. Ralph McInerny. South Bend IN: St. Augustine's Press, 1999.

_____. *Commentary on Aristotle's Physics.* Trans. Richard J. Blackwell, Richard J. Spath, and W. Edmund Thirlkel. Notre Dame: Dumb Ox Books, 1999.

———. *Commentary on Aristotle's De Anima.* Trans. Robert Pasnau. New Haven: Yale University Press, 1999.

Audi, Robert. "Direct Justification, Evidential Dependence, and Theistic Belief." In *Rationality, Religious Belief, and Moral Commitment,* ed. Robert Audi and William Wainwright, 139-66. Ithaca: Cornell University Press, 1986.

Augustine. "Soliloquies." In *Augustine: Earlier Writings,* ed. J.H.S. Burleigh 23-63. Philadelphia: Westminster Press, 1953.

Barad, Judith. *Consent: The Means to an Active Faith According to St Thomas Aquinas.* New York: Peter Lang, 1992.

Bonansea, Bernardino. "The Human Mind and Knowledge of God." *Franciscan Studies* 40 (1980): 5-17.

Bonaventure. "Selections from *Collationes in Hexaemeron.*" In *St Thomas Aquinas, Siger of Brabant, St. Bonaventure: On the Eternity of the World,* ed. Cyril Vollert, Lottie H. Kendzierski, and Paul M. Byrne, 113-17. Milwaukee: Marquette University Press, 1964.

Brady, Ignatius. "John Pecham and the Background of Aquinas's *De Aeternitate Mundi*." In *St. Thomas Aquinas 1274–1974*, ed. Armand A. Maurer, 141-78. Toronto: Pontifical Institute of Medieval Studies, 1974.

Brown, Stephen F. "Henry of Ghent's Critique of Aquinas' Subalternation Theory and the Early Thomistic Response." In *Knowledge and the Sciences in Medieval Philosophy*, ed. R. Tyorinoja, A. I. Lehtinen and D. Follesdal, 3:337-45. Helsinki: S.I.E.P.M, 1990.

Burrell, David B. "Aquinas and Islamic and Jewish Thinkers." In *Cambridge Companion to Aquinas*, ed. Norman Kretzmann and Eleonore Stump, 60-84. Cambridge: Cambridge University Press, 1993.

Celsus. *On the True Doctrine: A Discourse against the Christians.* Trans. R. Joseph Hoffmann. New York: Oxford University Press, 1987.

Chenu, M. D. *Toward Understanding Saint Thomas.* New York: Henry Regnery, 1964.

Clark, Gordon H. *Religion, Reason and Revelation.* Philadelphia: Prebyterian and Reformed Publishing Co., 1961.

Clifford, William K. "The Ethics of Belief" in *TheEthics of Belief and Other Essays* (Prometheus Books, 1999).

Colish, Marcia L. *The Mirror of Language: A Study in the Medieval Theory of Knowledge.* Lincoln: University of Nebraska Press, 1983.

Copleston, Frederick C. *Thomas Aquinas.* Harmondsworth, England: Penguin, 1955.

Craig, William Lane. *The Cosmological Argument from Plato to Leibniz.* London: Macmillan, 1980.

Cunningham, Francis A. "*Certitudo* in St. Thomas Aquinas." *Modern Schoolman* 30 (1953): 297-324.

Dales, Richard. "Time and Eternity in the 13th Century." *Journal of the History of Ideas* 49 (1988): 27-45.

———. *Medieval Discussions of the Eternity of the World.* Leiden: E. J. Brill, 1990.

Davies, Brian. *The Thought of Thomas Aquinas.* Oxford: Clarendon Press, 1992.

Dawkins, Richard. "You ask the questions." *The Independent* 12/23 (1998): 8.

Dod, Bernard G. "*Aristoteles Latinus.*" In *The Cambridge History of Later Medieval Philosophy*, ed. Norman Kretzmann, Anthony Kenny, and Jan Pinborg, 45-79. Cambridge: Cambridge University Press, 1982.

Elders, Leo. *Faith and Science: An Introduction to St. Thomas' Expositio in Boethii De Trinitate.* Rome: Herder, 1974.

Flew, Anthony. "The Presumption of Atheism." In *Contemporary Perspectives on Religious Epistemology*, ed. R. D. Geivett and B. Sweetman, 19-32. Oxford: Oxford University Press, 1992.

Fogelin, Robert J. "A Reading of Aquinas's Five Ways." *American Philosophical Quarterly* 27/4 (1990): 305-313.

Gilson, Etienne. *Reason and Revelation in the Middle Ages.* New York: Charles Scribner's Sons, 1938.

———. *The Christian Philosophy of St. Thomas Aquinas.* Trans. L. K. Shook. Notre Dame: University of Notre Dame Press, 1956.

Greco, John. "Is Natural Theology Necessary for Theistic Knowledge?" In *Rational Faith: Catholic Responses to Reformed Epistemology*, ed. Linda Zagzebski, 168-98. Notre Dame: University of Notre Dame Press, 1993.

Griffin, John Joseph. "The Interpretation of the Two Thomistic Definitions of Certitude." *Laval Theologique et Philosophique* 10 (1954): 9-35.

Guzie, Tad. "The Act of Faith According to St. Thomas: A Study in Theological Methodology." *Thomist* 29 (1965): 239-80.

Hall, Theodore. *Paul Tillich's Appraisal of St. Thomas' Teaching on the Act of Faith*. Rome: Catholic Book Agency, 1968.

Hankey, W. J. *God in Himself: Aquinas' Doctrine of God as Expounded in the Summa Theologiae*. Oxford: Oxford University Press, 1987.

Hibbs, Thomas. "Kretzmann's Theism Vs. Aquinas' Theism." *Thomist* 62 (1998): 603-622.

Hick, John. *Faith and Knowledge*. Ithaca: Cornell University Press, 1966.

———. "Faith." In *The Encyclopedia of Philosophy*, ed. Paul Edwards, 165-169. New York: Macmillan Company & The Free Press, 1967.

Hoenen, M. J. F. M. "The Literary Reception of Thomas Aquinas' View on the Provability of the Eternity of the World in De La Mare's *Correctorium* (1278–9) and the *Correctoria Corruptorii* (1279–Ca 1286)." In *The Eternity of the World*, ed. Josef Wissink, 39-68. Leiden: E. J. Brill, 1990.

Houser, R. E. "Trans-Forming Philosophical Water into Theological Wine: Gilson and Aquinas." *Proceedings of the American Catholic Philosophical Association* (1995): 103-116.

Jenkins, John I. *Knowledge and Faith in Thomas Aquinas*. Cambridge: Cambridge University Press, 1997.

———. "Faith and Revelation." In *Philosophy of Religion*, ed. Brian Davies, 202-227. Washington DC: Georgetown University Press, 1998.

John Paul II, Pope. *Encyclical Letter* Fides Et Ratio *of the Supreme Pontiff John Paul II to the Bishops of the Catholic Church on the Relationship between Faith and Reason* (1998), www.vatican.va/holy_father/john_paul_ii/encyclicals/documents/hf_jp-ii_enc_15101998_fides-et-ratio_en.html (accessed June 13, 2011).

Jordan, Mark D. "Theology and Philosophy." In *The Cambridge Companion to Aquinas*, ed. Norman Kretzmann and Eleonore Stump, 232-51. Cambridge: Cambridge University Press, 1993.

Kellenberger, James. "Three Models of Faith." In *Contemporary Perspectives on Religious Epistemology*, ed. R. D. Geivett and B. Sweetman, 320-58. Oxford: Oxford University Press, 1992.

Keller, Evelyn Fox. *Making Sense of Life: Explaining Biological Development with Models, Metaphors, and Machines*. Cambridge: Harvard University Press, 2003.

Kennick, W. E. "A New Way with the Five Ways." *Australasian Journal of Philosophy* 38 (1960): 225-33.

Kenny, Anthony. *The Five Ways: St. Thomas Aquinas' Proofs of God's Existence.* London: Routledge & Kegan Paul, 1969.

———. *What Is Faith?* Oxford: Oxford University Press, 1992.

Konyndyk, Kenneth J. "Aquinas on Faith and Science." *Faith and Philosophy* 12/1 (1995): 3-21.

Kovach, Francis J. "The Question of the Eternity of the World in St. Bonaventure and St. Thomas—A Critical Analysis." In *Bonaventure & Aquinas: Enduring Philosophers*, ed. Robert W. Shahan and Francis J. Kovach, 155-86. Norman: University of Oklahoma Press, 1976.

Kretzmann, Norman. "Infallibility, Error, and Ignorance." In *Aristotle and His Medieval Interpreters*, edited by R. Bosley and M. Tweedale, 159-94. Calgary: University of Calgary Press, 1991.

———. "Philosophy of Mind." In *Cambridge Companion to Aquinas*, ed. Norman Kretzmann and Eleonore Stump, 128-59. Cambridge: Cambridge University Press, 1993.

———. *The Metaphysics of Theism: Aquinas's Natural Theology in Summa contra gentiles I.* Oxford: Clarendon Press, 1997.

———. *The Metaphysics of Creation: Aquinas's Natural Theology in Summa contra gentiles II.* Oxford: Clarendon Press, 1999.

Kuksewicz, Z. "Criticisms of Aristotelian Psychology and the Augustinian-Aristotelian Synthesis." In *The Cambridge History of Later Medieval Philosophy*, ed. Norman Kretzmann, Anthony Kenny, and Jan Pinborg, 623-28. Cambridge: Cambridge University Press, 1982.

Lee, Richard A. "Peter Aureoli as Critic of Aquinas on the Subalternate Character of the Science of Theology." *Franciscan Studies* 55 (1998): 121-36.

Leo XIII, Pope. "On the Restoration of Christian Philosophy: *Aeterni Patris*" (1879), www.vatican.va/holy-father/leo-xiii/encyclicals/documents/hf_l-xiii_enc_0481879_aeterni-patris_en.html (accessed June 2011).

MacDonald, Scott. "Theory of Knowledge." In *Cambridge Companion to Aquinas*, ed. Norman Kretzmann and Eleonore Stump, 160-95. Cambridge: Cambridge University Press, 1993.

Marrone, Steven P. "Concepts of Science among Parisian Theologians in the Thirteenth Century." In *Knowledge and the Sciences in Medieval Philosophy*, ed. R. Tyorinoja, A. I. Lehtinen, and D. Follesdal, 3:124-33. Helsinki: S.I.E.P.M., 1990.

Marx, Karl, and Friedrich Engels. "Contribution to the Critique of Hegel's Philosophy of Right: Introduction." In *On Religion*. Chico, California: Scholar's Press, 1964.

Masiello, Rallph J. "Reason and Faith in Richard of St. Victor and St. Thomas." *New Scholastic* 48 (1974): 233-42.

McGrath, P. J. *Believing in God.* Dublin: Millington Press, 1995.

McInerny, Ralph M. "The Contemporary Significance of St. Bonaventure and St. Thomas." *Southwestern Journal of Philosophy* 5 (1974): 11-26.

————. "Analogy and Foundationalism in Thomas Aquinas." In *Rationality, Religious Belief and Moral Commitment*, ed. Robert Audi and William Wainwright, 271-88. Ithaca: Cornell University Press, 1986.

McKirahan, Richard. *Principles and Proofs: Aristotle's Theory of Demonstrative Science*. Princeton: Princeton University Press, 1992.

McLean, Michael. "An Exposition and Defense of St. Thomas Aquinas' Account of the Rational Justification of Religious Belief." Ph.D. dissertation, University of Notre Dame, 1981.

Mitchell, Basil. *The Justification of Religious Belief*. New York: Seabury Press, 1973.

Mohler, James A. *The Beginning of Eternal Life: The Dynamic Faith of Thomas Aquinas, Origins and Interpretation*. New York: Philosophical Library, 1968.

Noone, Timothy. "The Franciscans and Epistemology: Philosophy and Theology on the Issue of Universal Causality." In *Medieval Masters: Essays in Memory of Msgr. E. A. Synan*, ed. R. E. Houser, 63-90. Houston: Center for Thomistic Studies, 1999.

Owens, Joseph. "Aquinas and the Five Ways." In *St. Thomas Aquinas on the Existence of God: Collected Papers*, ed. John Catan, 132-41. Albany NY: SUNY Press, 1980.

————. "Faith, Ideas, Illumination, and Experience." In *The Cambridge History of Later Medieval Philosophy*, ed. Norman Kretzmann, Anthony Kenny, and Jan Pinborg, 440-59. Cambridge: Cambridge University Press, 1982.

————. "Aristotle and Aquinas." In *Cambridge Companion to Aquinas*, ed. Norman Kretzmann and Eleonore Stump, 38-59. New York: Cambridge University Press, 1993.

Pasnau, Robert. *Theories of Cognition in the Later Middle Ages*. Cambridge: Cambridge University Press, 1997.

Pecham, John. *Questions Concerning the Eternity of the World*. Trans. Vincent G. Potter. New York: Fordham University Press, 1993.

Pegis, Anton C. "Four Medieval Ways to God." *Monist* 54 (1970): 317-58.

Penelhum, Terence. "The Analysis of Faith in St. Thomas Aquinas." *Religious Studies* 3 (1977): 133-54.

————. *Reason and Religious Faith*. Boulder CO: Westview Press, 1995.

Persson, Per Erik. *Sacra Doctrina: Reason and Revelation in Aquinas*. Trans. Ross Mackenzie. Philadelphia: Fortress Press, 1970.

Plantinga, Alvin. *God and Other Minds*. Ithaca: Cornell University Press, 1967.

————. "Reason and Belief in God." In *Faith and Rationality*, ed. Alvin Plantinga and Nicholas Wolterstorff, 16-93. Notre Dame: University of Notre Dame Press, 1983.

————. *Warranted Christian Belief*. Oxford: Oxford University Press, 2000.

Pojman, Louis P. *Religious Belief and the Will*. London: Routledge & Kegan Paul, 1986.

Potts, Timothy. "Aquinas on Belief and Faith." In *Inquiries into Medieval Philosophy*, ed. J. F. Ross, 3-23. Westport CT: Greenwood Publishing Co., 1971.

Preller, Victor. *Divine Science and the Science of God*. Princeton: Princeton University Press, 1967.

Presa, W. K. "St. Thomas on Religious Belief." *Sophia* 19 (1980): 25-30.

Quinn, John F. *The Historical Constitution of St. Bonaventure's Philosophy*. Toronto: Pontifical Institute of Medieval Studies, 1973.

———. "Certitude of Reason and Faith in St. Bonaventure and St. Thomas." In *St. Thomas Aquinas 1274–1974*, ed. Armand A. Maurer, 105-140. Toronto: Pontifical Institute of Medieval Studies, 1974.

Reilly, George C. "St. Thomas and the Problem of Knowledge." *Thomist* 17 (1954): 510-24.

Riga, Peter J. "The Act of Faith in Augustine and Aquinas." *Thomist* 35 (1971): 143-74.

Ross, J. F. "Aquinas on Belief and Knowledge." In *Essays Honoring Allan B. Wolter*, ed. William A. Frank and Gerard J. Etzkorn, 245-69. St. Bonaventure NY: Franciscan Institute Publications, 1985.

Serene, Eileen. "Demonstrative Science." In *The Cambridge History of Later Medieval Philosophy*, ed. Norman Kretzmann, Anthony Kenny, and Jan Pinborg, 496-517. Cambridge: Cambridge University Press, 1982.

Sillem, E. *Ways of Thinking About God*. London: Darton-Longman-Todd, 1961.

Simmons, Edward D. "Demonstration and Self-Evidence." *Thomist* 24 (1961): 137-62.

Stump, Eleonore. "Aquinas on Faith and Goodness." In *Being and Goodness*, ed. Scott MacDonald, 179-207. Ithaca: Cornell University Press, 1991.

———. "Aquinas on the Foundations of Knowledge." In *Aristotle and His Medieval Interpreters*, ed. R. Bosley and M. Tweedale, 125-58. Calgary: University of Calgary Press, 1992.

Stump, Eleonore, and Norman Kretzmann. "Eternity." *Journal of Philosophy* 78/8 (1981): 429-58.

Sweeney, Eileen C. "Metaphysics and Its Distinction from Sacred Doctrine in Aquinas." In *Knowledge and the Sciences in Medieval Philosophy*, ed. R. Tyorinoja, A. I. Lehtinen, and D. Follesdal, 3:162-70. Helsinki: S.I.E.P.M., 1990.

———. "Three Notions of *Resolutio* and the Structure of Reasoning." *Thomist* 58/2 (1994): 197-243.

Tatian. *Address of Tatian to the Greeks* (ca. 160-170), trans. J. E. Ryland, Christian Classics Ethereal Library, www.ccel.org/ccel.schaff/anf02.iii.i.html (accessed June 2011).

Tertullian. *The Prescription against Heretics* (ca. 200), trans. Peter Holmes, Christian Classics Ethereal Library, www.ccel.org.ccel.schaff.anf03.v.iii.i.html (accessed June 2011).

Thorndike, Lynn. *University Records and Life in the Middle Ages*. New York: Octagon Books, 1971.

Tyrrell, Francis Martin. *The Role of Assent in Judgment: A Thomistic Study*. Washington DC: Catholic University of America Press, 1948.

Van Melson, A. G. M. "St. Thomas' Solution of the Problem of Faith and Reason." *Sapienta* 29 (1974): 125-34.

Van Steenberghen, Fernand. "Eternity of the World." In *Thomas Aquinas and Radical Aristotelianism*. Washington DC: Catholic University of America Press, 1980. (1-27).

Van Veldhuijsen, P. "The Question on the Possibility of an Eternally Created World: Bonaventura and Thomas Aquinas." In *The Eternity of the World*, ed. Josef Wissink, 20-38. Leiden: E. J. Brill, 1990.

———. "Richard of Middleton Contra Thomas Aquinas on the Question Whether the Created World Could Have Been Eternally Produced." In *The Eternity of the World*, ed. Josef Wissink, 69-81. Leiden: E.J. Brill, 1990.

Velecky, Lubor. "The Five Ways—Proofs of God's Existence?" *Monist* 58 (1974): 36-51.

———. *Aquinas's Five Arguments in the Summa Theologiae Ia 2, 3*. Kampen, Netherlands: Kok Pharos Publishing House, 1994.

Wallace, William A. *The Role of Demonstration in Moral Theology: A Study of Methodology in St. Thomas Aquinas*. Washington DC: Thomist Press, 1962.

———. *Galileo's Logic of Discovery and Proof*. Boston: Kluwer Academic Publishers, 1992.

Weisheipl, James A. "The Meaning of Sacra Doctrina in *Summa Theologiae I, Q.1*." *Thomist* 38 (1974): 49-80.

Wilcox, John R. "The Five Ways and the Oneness of God." *Thomist* 62 (1998): 245-68.

Wippel, John F. "The Condemnations of 1270 and 1277 at Paris." *Journal of Medieval and Renaissance Studies* 7 (1977): 169-201.

———. "Did Thomas Aquinas Defend the Possibility of an Eternally Created World? (The *De Aeternitate Mundi* Revisited)." *Journal of the History of Philosophy* 19 (1981): 21-37.

———. "Thomas Aquinas, Henry of Ghent, and Godfrey of Fontaines on the Reality of Nonexisting Possibles." In *Metaphysical Themes in Thomas Aquinas*, ed. John F. Wippel, 163-89. Washington DC: Catholic University of America Press, 1984.

———. "The Latin Avicenna as a Source for Thomas Aquinas's Metaphysics." *Freiburger Zeitschrift fur Philosophie und Theologie* 37 (1990): 53-59.

———. "Thomas Aquinas on What Philosophers Can Know about God." *American Catholic Philosophical Quarterly* 66 (1992): 279-98.

———. *Medieval Reactions to the Encounter between Faith and Reason*. Milwaukee: Marquette University Press, 1995.

Wolter, Allan B. *The Philosophical Theology of John Duns Scotus*. Ithaca: Cornell University Press, 1990.

Wolterstorff, Nicholas. "The Migration of the Theistic Arguments: From Natural Theology to Evidentialist Apologetics." In *Rationality, Religious Belief, and Moral Commitment*, ed. Robert Audi and William Wainwright, 38-81. Ithaca: Cornell University Press, 1986.

Wykstra, Stephen. "Toward a Sensible Evidentialism: On the Notion of 'Needing Evidence.'" In *Philosophy of Religion: Selected Readings*, ed. William Rowe and William Wainwright. New York: Harcourt Brace Jovanovich, 1989.

INDEX